THE SPORTS SUCCESS BOOK

THE SPORTS SUCCESS BOOK

The Athlete's Guide
To Sports Achievement

Karl Morrow Woods

COPPERFIELD PRESS
Austin, Texas
1985

Opposite: Magic Johnson (courtesy of the Los Angeles Lakers).

796
woo

Copperfield Press
Post Office Box 15025
Austin, Texas 78761

THE SPORTS SUCCESS BOOK
Copyright © 1985 by Karl Morrow Woods

First Edition

1   2   3   4   5   6   87   86   85

Library of Congress Cataloging in Publication Data

Woods, Karl Morrow, 1951-
  The sports success book.

  Companion vol. to: The sports success workout book.
  Bibliography: p.
  Includes index.
  1. Sports—Psychological aspects.   2. Achievement motivation.
3. Professionalism in sports.   4. Athletics.   5. Intramural sports.   I. Title.
GV706.4.W66   1985   796'.023   84-19832
ISBN 0-933857-00-4
ISBN 0-933857-01-2 (pbk.)

Production Data:
Editing: Maude Cardwell
Cover Design: Suzanne Pustejovsky
Typesetting and Production: The Composing Stick,
Austin, Texas
Manufacturer: BookCrafters, Inc.
Chelsea, Michigan

To my
Mother and Father —
Nancy Morrow Woods and
Herschel E. Woods

Acknowledgments

I AM INDEBTED TO ALL OF THE PEOPLE WHO CONTRIBUTED TO THE EVOLU-
tion of this book. My family gave me their prayers, their love, and
their encouragement. Pat and Elizabeth Aston Sullivan supported me
with their friendship and editorial assistance. Maude Cardwell provided
patient, intelligent editing that turned a sea of words and paper into a
readable, publishable book. Malcolm Riker offered his enthusiasm
and spiritual guidance. Thank you all!

I would also like to thank my friend and agent Ray Bard for his confidence and for his work in placing the book. I am grateful to my
friends in the Austin Writers' League for everything they added to the
book and are adding to my writing career, especially Jeannette
Varner, Bonnie Skaar George, Carol Thurston, Bob Rafferty, Texe
and Wanda Marrs, James L. Haley, and Ray Bard.

The following individuals contributed to my sports education and
were especially generous with their time, interviews, advice, or en-
couragement: Fred Akers, Holly Bashford, Bob Bass, Johnny Bench,
Lorraine Borman, Jack Boston, Ellington Darden, Ed Farnham, Kim
Gillespie, Steve Garvey, Cliff Gustafson, Karen Hunter, Rich
Lawrence, Charles Laws, Bob Lilly, Donna Lopiano, Bob Mathias,
Moses Malone, Ray Meyer, Ann Meyers, Al Miller, Charles Moser,
Billy Olson, Tom Osborne, Ray Overton, Vince Papale, Chris Plonsky,
Elaine Rundle, Otis J. Sanders, Jr., Laura Sharp, Linda Sharp,
Tommy Sherrill, Greg Sherwood, Ken Skaggs, James Street, Gene
Sullivan, Gail Tooley, Derrick Wilson, and Tom Winchell. I am deeply
grateful for their assistance.

I would like to thank the sports organizations, associations, and
corporations and the colleges and universities that responded with
information, photographs, and advice. I would also like to thank Ken
Litchfield and David Goodin of Maverick Graphix in Austin, Texas,
for the excellent photographs they provided for this book and for *The
Sports Success Workout Book*. Finally, I am indebted to my typists
Ann Shaughness, Janet Messer, and Pamela Jenson.

CONTENTS

Introduction

"WHEW, COACH! I WISH I COULD JUST TAKE A CONDITIONING PILL!"

Every coach has heard his athletes express a wish for magic pills or potions as they face the last laps or the last drills that loom ahead. The coach himself might wish there were an easier and faster way to whip a team into shape and to stay two or more steps ahead of the competition. The drive to be better, to be stronger, or to be faster probably began long before the first Olympic Games in Greece. And since that time the quest has continued as coaches and athletes have sought the common denominators for athletic success and achievement.

Consequently, today's list of self-help sports books is long and encompassing. Athletes can find book after book explaining how to run longer and faster, how to throw harder and straighter, and how to jump higher and farther. There are positive-attitude books that extol everything from meditation to hypnotism. The single task or tasks that supposedly lead to athletic success—the winning formulas—are wrapped in handy packages that athletes can use the way they would any other piece of equipment. A pregame inventory is simple: "Shoulder pads, helmet, cleats, positive attitude. . ."

But achieving success in any sport is not a simple, task-oriented project. Running faster, being stronger, or thinking more positively will seldom lead an individual beyond high school athletics. And even a reliance on natural talent and hard work is no guarantee against a short athletic career and dissatisfaction. Long-term success in sports is just as often a product of *good career management* as of athletic ability. For too many individuals, the route to athletic excellence is haphazardly based on shaky conceptions and wishes for good luck. Their lack of sports knowledge and experience holds them back and prevents them from reaching their full athletic potential. *What athletes need to know is how to manage their sports careers.*

The Sports Success Book provides that information. It is a complete guide for long-term athletic success and achievement, explaining how any athlete can take control of and successfully manage his or her total sports career. It answers such questions as: How can an athlete excel in junior high and high school sports? How can he or she earn a college scholarship? What are the keys to success in a major college sports program? How can an individual qualify for the United States Olympic Team? What can athletes do to improve their chances of competing in a professional sport? The important aspects of training and conditioning are covered in Appendix A. Strength, flexibility, speed, endurance, skills, and injury prevention are explored and discussed in detail.

The Sports Success Book was written for every junior high and high school student who wants a better chance of reaching his or her full athletic potential, for the thousands of individuals who have hopes of being awarded athletic scholarships and of excelling in intercollegiate athletics, for the individuals whose goals include competing in professional sports, and for all the athletes working their hearts out to qualify for the U.S. Olympic Team. *The Sports Success Book* was written for young athletes in every sport who believe in themselves, who dream of athletic excellence and success, and who want to transform those dreams into reality.

THE SPORTS SUCCESS BOOK

Reggie Jackson opened the 1985 baseball season with 503 career home runs (courtesy of the California Angels).

Chapter 1
What Makes an Athlete Great?

EVERY DAY, SUCCESSFUL ATHLETES IN HIGH SCHOOL, COLLEGE, AND PRO-
fessional sports compete at the highest levels against the best competition and continue to work toward the realization of their full athletic
potential. At the same time, other athletes seem to be getting nowhere;
their sports programs are filled with starts, stops, and half-hearted
efforts. For them, success is only a dream, but for the top athletes,
success is as real as a Dallas Cowboy touchdown or a Reggie Jackson
home run.

What makes an athlete great? The answers to this question are often
as different as golf and tennis. Athletes have a variety of ideas about
the keys to sports success, and their training and conditioning programs reflect their views. What seems to work one week may fail the
next. What works with one athlete may fail with another. If a new
technique suddenly comes on the scene and seems to bring success,
athletes will rush to use it. All of the possible combinations are
tried and discarded and tried again. The misinformation, myths, and
misconceptions that float through the sports world merge into a whirl-
pool of inefficiency from which only a few athletes are able to escape
and realize their full potential. The questions remain: What makes
an athlete successful? Why is it that some people end up in the main-
stream of sports, while everyone else is sent to the stands to watch
and cheer? Is it all that hard work and conditioning? Is it superior, natural talent and ability? Or is it just old-fashioned good
luck?

The best way to answer these questions is to see how several of
today's top athletes have achieved success by taking charge of their
sports careers. The 1981 National Conference championship football
game between the Dallas Cowboys and the San Francisco 49ers is a
good place to start because it provides a perfect introduction to the
career of Joe Montana.

The game had been a cliff-hanger from the start; the season was
suddenly boiled down to sixty minutes of football, with the winning

team advancing to the Pontiac Silverdome and Super Bowl XVI. By the midpoint of the fourth quarter, Dallas had pulled ahead, 27 to 21, and the Cowboy fans began to relax. Across the field, the San Francisco fans were worried. Their team had been beating themselves all afternoon; the Niners had had six turnovers and had given up the lead three times. Dallas was winning the breaks as well as the game. But on the field, the 49ers seemed untouched by the excitement that surrounded them. They had just gotten the ball, and despite the bad news (six points down, eighty-nine yards from the goal, and 4:51 remaining), it was business as usual. No wonder: they had three time-outs left and Joe Montana at quarterback.

In college, Joe Montana was nicknamed the "Comeback Kid." As a Notre Dame quarterback, he had shown an unshakable nerve in leading his team to six come-from-behind victories against equally good opponents and storybook odds. During his last college game, the 1979 Cotton Bowl, Montana and company overcame a minus-six-degree chill factor, a twenty-two-point deficit, and the Houston Cougars to pull off one of the most surprising rallies in college football. The comeback started with a blocked punt that led to a touchdown. With the fans on their way to the exits and only 4:15 remaining, Montana scored Notre Dame's fourth touchdown on a two-yard run. He passed for the two-point conversion to bring the score to 34-28. In an incredible finish, Notre Dame got the ball back, and Montana's last pass as a college quarterback tied the game just as the final gun sounded. The extra point kick was good, and the Fighting Irish won 35 to 34.

If history repeats itself, it did so for Montana during the 1981 National Conference championship game in San Francisco. The eighty-nine-yard drive against the Dallas Cowboys took just over four minutes and ended with a touchdown pass from Montana to split end Dwight Clark. The kick for the extra point was good, and the 49ers were on their way to Super Bowl XVI and a game with the Cincinnati Bengals. San Francisco won the game, 26 to 21, and Montana was voted the game's Most Valuable Player. Three years later, in 1985, Montana led the 49ers to their second Super Bowl victory with a 38-16 win over the Miami Dolphins. Montana was again voted the game's MVP.

Success for Joe Montana was in many ways a dream come true. Today, he is a superstar with a long string of sports successes that began back in his hometown of Monongahela, Pennsylvania. As a youngster, Montana was a constant competitor. His interest in sports, his determination, and his leadership ability gave him the All-American Kid qualities that seemed as natural to him then as his pinpoint passing does today. His father was the first to encourage him to participate in sports, and he became his biggest fan and probably his best teacher.

Joe Montana (copy-
right © Michael
Zagaris).

Montana played football, baseball, and basketball, and he was good at all three sports. Football, however, attracted him the most, and he set his mind on excelling as a quarterback. Montana recalled his decision for a cover story in *Newsweek*: "I never thought about playing anything but quarterback. That's the position they talk about on TV, the one you dream about when you're running in your yard." Once, for a high school game, he was asked to play safety. He practiced poorly on purpose so that he would be moved back to quarterback. "Heck, that's what I am," he said flatly. "A quarterback."[1]

[1]Copyright 1982 by Newsweek Inc. All Rights Reserved. Reprinted by Permission. (See Foot-notes, page 230.)

Montana seems to be a natural athlete and even a natural quarter-back, but what goes unnoticed by everyone today are the hours and weeks and years of practice. The thousands of passes that were thrown to the neighborhood kids and at a tire swinging on the end of a rope are overlooked by everyone but Montana and his dad. Montana's father saw to it that his son had plenty of opportunity to practice in the backyard and to play in organized leagues. Those years of coaching and encouragement paid off, and Montana learned the skills and leadership qualities that are the trademarks of his game today.

About a half-dozen years before Joe Montana was born, Johnny Bench made a decision to be a major league baseball player. In Ira Berkow's book *Beyond the Dream: Occasional Heroes of Sports,* Bench explained his motivations and his early baseball goals: "Since I was four or five years old, that's all I wanted to be, a major league baseball player. I watched Mickey Mantle on television. He had been like me once, a kid from a small town in Oklahoma. I wanted to be a star like him, playing in all the great ball parks. And I wanted to have lots of money so that I could retire and go to Europe and ski, or go camping when I wanted, or play golf all over."[2]

Johnny Bench played major league baseball for sixteen seasons; in the process, he reached his childhood goals long before he retired in 1983. For most of those years, Bench led the Cincinnati Reds from one of the most important but least glamorous positions: catcher! When all the strains of that position are considered, catching for a major league team might be likened to pulling hazardous duty in a war zone. The equipment a catcher needs should serve as a fair warning of the hazards. Along with the regular uniform, a catcher wears a padded mask with steel bars across the face, a throat guard, a heavily padded chest and stomach protector, and steel shin guards. To catch the ball, he uses a padded mitt that could double as a bumper on a small economy car. His list of job responsibilities is awesome: crouch behind home plate for nine innings with a bat whizzing overhead; set the infield; call the pitches; catch the ball; throw out the base runners; catch the pop-ups and foul-tips; snag the bunts; and get a hit when batting.

Johnny Bench is one of the greatest catchers in baseball history. He played on four World Series teams and won the Series twice. He was the first catcher in major league baseball to win Rookie of the Year honors, and he won the National League's Most Valuable Player award two times. Bench hit a career high of forty-five home runs in a single season, and he led the league twice in home runs and three times in RBIs. His career batting average is .270.

Johnny Bench's life story is a perfect answer to the question, What makes an athletes great? Bench grew up in Binger, a small town in Oklahoma. His father had been a semi-pro catcher and wanted his three sons to excel in baseball, but Binger was so small Bench's father had to organize the Little League so his boys would have a team. With his father coaching him, Johnny learned to throw from a crouched position; he had to be able to hit all three bases with precise, rifle-shot throws. He practiced for hours catching pop-ups and snagging bunts. During the season, he watched the major league games on television and followed the careers of the best players.

Bench set his mind on a major league career and never changed it. In recalling his decision years later, he remembered his early confidence and determination. "In the second grade they asked us what we wanted to be. Some said they wanted to be a farmer. Some said a rancher or cowboy. I said I wanted to be a ballplayer, and they laughed. In the eighth grade they asked the same question, and I said ballplayer, and they laughed a little more. By the eleventh grade no one was laughing."[3]

The years of practice paid off. Johnny developed his throwing skills so well that in high school he played both pitcher and catcher (but not at the same time). He had a .675 batting average and was one of the best high school ballplayers in the nation. The Cincinnati Reds drafted Bench, and after a short minor league career, he became the Reds' starting catcher. Sixteen years later, after playing catcher and both first and third bases, Bench retired with his greatest honor still to come: induction into the National Baseball Hall of Fame.

There are hundreds of athletes who have managed their careers in such a way as to reach their full athletic potential. But one athlete today is living such an amazing success story that he is changing the whole complexion of the National Hockey League.

Ice hockey is a sport with blazing speed, slap shots, hat tricks, penalty boxes, blue lines, and black pucks. It is a fast-paced, action-packed sport that is the national passion of Canada. But for most Americans below the Canadian border, it has been a sport that somebody else watches and few people understand. Now, all of that is likely to change, if Wayne Gretzky has his way. And that is exactly what is happening on ice rinks all across North America. Wayne Gretzky is a superstar Canadian hockey player for the Edmonton Oilers, who is revolutionizing hockey with his brand of high-speed skating, passing, and shooting.

What is so great about Gretzky? Well, when he started the 1981-82 season, only two players in the history of the National Hockey League

Wayne Gretzky won his fifth consecutive scoring title during the 1984-85 NHL season. Gretzky scored seventy-three goals and had a record 135 assists for a total of 208 points (courtesy of Karhu-Titan).

had scored fifty goals in the first fifty games of the season. Gretzky scored fifty goals in the first thirty-nine games. When the season ended, he had rewritten the hockey record book by scoring ninety-two goals and 212 total points. *Sports Illustrated* recognized Gretzky's accomplishments by naming him Sportsman of the Year. And during the 1983-84 season, Gretzky was just as awesome. He scored 205 total points during the regular season and thirty-five total points during the playoffs, leading the Oilers to their first NHL championship by helping to defeat the New York Islanders in the Stanley Cup finals.

What produced Gretzky's incredible accomplishments? First of all, his father had him on ice skates before he was three years old. His father had played hockey as a youngster and knew the type of training and preparation necessary for success. Wayne practiced for hours on a homemade ice rink his dad built; he improved his skating, developed his puck handling, and practiced shooting from every angle. Young Gretzky learned fast; at the age of five, he was competing successfully against boys almost twice his age. He followed his favorite pro teams and learned as much as he could about hockey. At the age of seventeen, he turned pro and continued toward stardom. Today after being voted the NHL's Most Valuable Player five seasons in a row, Gretzky is considered a Canadian national treasure. He is endorsing more than half-a-dozen products and has even made a movie about his life. Being the best player in the NHL has plenty of other rewards, including an income of more than one-million dollars a year.

The Building Blocks of Athletic Success

The athletic careers of Montana, Bench, and Gretzky contain individual differences, but several basic similarities can be found that helped them and other top athletes to succeed while thousands of others were quitting their sports programs. These career similarities are discussed below.

1. A competitive, energetic childhood. A child's participation in games and in physical activities like racing and wrestling helps to form the foundations of his or her future sports successes. Competitive, energetic play develops coordination, confidence, self-assertiveness, sociability, and intelligence. Both males and females are likely to have a strong desire to compete in sports if as children they are encouraged to participate in competitive, energetic play. Parents who are successful athletes will oftentimes have children who are also successful athletes partly because the parents encouraged their children to excel in competitive situations. These parents will invent situations that require the children to meet high standards in games and physical activities. If a child has a rich exposure to competitive situations and energetic play, he or she will begin developing the physical abilities and the personality traits that will enhance the learning of specific sports skills. As children, Montana, Bench, and Gretzky were encouraged to participate competitively and energetically in play and other activities that set the stage for their successful sports careers.

2. Family participation and sports instruction. James Scott Connors was learning tennis from his mother when he was four years old. After more than a decade-and-a-half of his mother's coaching and encouragement, Jimmy became a UCLA All-America and won the 1971 NCAA singles championship. Similarly, Nancy Lopez began playing golf with a club she borrowed from her mother, and with her father's instructions, she won her first tournament one year later — at age nine. She won the U.S. Golf Association's junior tournament when she was fifteen, the 1976 AIAW golf championship while on scholarship at Tulsa University, and nine LPGA tournaments during her rookie season on the pro tour.

Many parents overlook the importance of their participation and instructions in their children's athletic development and allow their children to learn their early sports habits and skills without the benefits of formal instructions or organized lessons. A lack of early super-

Nancy Lopez (courtesy of the Ladies Professional Golf Association).

vision can lead to the adoption of bad habits and incorrect skills that may mask a child's true potential by making him or her seem unsuited for competition or uninterested in sports participation. On the other hand, when a child's sports participation is supervised and he or she receives positive recognition from one or both parents or other family members, he or she will be more excited about athletics and will try harder to excel. As a result, the sports instructions and encouragement children receive from their parents and from organized lessons help to develop the basic sports skills and habits that will enable them to have continuous improvement and to move successfully to higher levels of competition.

Mary Decker Slaney
(courtesy of
NIKE, Inc.).

3. Personality development. The long-term success of Montana, Bench, Gretzky, and hundreds of other top athletes can be attributed directly to their personality development. Because of certain psychological factors, they were able to dedicate themselves to years of sports practice while their peers were participating in sports only in a casual fashion. The chief psychological factor in their success is their positive self-concept. An individual's self-concept is the total package of views he or she holds to be true about himself or herself. Montana, Bench, and other top athletes were able to succeed because their self-concept was that they were dedicated athletes deserving of success. The importance of personality in athletic development and its contribution to athletic success are explained in detail in Chapter 3.

4. Sports achievement and attraction. Mary Decker began running competitively when she was in the sixth grade. She set her first half-mile record, 2:12.7, at age thirteen. At fifteen, she was a world-class athlete and one of the top middle-distance runners in the United States. Since then, she has been setting and resetting records right and left. In July of 1982, Decker set a new women's world record in the mile run with a blistering 4:18.08. In a similar fashion, Tracy Austin was considered a world-class tennis player long before she turned pro at sixteen. As an amateur, she won almost every tennis tournament she entered and even appeared on the cover of *World Tennis* magazine at the age of four.

For both of these athletes and for hundreds of others, their sports achievements led to additional achievements and successes and, finally, to what seemed to be an unlimited athletic future. Sports achievements can be attributed almost entirely to a high level of coaching received by athletes and to the many hours of practice they devote to improving their sports skills. When athletes excel in sports, they are attracted by the attention they receive, and in consequence, participate more seriously; their desire for achievement grows and leads them toward greater successes and increased participation.

5. Constructive, goal-setting behavior. The decisions an athlete makes regarding goals and accomplishments will help to determine the direction of the athlete's entire sports career. Before Billie Jean King was a teenager, she made a decision that she would someday be one of the best tennis players in the world. As a result of that decision, she practiced almost every day, won her first Wimbledon title at age seventeen, and went on to an extraordinary tennis career.

The importance of constructive goal-setting behavior in building athletic greatness is obvious. A tremendous amount of planning and preparation is needed to enable an athlete to excel in any sport. The casual participants who do not establish their goals drop out as they fall behind the athletes who know what they want to accomplish and are working to make those accomplishments a reality. Constructive goal-setting behavior helps to build athletic greatness by giving athletes the direction and intensity they need to achieve their full athletic potential.

6. Intelligent, inspirational coaching. Every successful athlete can review his or her sports career and remember several coaches who had a tremendous, positive impact on his or her sports participation. Perhaps the athlete will remember the coach who offered special attention or instruction. The athlete may remember the coach who provided inspiration and motivation at a critical time when giving up and dropping out seemed to be the thing to do, or the athlete may remember the coach who made him work harder and pushed him further than he had ever gone before. Whatever the reason, top athletes are able to cite several examples of how they responded to their different coaches and how those coaches were able to help them excel. Intelligent, inspirational coaching will almost always make the difference between a second-place finish and a championship performance. The importance of good coaching is discussed further in Chapters 4 and 5.

7. Sports study and understanding. Larry Bird is arguably the best

Texas Coach Jody Conradt won Coach of the Year honors in 1980 and 1983. Intelligent, inspirational coaching is an essential ingredient in developing athletic greatness (photo by Susan Camp, courtesy of Women's Athletics, University of Texas).

all-around player in the National Basketball Association. He can do it all—score, play defense, rebound, block shots, make the plays, and lead the team. His perception of the action, his anticipation, and his reactions are incredible. Throughout a game he knows where all the players are and anticipates what they are going to do. As opportunities develop, Bird reacts accordingly; he may go for the basket himself, pass off for a quick assist, steal a pass, or block a shot. His contributions to the Celtics have made him one of the best playmakers in basketball.

This ability to comprehend the total flow of a game's action, to anticipate what is likely to happen, and to react as the action dictates is developed over time as an athlete gains a broader knowledge and a better understanding of all of the aspects of a sport. Anytime an athlete's sports knowledge is limited to only his personal responsibilities, then his total performance will be limited as well. But when an athlete understands a sport completely, he can turn his attention to what is happening in the game rather than having to concentrate totally on what he is doing. He can look for opportunities to control the action and make things happen. A thorough understanding of a sport comes

Larry Bird (courtesy of the Boston Celtics).

from analyzing actual competition, from reading books and articles about the sport, and from discussions of the sport with knowledgeable coaches and players.

Like Larry Bird, most successful athletes have a complete understanding of their sports that enables them to focus on the action and compete aggressively with no inhibitions about making mistakes and blowing games. As a result, they have higher personal goals, their accomplishments are greater, and they are more likely to succeed.

8. Continued conditioning and skill development. Successful athletes are in a constant battle to sharpen their skills and conditioning and to prevent them from deteriorating. After his fourth season as an outstanding running back with the Dallas Cowboys, Tony Dorsett knew that he could improve his performance and make a bigger contribution to the team. During the off-season Dorsett rekindled his desire to excel; he worked out regularly and reported to training camp in top condition. As a result, during the 1981 season, he carried the ball with more authority, fumbled less, and could be considered a genuine scoring threat each time he got the ball. At the end of the season, he had had his best rushing year, carrying the football for 1,732 yards, and he had led the Cowboys to the National Conference championship game.

In much the same way, Jimmy Connors became a better tennis player and rode his new style of playing to the 1982 Wimbledon singles title. There was no doubt in 1982 that Jimmy Connors was one of the best tennis players in the world, but his steady baseline play and his highpowered, two-handed backhand had not won him many of the major tournaments in the 1981 season. Several months before Wimbledon, Connors regrouped his tennis skills and taught himself a more aggressive style of play by improving his serve and following it to the net. At Wimbledon, in the championship match against John McEnroe, Connors's new serve-and-volly game was ferocious; he would rush the net, force the play, and win the point. His game was tremendously improved over his past few Wimbledon appearances. As a result, he earned his second All England Club title since first winning Wimbledon in 1974.

Athletes have to continually improve their conditioning and skills. Anytime individuals rely on agility and coordination alone, they will soon be outplayed and fall behind. Successful athletes make the most of every opportunity they have to improve.

9. Continued sports experience and success. An athlete builds his career in much the same way a boxer builds his record to earn a match against the champion in his weight class. A boxer has to have a long string of victories against good opponents to have any hope of earning a title shot. In the same way, the best athletes are always moving toward higher levels of competition. An athlete succeeds in high school, then in college, and then in the pros. Success leads an athlete to more serious participation and encourages him or her to have higher ambitions and more rewarding goals.

All nine of the above success factors contribute to an athlete's total sports achievement. It is not enough for you to see how Joe Montana or Nancy Lopez became successful without also comparing their lives and experiences with your own. There is, of course, no way for you to relive your past and change your early experiences, but, if you find a substantial lack of positive influences in one or more of the nine areas discussed, you can begin to make adjustments today that will compensate for any deficiencies. For example, an individual may be highly motivated to succeed in a sport and, as a consequence, do so in spite of his or her parents' lack of interest in athletics. Another athlete, faced with repeated early failures because of poor training, may have so strong a self-concept that he will not quit without first making an all-out effort. And often, an individual who decides to get serious about a sport at an older age will, with the aid of expert instruction and an exaggerated workout schedule, make up for a lack of early experience. Once you understand how these nine success factors lead an individual toward athletic excellence, you can begin to take charge of your sports career and set your own course toward the achievement of your full athletic potential.

Steve Garvey: It's Purely Dedication[4]

Soon after the 1983 baseball season opened, Steve Garvey set a new National League record when he played in his 1,207th consecutive game. On the way to that milestone, in 1974, he was voted the National League's Most Valuable Player. Garvey has maintained a lifetime batting average of .300, has appeared in nine All-Star Games, and has clearly established himself as one of the premier baseball players in the game today. In an interview, Garvey spoke of his career in baseball and of the route to sports success.

QUESTION: What feelings did you have as a youngster that caused you to make a commitment to sports?

GARVEY: I was really a big fan of football, basketball, and baseball. As a child, I would go out in the morning and stay until the sun went down, playing as much as I could. I was an organizer; I tried to get as many games going during the week as possible. Baseball was probably my best sport because I seemed to have more Godgiven talent. I just enjoyed it. I enjoyed all the aspects of baseball; the running, the hitting, the catching, and the throwing. Baseball involves more of a total use of your body, and that was the most appealing aspect to me—along with being a team sport where I could have a lot of interaction with friends and teammates.

Probably, as we all do, I had dreams of becoming a major league player. But I was a realist; I knew that I needed a college education and that coaching would be a good vocation for me. I really didn't have any commitments one way or another until I went to college. I thought I'd probably be more successful in baseball, but I played both football and baseball. I was offered a contract with the Dodgers, and of course, they being my favorite team, I signed with them.

QUESTION: Do you feel that it is better for an athlete today to go into a college program rather than going straight from high school into the minor leagues?

GARVEY: In the long run, yes. The additional education and the quality of baseball on the college level make it more appealing and, I think, better for the athlete. I was fortunate to be able to go to college and play two years of college baseball. After that, when I did sign with the Dodgers, I stipulated in my contract that I had to attend the remaining three terms of college, and it worked out for the best. I graduated in four-and-one-half years.

QUESTION: Can an athlete who is not a "natural" make it through hard work and dedication?

GARVEY: I think so. I've seen a lot of players that just don't have the polished skills or the great speed or strength, but they have worked hard to become very, very good competitors and highly successful people.

QUESTION: As you prepared for a professional career, do you feel that you worked harder than your teammates who were in college or the minor leagues?

GARVEY: I don't know—everybody worked hard. I was fortunate to have good hand-and-eye coordination and to have been successful. I put in the extra work that was needed. A lot of guys worked as hard; probably nobody worked harder. I think it all paid off.

QUESTION: What does it take to make it in the long run from high school, through college, and into the pros? In looking back, would you have any advice for athletes who are just beginning?

GARVEY: I think it's purely dedication—a willingness to make all of the sacrifices, to play as much as possible, to be as coachable as you can be, and to learn and apply the coaching techniques and individual techniques that can help you become a better player.

I would tell a young athlete to get as much enjoyment out of playing as possible and to try to develop himself

Steve Garvey was voted the Most Valuable player of the 1984 National League Championship Series (courtesy of the San Diego Padres).

physically, mentally, and spiritually, because this is the time when he really develops his standards, his principles, and his habits. The harder we work, the more it becomes a habit, and we learn that hard work turns into success and that whatever we achieve in life will be relative to our standards, our principles, and our preparation.

Are Athletes Born or Made?

Heredity and sports success have been linked together for years. This issue is important because it affects the way many individuals value their own athletic ability and the way some parents support and encourage their children to participate in athletics. The subject is often hotly debated: How much of an athlete's performance is the result of heredity, and how much is the result of his or her environment?

Nowhere is the idea of a natural-born athlete more vigorously supported than in the sport of horse racing. Each year, horse owners spend millions of dollars to breed the best mares with top horses like Secretariat, Spectacular Bid, and Seattle Slew. The idea is simple enough: breed the best bloodlines available in order to produce winners. At race time, millions more are spent as bettors try to estimate the speed and endurance the racehorses may have inherited from their famous and not-so-famous parents and grandparents. The fact is, however, that speed does not always beget speed; in looking at the most famous sires and their immediate offspring, one sees more also-rans than champions. And each year a number of "nobody" horses will pop up and surprise everyone. Before he reached his peak, John Henry, the 1981 Horse of the Year, was written off as a loser and sold for $1,100. But in 1984, he was the first thoroughbred to surpass the five-million-dollar mark in career winnings.

There is no doubt that a horse has to be born with the capability for speed and endurance in order to compete in the top levels of racing, but there are hundreds of ways to lose races between the first day of training and the Kentucky Derby. Such things as nutrition, veterinary care, conditioning programs, the horse's schedule, and the jockey and race-day track conditions can make a tremendous difference in the animal's ability to run with the best. The effect of the environment on human athletes is equally obvious. Regardless of an athlete's heredity, there are hundreds of positive and negative environmental factors that will influence his training and his success.

Several studies conducted in recent years have sought to determine the impact heredity has on athletic ability. Researchers have isolated several physical characteristics that enhance athletic ability. These characteristics include the body's ability to deliver oxygen to the muscles; bodily proportions, such as the length of an individual's arms and legs; muscle-fiber makeup; intelligence; and coordination. All of these physical characteristics contribute to an athlete's total success, but they are only parts of a whole; they are the raw materials of success. Without the contributions of the environment, such as conditioning and skill improvement, and the development of a sincere desire to excel in sports, an athlete's physical characteristics are of little value.

The question of natural ability is raised anytime athletes exhibit exceptional skills in their sports. Researchers have divided sports skills into two groups: specific and general. Specific skills are those that apply to only one sport, such as throwing a baseball, serving a tennis ball, and punting a football. General skills are those that transfer from one sport to another, such as running and jumping. The physical characteristics mentioned above can help athletes perform both specific and general skills, but without the proper training and conditioning, they cannot produce athletic excellence. This is nowhere more obvious than in professional sports. Today's professional sports competitors are gifted, talented individuals with exceptional physical characteristics, but they are not natural-born athletes who can do everything that there is to do in sports. For example, the best baseball players are not prepared to compete in pro soccer or basketball. The top golfers and tennis players cannot pull on ice skates or shoulder pads and compete in professional hockey or football. All of these athletes are specialized in their particular sports. They are not athletic supermen, but highly trained individuals who have succeeded by developing the talents that they have and channelling them into sports where they are the best suited for competition.

Most researchers agree that an individual's heredity establishes the upper limits of all of his or her talents and abilities and that the individual's environment determines how close he or she will come to reaching those limits. Musical aptitude is an excellent example. Many individuals have inherited the ability to hear and reproduce muscial sounds, but only a small number of people will reach the upper limits of their musical aptitude. Those who do so will reach their limits only after years of practice. Unfortunately, as far as musical ability goes, if an individual cannot reproduce musical sounds, he or she probably will not become much of a musician. Similarly, athletes who reach the upper limits of their athletic ability will do so after years of practice. Fortunately, however, athletic ability is not as restricted as musical ability. In athletics, if an individual does not have the ability to excel in one sport, that does not mean that he or she cannot excel in other sports. The specific skills required for different sports make each sport unique. Once an athlete determines what seems to be his "inherited potential" and what sport or sports he seems to be best suited to play, he can then capitalize on his environment (such as coaching, conditioning, and skill development) and work toward the realization of his full athletic potential.

The answer to the question "Are athletes born or made?" is that great athletes rely on *both* heredity and environment for success. Athletic greatness is a result of inherited characteristics and environmental factors coming together to produce superior performances. But what an athlete must realize when heredity and environment are compared is that *environment is the more important factor* in determining long-term athletic success. It is the training, the coaching, and the hard work, rather than heredity, that makes the difference between an also-ran and an all-star.

What Makes an Athlete Great?

Three overriding factors contribute to long-term athletic success and produce athletic greatness (see the chart on page 19). In order of importance these factors are: *personality, opportunity* (representing environment), and *heredity.* Heredity is an overriding factor in the achievement of athletic success because it establishes the upper limits of an individual's ability. Opportunity is an overriding factor because athletes have to have the necessary time, the sports facilities, the training, and the equipment to develop their abilities and interests. Most individuals have inherited about an average amount of athletic ability and also have at least an average amount of opportunity to participate in several sports.

Occasionally, however, individuals who may appear to have less than an average amount of athletic ability or who may have had less than the average amount of opportunity to participate in sports become successful, superstar athletes who excel despite these or other disadvantages. Glenn Cunningham's story is perhaps the most famous example. After his feet and legs were severely burned and he was told by doctors that he would never run again, Cunningham set his goal to be a champion runner. By 1934, he surpassed that goal and held the world record in the mile run.

This example and many similar ones demonstrate that the most critical of these three facts is personality — or in other words — the psychological makeup of the athletes themselves. Admittedly, there are athletes who appear to have inherited a wheelbarrow load of natural ability or who may have had more time and better facilities to practice and improve themselves. But even in the case of these athletes, their personalities allow them to be dedicated to the development of whatever natural talent they have and to make the most of their sports opportunities. Great athletes are great because their personalities have allowed them to consciously or unconsciously take control of their sports careers and to approach the upper limits of their full athletic potential.

Every athlete in sports today can take control of his or her own sports career and do the same.

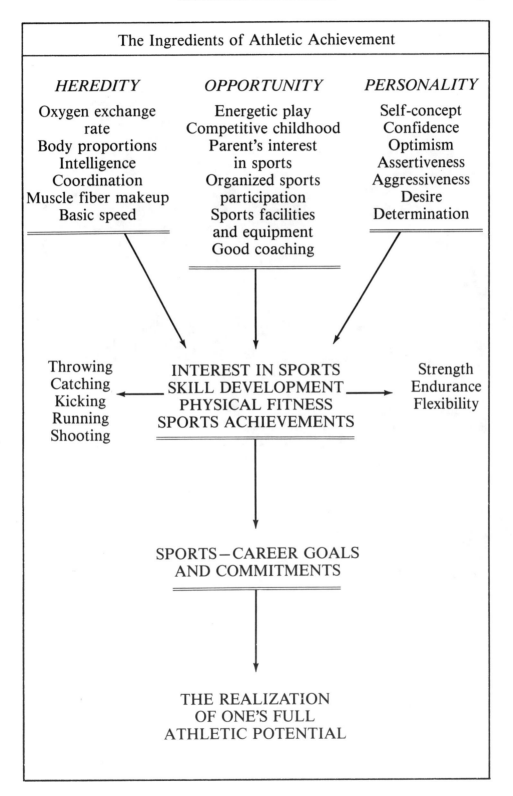

The Ingredients of Athletic Achievement

HEREDITY

Oxygen exchange
rate
Body proportions
Intelligence
Coordination
Muscle fiber makeup
Basic speed

OPPORTUNITY

Energetic play
Competitive childhood
Parent's interest
in sports
Organized sports
participation
Sports facilities
and equipment
Good coaching

PERSONALITY

Self-concept
Confidence
Optimism
Assertiveness
Aggressiveness
Desire
Determination

Throwing
Catching
Kicking
Running
Shooting

INTEREST IN SPORTS
SKILL DEVELOPMENT
PHYSICAL FITNESS
SPORTS ACHIEVEMENTS

Strength
Endurance
Flexibility

SPORTS—CAREER GOALS
AND COMMITMENTS

THE REALIZATION
OF ONE'S FULL
ATHLETIC POTENTIAL

Tom Landry (courtesy of the Dallas Cowboys).

Chapter 2
Managing Your Sports Career

A HEAD COACH HAS A LONG LIST OF CRITICAL DECISIONS THAT HAVE TO BE made regarding every aspect of his team's success. There are too many variables that change from season to season and week to week to make coaching routine. Experience may streamline his coaching style, but a head coach's concerns for details and specifics will not be diminished. How many quality players does he have? Does the team have speed and size and strength? The questions also cover injuries, skills, conditioning, flexibility, and attitudes. A head coach has to make judgments about the competition and balance an unlimited number of strengths and weaknesses to get his team ready to play each new opponent.

An athlete is in control of his or her own sports future in the same way that a head coach controls the future of his team. Your long-term success hinges directly on how quickly and effectively you take control of and manage your sports career. *All of the efforts of the best coaches and the best athletic departments will be ineffective if you have not made a commitment to sports achievement and have not accepted the responsibility for your own success.* With the help of your parents and coaches, you have to evaluate your potential, set your goals, and then follow through. This chapter discusses several management decisions that will help you plan your sports career.

Why Play Sports Anyway?

The first step in managing your sports career is to understand your reasons for participating. To be successful, you have to know why you are playing, because, whatever your motivation, it will affect the outcome. Most individuals begin playing organized sports with a wait-and-see attitude. Their friends are playing, and it seems to be the thing to do. The majority of athletes continue in sports without really considering or realizing why they are participating or what they even expect to accomplish. The list below contains several common reasons that may describe why you are participating in athletics.

★ You enjoy the participation.
★ You enjoy the competition.
★ You feel peer pressure and want to be popular.
★ You want to compete in several sports.
★ You want to achieve certain sports goals.
★ You want to maintain physical fitness.
★ You want the prestige of playing.
★ You want to earn the respect of parents, coaches, or others.
★ You want the chance to become a top athlete.
★ You want the opportunity to earn a scholarship.
★ You hope your participation will lead to a future career (pro sports, coaching, etc.).
★ You are expected to participate.
★ You want to participate.

As you decide how many of these reasons (or any others) apply to you, you might use one of the last two reasons as the heading of your list. Obviously, when you are participating because you want to take part, your results will be different than when you are participating because you are expected to take part.

Your understanding of why you are participating is the seed from which all growth and improvement will come. It will make a great deal of difference if you realize that you are getting up at five in the morning to swim three miles because you have set some specific sports goals, instead of doing it because it "builds good character." The success of a long off-season program will depend on your understanding of why you are out there knocking yourself out while your friends are enjoying their freedom.

As you go through this chapter, take some time to consider all of your reasons for participating in athletics. If you are playing sports for the fun of it, to be part of a team, or just for kicks, that is fine—get after it. On the other hand, if you are playing to develop yourself and you have set some specific goals that include being the best athlete you can be, then recognize that fact and begin to use it to your advantage.

Bob Lilly: Football Should be Fun[1]

During his fourteen-year career with the Dallas Cowboys, Bob Lilly played in seven Pro Bowls and established himself as one of the greatest players in the game. His brilliant career was capped on August 2, 1980, when he was inducted into the Pro Football Hall of Fame. In an interview, Lilly spoke of his love of sports, why he played football, the route to the pros, and the importance of college.

LILLY: I really wanted to play football; I thought it was great. I had a good knowledge of the game because I'd been watching it since I was about seven or eight years old. I looked up to all the athletes and thought it was a great sport. I played basketball, too. I enjoyed all sports; they were really my recreation. As I got older, as a junior and a senior in high school, I did have visions of getting a scholarship because I had grown to six-foot-four and weighed over 200 pounds; so I thought I had a good chance of going to college. But getting a scholarship didn't really change my feelings toward the game; I still played because I liked it.

I think that football should be played, in the early years at least, for fun, without any thoughts of going to college or playing pro football. It should be played because you enjoy it. It's wholesome, and I think it is good for your body. A person has to assess his qualifications as he gets older and sees that he has the ability and potential to play in college. There are many avenues you can take: a junior college, a small college, or a major college. When you see that you have the potential to play in college, that is the time to increase your weight program and to do what you can to improve yourself.

I think that, when you are in college and playing football, you should get an education. If an athlete is talking to the pro scouts and feels he has the ability, he can start think-

Bob Lilly (courtesy of the Dallas Cowboys).

ing in terms of pro football. But the Number 1 reason to go to college is to get an education. Only after being drafted would I concern myself with agents and money; that would be getting the cart before the horse. Football should always be fun. It's fun in the pros or in college or in high school; that doesn't change. The people who are going to make it are going to enjoy the practices and enjoy the work.

The Players and the Playmakers

When coaches talk about their athletes, they often divide them into two groups: the players and the playmakers. The playmakers, like Lawrence Taylor and Magic Johnson, seem to have a knack for their sports; they are usually in the right place at the right time, ready to mix it up and make something happen. The players, on the other hand, are always more conservative; they are seldom in the thick of the action and rarely make big plays or come through in the clutch. The difference in their styles of play can be seen in their levels of self-confidence, their desire to excel, their attitudes toward success and failure, and the goals they have set for themselves. Any athlete may compete at different times as either a playmaker or a player, depending on the confidence and the desire he or she has at the time to contribute to the final outcome of each game or meet.

Playmakers have high goals for themselves and are motivated toward success. They have a strong desire to excel in their sports, and they have a high degree of confidence that they can contribute to their own success and the success of their teams. In all sports, athletes have a specific assignment on each play or point and a general responsibility to contribute to the overall team effort. If athletes are playmakers, they will not only be concerned with completing their personal assignments, but they will try to participate in the total action of each play. Playmakers will take calculated risks, play as aggressively as possible, and look for opportunities to make things happen and to make breaks for their teams. Because they are high achievers, playmakers expect to succeed at the things they do; they are usually team leaders and are highly respected by their teammates and coaches for their contributions to the team's success.

The players, unlike their counterparts, are not highly aggressive and are not likely to control the action and make things happen. They are competing with a fear-of-failure attitude or a fear-of-success attitude that causes them to have low individual goals and makes them compete below their actual level of ability. Unlike the playmakers, they lack either the self-confidence or the desire to make any major contributions to the team's success.

Fear-of-failure players lack confidence in their overall ability. They are afraid that no matter how hard they try they are going to fail, and, therefore, they do not make a genuine effort to succeed. A fear-of-failure athlete will play a conservative game, avoid taking many risks, and concentrate all of his or her efforts on personal assignments in the game. These athletes are usually intimidated by their coaches and competition, afraid of being injured, and worried about causing their teams to lose. Their fears prevent them from playing heads-up ball, from getting into the flow of the action, and from looking for big-play opportunities.

While the fear-of-failure players lack the confidence that would enable them to succeed, the *fear-of-success players* lack the desire to excel and want to avoid the responsibility that comes from being top-notch athletes. In fact, fear-of-success players have the confidence

Carl Lewis at the 1984 Summer Olympics (courtesy AP/Wide World Photos).

that they could make bigger contributions to their teams by putting out a 100-percent effort, but they are afraid that they will be expected to play that well time and time again. These athletes do not want to cause their teams to lose, but they feel uncomfortable in leadership positions and especially uncomfortable when other people are depending on them for the team's success. Unlike the playmakers, fear-of-success athletes rarely make second efforts and never challenge themselves to excel or to become complete successes.

Playmakers and players can be seen in all sports. In football, playmakers will try to cause fumbles, intercept passes, sack ballcarriers, and block punts. Playmakers in basketball will mix it up, tie up the ball, and jump at the chance to steal a pass. The players are more reserved; when they recover a fumble or grab a rebound, it is often by happenstance. In baseball, a coach will have to push a fear-of-failure player off the base to get him to steal. But a playmaker cannot wait for a chance to steal a base, run out a bunt, or hit for the fences. If a playmaker has two strikes against him, he will hang in there ready to swing, fully expecting to get a hit. A fear-of-failure player will probably cause himself to strike out or be surprised if he gets a hit. In track, fear-of-success athletes will never run a 200-meter or 400-meter race with a 100-percent effort; they will always save enough to get through the race and later remind themselves that they could have done better if they had really wanted to work that hard. In tennis, a fear-of-failure player will spend more time hoping her opponent will double fault, rather than concentrating on making a good return herself. A playmaker, however, cannot wait for the change to turn a hard serve into a crisp passing shot.

Coaches may unconsciously encourage one or the other types of play with the instructions they give their athletes. For example, a coach might say, "Don't strike out" or "Don't miss that kick." When the instructions are "don't do this" or "don't do that," the athletes will worry about failing instead of planning to succeed. However, if a coach's instructions are positive — "Play your best" or "Watch the ball and swing through it," — the athletes will be more likely to concentrate on the actions that produce success and will make good things happen in competition. Team members can best encourage each other to be playmakers with statements that stress fundamentals, reminding each other to "stay in position," "play heads-up," or "follow the ball."

There are several things that you can do to help yourself become a playmaker instead of just a player in a sport. First, you should fully develop your athletic skills and your knowledge of a sport. If you are worried that you cannot return an opponent's serve, cannot sink long putts, cannot remember your assignments, cannot bunt well, or cannot catch passes consistently, you will be preoccupied during all or part of the contest and will not be able to concentrate on giving your best effort. If, however, you know that you can play well enough to participate aggressively in the action of each play or point, it will improve your confidence. It is this confidence that will allow you to concentrate on the action and to start looking for opportunities to make things happen and to contribute to the final outcome.

There will be times when athletes are equally matched or overmatched, and their self-confidence will drop. In such a situation, you will have to consider the final outcome as the only indicator of success or failure. Playmakers may be beaten several times, they may strike out three times in a row, or they may blow all of their free throws — but they will not let these setbacks determine their total performance. Because they view the final outcome as the indicator of success, they can continue working toward success and contributing to the team's effort regardless of any setbacks.

You can also be a playmaker in your overall athletic career. Poor conditioning, long workouts, individual defeats, and minor injuries can bring about the end of an athlete's career if he loses sight of his reasons for participating in a sport. Because playmakers have a strong desire to succeed, they will look beyond the individual defeats, the long hours of practice, and the sacrifices required, and will keep their sights on their overall athletic goals, such as excellence in high school sports, a college athletic scholarship, a pro career, or a coaching job. This type of positive, long-range orientation will be a major factor in helping you achieve your sports goals.

As the manager of your sports career, you need to analyze your participation. Are you a playmaker or just a player? If you find that you are fighting off negative thoughts and worrying about mistakes and

John Elway (courtesy of the Denver Broncos).

failures, look for the source of your anxiety. If you are always holding back, afraid to excel, and afraid to put out a 100-percent effort, examine your motivations for playing. You may need to develop more meaningful goals and the desire to reach those goals. You may also need to improve your confidence by spending more time working on your skills and getting into better condition through a complete running and weight-training program. You can become a playmaker by concentrating on a successful outcome in all your sports activities and, then, by doing all you can to make that outcome a reality.

Sports Specialization

An athlete's decision about which sport or sports he or she will compete in is one of the most crucial career decisions that must be made. Because the demands of competition always increase, an athlete must consider specializing in a single sport which offers him or her the best opportunities to excel. Specialization speeds the development of specific sport skills, builds good practice attitudes and habits, increases an athlete's knowledge and understanding of a sport, exposes the athlete to the best available competition, and provides the athlete with the greatest opportunities for long-term success. As Chapter 1 points out, today's professional athletes have succeeded because of their high degree of expertise in one sport. Even in college, most athletes compete in only their best sport. The high school superstars, who may have lettered in several sports, usually concentrated on one sport in college or combine a team sport with track events.

There are, however, several disadvantages to specialization. The first disadvantage is burn-out. The many hours of practice and competition can be too much for some athletes and cause them to want to quit the sport completely. The second disadvantage of specialization is that it prevents athletes from discovering other sports which they might find more enjoyable or might be better equipped to play. The third disadvantage deals with forced specialization. If someone other than the athlete makes the decision to specialize in a sport, it can cause the athlete to reject athletics altogether and to lose all interest in sports. But the positive gains usually outweigh the negatives. And even when an athlete changes sports after a period of specialization, all is not lost, because the general skills that are improved and the good practice habits that are developed will transfer to other sports and give the athlete a head start in those sports.

Single-participant sports, such as golf, tennis, or gymnastics, usually require earlier specialization than is required for team sports. This is

**All-America Kath-
leen Cummings. In
the single partici-
pant sports, like
tennis, specializa-
tion is necessary to
enable an athlete to
reach his or her full
potential (photo by
Susan Camp, cour-
tesy of Woman's
Athletics, University
of Texas).**

so because, for single participant sports, five or six or more full years
of practice are generally needed to bring an athlete to the upper limits
of his or her full potential. If, for example, an athlete begins serious
golf specialization at age ten, he will begin reaching the upper limits of
his full golf potential when he is about sixteen or seventeen. A serious
misjudgment can be made when an individual predicts his potential
after only one or two seasons of haphazard participation in a sport.
Early specialization in a single-participant sport is the best way to provide ample time for specific skill development and to get an athlete
moving toward the realization of his or her full potential.

Specialization in a team sport, however, is not usually necessary or
desirable until an athlete is at least a junior or senior in high school. At
age fifteen, a football player may suddenly grow six inches and
become a better basketball prospect. If he has already specialized in
football, he will be considerably behind in developing his basketball
skills. The reason for delayed specialization in a team sport is that

most athletes will not have a good idea of their potential until they have had several years experience in several sports. A broad experience with a number of sports will prevent athletes from becoming locked-in to a sport they may not be suited to play when they are older.

As you are deciding when and how to specialize you should consider what your best sport or sports are as well as your overall athletic goals. You must also consider the total opportunities for success that each sport offers. A talented football player who is also a good golfer may decide to specialize in golf because he feels that he will have less chance of injury in golf and a longer period of time in which to develop his skills for a pro career. An athlete who is good in both basketball and baseball may choose baseball because of the minor league opportunities available in baseball. An athlete who plays both soccer and football may decide to stick to soccer because of the expected growth of soccer in the next ten years.

The question of specialization should definitely be decided before an athlete is a senior in high school. This is especially important if an athlete has hopes of a college scholarship. When a college coach is considering an athlete for a scholarship, he will base his final decision almost entirely on the athlete's senior season. For this reason, an athlete should plan to specialize in one sport during his senior year and should follow a complete off-season program both before and after his last year in high school. In doing this, he will be able to have a top-notch senior season, and at the same time, he will be improving his skills and getting ready for his first year as a college athlete. A college coach does not really care if an athlete is a four-sport letterman or not. He is looking for individuals who can play the sport he coaches and play it better than anyone else. The number of points an athlete averages in basketball will not bring more football recruiters to scout his football games. The same is true in other sports: basketball coaches want basketball players; baseball coaches want baseball players; tennis coaches want tennis players.

Specialization for an all-around athlete is sometimes hard because so many people expect him or her to play several sports. In his senior year, when a football player needs to be in training for his first college season, the basketball coach or baseball coach may come around and try to convince him to play one more season for the school. They will tell the athlete that the team needs him to have a shot at the city title. This pressure will make it hard for him not to play. But an athlete has to make his decision based on what is best for him. If a football player wrecks his knee in baseball, he may lose his scholarship, or he may not be ready to play college football because of a long baseball season. During the football season, a senior basketball player should skip football altogether and practice his roundball skills. Specialization in the single participant sports is even more important than team sport specialization because competition for scholarships in the single participant sports is usually heavier than for scholarships in the team sports, especially at the major colleges. The number of touchdowns a tennis player or golfer scores during the football season will not help him get a tennis or golf scholarship.

The question all athletes have to ask is: "How can I best invest my sports time?" If you want to be a four-sport letterman in high school, that is fine. But if you want to earn a scholarship to one of the best colleges in the nation, a place on the U.S. Olympic Team, or a chance to play a sport professionally, you need to begin zeroing in on one or two sports and, finally, to specialize in the sport that offers you the best opportunities to reach your goals.

A Short Course in Nutrition[2]

As the manager of your sports career, you are responsible for seeing that you eat a well planned, balanced diet. Even if you do not cook your own meals, you should select your foods wisely and offer suggestions as to what your meals should include. The following information from the U.S. Department of Agriculture and the Food and Drug Administration will help you do both.

Your diet should supply your body with seven basic nutrients: protein, carbohydrates, fats, vitamins, minerals, fiber, and water. All of these nutrients are essential for maintaining life, for growth and repair of tissue, for meeting the body's energy needs, and for aiding elimination.

Proteins are necessary for such functions as building and repairing body tissue, for the production of antibodies, enzymes, hormones, and hemoglobin, and for use as a reserve energy source. About 10 to 15 percent of the total calories in your diet should be in the form of protein. Most people consume two to three times as much protein each day as their bodies actually need to function

properly. Athletes *do not need to increase* their protein intake above the normal recommended levels. When more protein is eaten than the body actually needs, the extra protein will be converted to body fat. Meat, fish, eggs, poultry, milk, and cheese are high quality sources of protein. Additional sources include dry beans, dry peas, nuts, and peanut butter.

Carbohydrates supply energy as the body's primary fuel. Digestion turns carbohydrates into simple sugars that are converted by the liver into glycogen and glucose (blood sugar). Carbohydrates that are not used for immediate energy needs are stored in the body as fat. Cereal grains, potatoes, many fruits and vegetables, sugar cane, and many processed foods such as breads, baked goods, and spaghetti are major sources of carbohydrates.

Fats are a source of reserve energy and are essential to the body for proper growth. Sources of fat include butter, margarine, cooking and salad oils, and fat particles in meats and dairy products. Excessive amounts of fats in the diet can lead to a variety of health problems.

Vitamins play an important role in body processes such as converting energy from foods, promoting healthy tissue growth, and aiding the normal function of the nerves and muscles. A well balanced diet will provide a good supply of the vitamins needed by the body each day.

Minerals help the body perform numerous vital functions and maintain healthy tissues. Calcium is the most abundant mineral in the body and helps maintain strong teeth and bones. Other minerals include phosphorus, iodine, magnesium, copper, and zinc. Iron is necessary for the blood to carry oxygen and carbon dioxide to and from the cells.

Fiber is added to the diet from such sources as the stems of salad greens, celery, wheat bran, and apple skins. Fiber is necessary for normal action of the intestinal tract and for the removal of waste from the body. Research indicates that a good supply of fiber may protect the body from a number of non-infectious health problems, such as cancer of the colon.

Water makes up about two-thirds of the body and is essential for life. Water is taken into the body from many sources such as fruits, vegetables, meats, and even breads. The body needs about sixty-four ounces of water each day.

The Four Food Groups. If you will select your food from the four food groups every day, you will be eating a balanced diet. The U.S. Department of Agriculture makes these recommendations: *Meat group*—two or more servings per day. Count as one serving: two to three ounces of meat, fish, or poultry; one egg; one-half cup of cooked dry beans, dry peas, or lentils. *Vegetable-fruit group*—four or more servings per day. Count as one serving: one-half cup of vegetables or fruit; or a portion as ordinarily served, such as one medium apple,

banana, orange, or potato. *Milk group*—four or more servings per day for teenagers, two servings or more for adults. Count as one serving: one eight-ounce glass of milk; one-and-one-half cups of ice cream; a two-inch cube of Cheddar-type cheese; or one-and-one-half cups of cottage cheese. *Bread-cereal group*—four servings or more per day. Count as one serving: one slice of bread; one ounce of ready-to-eat cereal; three-fourths cup of cooked cereal, rice, noodles, or spaghetti. *Other foods*—include unenriched, refined breads, cereals, flours; butter, margarine, vegetable oils, other fats.

Planning your meals. The following suggestions offer a balanced diet with a variety of foods:

Breakfast

Fruit or juice—fresh, canned, or frozen

Cereal—ready-to-eat or cooked

Protein—meat, eggs, bacon, ham, or sausage

Bread—hot cakes, waffles, French Toast, or toast

Beverage—milk is the best choice

Lunch and Dinner

Soup or salad with dressing

Protein—one or more servings per meal

Vegetables—select two or more per meal

Bread or rolls—with butter or margarine

Dessert—fresh fruit, cookies, cake, ice cream, etc.

Beverage—milk is the best choice

The recommended daily dietary allowances vary for males and females, and the recommendations increase for both male and female athletes depending on how active they are during the day. For example, an athlete may need 1,000 to 4,000 additional calories per day during a strenuous training period. The body's needs for protein, carbohydrates, fats, vitamins, minerals, and water will all increase as well.

To fill these needs, it is important that you eat a balanced diet and expecially important that you eat a good, balanced breakfast. During the night your body has fasted; in the morning it's ready to be fed. Don't get in the habit of having a snack and a bottle of pop for breakfast or lunch or supper. If you don't have time for breakfast, start getting up earlier. If no one will fix balanced meals for you, learn to fix them yourself. You are responsible for your own success both in and out of sports; eating a well planned, balanced diet will only increase your chances of reaching your goals.

Female Athletes: Write Your Own Winning Ticket

During the early 1970s less than 100 colleges offered athletic scholarships to women; today that number is closer to 700. This increase represents a far reaching acceptance of girls and women in sports at all levels of competition and has been brought about by numerous cultural and institutional changes. On the cultural side, attitudes have changed over the past few decades as more female athletes have competed in different sports and as the myths concerning female athletes and sports competition have been chipped away. Beliefs that girls and women are not interested in sports, that female bodies are not suited for sports competition and are prone to athletic injuries, and that female athletes should only compete in certain sports are all opinions of the uninformed or uneducated. Dozens of institutional changes such as better funding, coaching, equipment, and facilities have helped open the way for women to participate and excel in athletic competition.

An important consequence of these changes and of the increased opportunities for female athletes is that the quality of the sports competition itself is improving. The execution of sports skills, the speed and strength of the athletes, and their overall performances are being built to higher and higher levels. No longer can a female athlete approach her sport or sports with a haphazard attitude toward improvement and expect to come out a winner. The same type of intelligent, organized sports-career management that produced the great male champions of the past and present is necessary now to produce the female champions of the future. All of the sports-success strategies and sports-career management techniques explained in this book are applicable to male and female athletes. The dedication, planning, and preparation required to become a top-notch athlete knows no sex bias.

Success brings success. A female athlete can create her own opportunities by working hard and being successful in a sport. Ann Meyers'[3]

Ann Meyers (courtesy of Ann Meyers).

athletic career is a perfect example of a female athlete writing her own ticket to the top of the sports world. Ann grew up in a family with eleven children, and she was encouraged by everyone to participate in sports. She practiced her sports skills against both her brothers and sisters (her older brother Dave became a UCLA All-America and a forward for the Milwaukee Bucks in the NBA). Ann became an outstanding high school athlete and, at five foot nine, 130 pounds, one of the nation's top basketball recruits. Ann attended UCLA and with her steady ballhandling became the team's leading playmaker; she averaged almost eighteen points per game and was voted an All-America forward four years running. During her senior season in 1978, Meyers led the Bruins to the national championship. That same year, she was voted the UCLA Athlete of the Year, and her jersey was retired to both the National Basketball Hall of Fame in Springfield, Massachusetts, and the UCLA Hall of Fame.

Over the years, Ann Meyers has made the most of every opportunity she has had to play basketball. She was a star on the 1976 U.S. Olympic basketball team that won the silver medal in Montreal, she was a sensational player for the New Jersey Gems of the Women's Professional Basketball League, and she is the only woman to sign a contract to play in the National Basketball Association. Meyers has capitalized on her other sports opportunities as well. She is a sports broadcaster for CBS, ABC, and ESPN. And even with her television career, she has not given up active competition. For three years in a row, 1981, '82, and '83, Meyers competed in and won the women's superstars title on the ABC sports program *The Superstars*.

When Ann Meyers began playing basketball and other sports against her brothers and sister in the 1960s, there were few opportunities for women even to play on organized teams. But she stayed at it, shooting, dribbling, and sharpening her skills, never imagining the rainbow of opportunities that would open up to her as she met and excelled beyond each new challenge.

Today, the opportunities for girls and women in sports are wide open. You can begin writing your own ticket by setting your goals and working to reach them with the management techniques outlined in this book. In the process of achieving your full athletic potential, you will have plenty of opportunities to reach your goals and, like Ann Meyers, to showcase your athletic abilities.

What If You Lose?

Every athlete has lost at one time or another. And every athlete has had setbacks, failures, and disappointments. Babe Ruth struck out more often than he hit home runs. The Dallas Cowboys have lost three of five Super Bowls. Muhammad Ali won and lost the heavyweight championship three times. No matter how good you become, there will always be wins and losses, peaks and valleys. The important thing is how you feel about yourself after the losses and the disappointments and what you do to overcome them. It's easy to be a good winner — anyone can hold his or her head high after a big victory. The challenge lies in overcoming the defeats and disappointments and achieving your goals just the same.

When you make the decision to compete seriously in athletics, you take on three principal responsibilities: 1) to do everything you can in practice and training to develop your skills and abilities to the highest possible level; 2) to make the greatest effort you can in actual competition to perform your best and win the contest; and 3) to practice good sportsman- ship at all times. No one can ask you to do more. In fact, if you fulfill these three responsibilities completely while striving for excellence in everything you do, you will always *be able to hold your head high and feel good about yourself; regardless of your win/loss record, your sports career will be a success, and you can be just as proud of your accomplishments as any world champion can be of his or hers.*

Why Most Atheltic Careers Are Benched

An understanding of why most athletes fail to achieve their full athletic potential will help you to better manage your athletic career. Few top-notch competitors quit a sport because they are tired of being successful. In fact, the opposite is often the case, with former superstars refusing to retire even when it is obvious that they cannot compete as well as they once did. Most athletes, however, drop out of their sports programs because they feel that they are just "average" and that they can no longer compete with other athletes at their cur- rent level or at the level just above. Their willingness to leave organized sports competition before they reach their full athletic potential is often the result of having been caught in one or more of the three mental traps discussed below. Learn to recognize these traps and avoid the negative impact they can have on your athletic career.

1. Pedestalitis. Americans love their sports heroes and tend to quickly place them on a gleaming pedestal. In an age in which there are few frontiers left to conquer and even fewer Charles Lindberghs to admire, the sports arenas have produced heroes and heroines for each generation. The mass media bring these individuals into the homes and lives of everyone. Athletes are grouped with actors, actresses, and singers; together, they are all elevated to the top of the proverbial pedestal.

It is okay to admire an individual for his or her accomplishments as long as the person's limitations are kept in view. Pedestalitis occurs when an individual is so enamored with a superstar that he or she begins to imagine that the hero has miraculous talents and abilities that transcend human nature. Consequently, when the individual begins to judge his own abilities against those of the hero, he comes up short. This practice leads to a "why bother" attitude because the individual believes that he cannot do as well as the hero. Other people, such as parents or friends, may encourage pedestalitis by talking about how good an athlete has to be to "make it". They may blow size, speed, natural ability, and good luck out of proportion. Before long, the aspiring athlete sees him or herself as incapable or unworthy of such grand success as the hero has achieved, and then chooses the life of a fan over that of a participant.

The cure for pedestalitis is to judge yourself against your own level of competition. You should never allow yourself to become contaminated by the idea that success is only for a chosen few. The view of pedestalitis, that there is no room at the top, only serves to stop individuals from trying to be all that they can be.

2. A wait-and-see attitude. This trap is a spin-off of pedestalitis and a throwback to the fear of failure. It starts when an individual views the task of becoming a top athlete as an awesome affair. He is overcome by a fear of failure and dreads the embarrassment of anyone knowing if he fails to reach his athletic goals. As a result, such a person decides *not* to set any goals and to simply wait and see how good he becomes. The idea is simple enough: Without any goals, he cannot fail, and by continuing to participate, he might get lucky and make it. A typical wait-and-seer may work hard and appear to be dedicated to athletics. The individual may be an excellent athlete and may receive positive encouragement from his coaches and family, but he lacks the self-confidence to commit to any long-term goals.

An athlete who is content to wait-and-see brings an early end to his or her sports career in two ways. First, without any long-term goals, his physical preparation will suffer because he will not have any specific standards to meet. Even if he works hard and appears to be making progress, his intensity and consistency will gradually decline. Consequently, he will not be physically ready when the competition gets tougher. The second catch is the killer. Without far-reaching goals, the wait-and-seer is not mentally ready to succeed and will have no burning desire to continue once he or she hits the wall. Because he is setting himself up to fail, he will be mentally ready to throw in the towel. "I knew it," he will say. "I knew I couldn't make it; I knew it would get too hard." At this point, he will simply quit instead of working through the difficulty and continuing toward success. The wait-and-seer might have been good enough to continue playing at higher and higher levels of competition, but he was not prepared to make the effort.

The cure for a wait-and-see attitude is to adopt specific goals and to commit to them. If there is a suppressed desire to excel in athletics and that desire is encouraged, it will bloom and push you toward success.

Giving in to a fear of failure is simply failure in itself.

3. A lack of knowledge and initiative. This shortcoming is one of the most common reasons people fail to achieve their goals or to reach their full potential in all areas of life. What compounds a lack of knowledge and initiative is that these people are usually unaware that they do not have all the facts or that they have not made a complete effort to succeed.

In sports, a lack of knowledge and initiative can be seen in the athletes who depend totally on their coaches to make them successful. These people do not study their sports or practice their skills on their own, and they do not take the initiative in practices or games to look for ways to improve. Rather than do these things for themselves, these people want their coaches to do it all for them. A coach can help his or her athletes improve their sports knowledge and their physical conditioning. But the final responsibility for self-development rests with each individual athlete. The individual has to be responsible for going that extra distance. No coach or athletic department can make an athlete learn more about his or her sport. No coach can get a kid to put out 100 percent, unless he is willing to put out 100 percent for himself. No coach or school system can carry an individual to fame and fortune. Anytime an athlete lacks the initiative to improve his knowledge of his sport or to improve himself physically, he will be doomed to failure. Regardless of his ability, his competition will one day pass him by, and he will have nothing to do but drop out of his sports program.

There are no valid reasons for you to suffer from a lack of knowledge and initiative, and the cure for this mental trap is simple and obvious. What is hard about it is for people to realize that they have this shortcoming. The great thing is that you are responsible for your own success and by taking the initiative to learn all that you can about your sport(s) and to improve yourself as much as you can physically, you will most likely achieve everything that you want to achieve in sports and become the kind of athlete that you want to become.

Managing Your Sports Career—What Does It Mean?

Managing your sports career means doing everything necessary to achieve your full athletic potential. It means that you understand the many factors that make athletes successful and that you know what your own abilities are. It also means that you know how to change your sports program, such as training and conditioning, when necessary, to have a better opportunity to reach your true potential. You can begin successfully managing your sports career by answering the

following questions:
1. What are the nine building blocks to athletic success that are discussed in Chapter 1? Explain each of these.
2. How do heredity and environment contribute to athletic success?
3. Why do you want to participate in athletics?
4. Are you a player or a playmaker?
5. What is the difference between a success-type athlete and a fear-of-failure or a fear-of-success athlete?
6. How should you approach sports specialization?
7. How can you avoid the three mental traps?
8. What are your athletic goals? (See Chapter 3.)

This is not a test. But if you are sincere about succeeding in athletics, you should take the time to know and understand your answers to these questions. Write your answers out and review them from time to time.

Billie Jean King and Chris Evert Lloyd (AP/Wide World Photos).

Chapter 3
Personality and Athletic Success

AN ATHLETE'S PERSONALITY IS THE MOST IMPORTANT FACTOR IN DETER-mining his or her long-term athletic success. Personality is the psychological makeup of the individual which determines the individual's traits, thoughts, and interests and which determines the individual's motivational, emotional, and behavioral dispositions. As a result of their personalities, successful athletes maintain a consistent level of motivation and dedication that enables them to reach their goals. Their success is not a "maybe I will or maybe I won't" proposition; it is the result of an orderly process in which they act out behavior that carries them toward greater achievement and toward their full athletic potential. Their personalities establish their expectations, influence their goals, and finally, dictate their behavior. Personality is the driving force that propels athletes toward sports success and excellence.

Do You Have an Athletic Personality?

It is important for every athlete to take a close look at his or her personality and to understand how it influences behavior. College coaches do this all the time with the athletes they recruit, and they are not shy about getting the information they need. After hearing the high school coach's opinions of the athlete's physical ability, his family background, and his scholastic performance, the college coach will focus his questions on the athlete's personality: Is the athlete aggressive? Is he a leader? Does he get along with his teammates? Is he coachable? Is he goal-oriented? Is he responsible? An athlete's personality is a key to his or her style of play. A college coach wants to recruit athletes whose personalities and physical abilities will add to the total team effort and help the team win.

Dozens of studies have been conducted to determine whether there is a specific "athletic personality." Researchers have studied many groups: athletes versus nonathletes, male athletes versus female ath-

Planned success. Kitty and Peter Carruthers set their goals high and then laid the plans that would make them world-class athletes. After years of training, they faced their ultimate challenge at the 1984 Winter Olympic Games. Kitty and Peter skated away with the silver medal (copyright© by Howey Caufman).

letes, white athletes versus black athletes, and champion athletes versus nonchampion athletes. The following section contains a review of information that has been collected over the past three decades.

1. Differences between athletes and nonathletes. Studies comparing the personalities of athletes and nonathletes reveal certain tendencies among athletes. Both male and female athletes generally rate higher than nonathletes in the following trait areas: self-confidence, achievement, sociability, extraversion, dominance, leadership, aggressiveness, emotional stability, and adventurousness. These traits are considered to be positive characteristics in American society and are associated with a success-type of personality. Because sports participation provides many opportunities for individuals to excel in relation to their peers, it is natural that a high achiever with self-confidence and an aggressive personality will be comfortable in competitive sports situations. Individuals who are not attracted by the competition or the opportunity to excel will usually prefer other activities.

2. Differences between male and female athletes. Comparisons between male and female athletes have found few personality differences. Studies indicate that female athletes are just as likely to have a high number of success-type personality traits as their male counterparts.

3. Differences between black and white athletes. Comparisons of successful black and white athletes have failed to reveal significant personality differences. Personality traits seem to be the same in all high achievers regardless of race.

4. Differences between champion athletes and nonchampion athletes. Studies of champion athletes and nonchampion athletes indicate that world-class athletes normally have a higher drive to excel and are able to generate a more consistent singleness of purpose that allows them to be dedicated to the long-term quest for athletic excellence. Top athletes are usually more coachable and are more inclined to coach and motivate themselves when necessary. These athletes also appear to have stronger success-type personality traits than do nonchampion athletes.

These comparisons provide added support for the chart on page 19 that lists the ingredients of athletic success as heredity, opportunity, and personality. As stated in Chapter 1, an athlete's personality is the most critical of these three factors in determining his or her long-term success. *The important realization for an athlete is that his or her personality is a learned phenomenon, that it can be changed over time, and that he or she is not locked-in to a particular type of personality or behavior.* Everyone can take charge of his or her future by developing personality traits and roles that are consistent with desired goals and career plans. To help you do this, this chapter will show you how to mold your personality so that it reflects your true potential in and out of athletics and maximizes your chances of realizing that potential.

Ten Success Traits: How do You Compare?

The answer to why some people succeed and others fail can almost always be found when the personalities of the individuals are compared and examined in detail. Personality is the psychological makeup of an individual that controls his behavior and shapes his future. An individual's personality traits are learned patterns of behavior. The strength of each trait will vary depending on the experiences that shaped the individual's personality. When all self-made successes are considered, the more successful a person is (both in and out of athletics), the more likely it is that he or she will have a majority of the ten success traits discussed below.

1. Self-confidence. Self-confidence is a conscious faith in one's ability to perform specific tasks successfully. It is derived from the personal assurance an individual has that he can meet or exceed the demands that will be placed on him in a particular situation. In athletics, self-confidence grows from a deeply-held belief that an athlete can learn the skills, strategies, and techniques of his or her sport(s) and can respond in competition with a satisfactory-to-excellent performance. Self-confidence allows an athlete to grow in a sport, to develop better skills, and to achieve greater successes.

2. Ambition. Most successful athletes have a tremendous need to excel, to improve, and to succeed. Desire for achievement and prestige are a part of this trait. The ambition for greater accomplishment grows from a personal feeling which tells an individual that he is special, that he is unique, and that he deserves to be better than average. An individual's ambition to succeed is also the result of an awareness of the rewards of success and the belief that he or she deserves those rewards and is capable of earning or winning them.

3. Discipline and dedication. The nature of athletics requires that an athlete defer his rewards until sometime in the future when he is "good enough" to reach his goals. A tremendous amount of discipline, dedication, and patience is required for a person to be able to follow through with the necessary training and conditioning to achieve his or her full athletic potential.

4. Aggressiveness. Aggressiveness is a willingness to compete in an all-out fashion without holding back anything. Aggressiveness does not include a desire to cause injuries to others or to bend or break the rules; it is simply the feeling that, when a total effort is needed for success, the athlete will produce that effort. Aggressiveness is characterized by hard-nosed play, second and third efforts, and an unwillingness to give up until the task is completed successfully.

5. Mental toughness. Mental toughness allows an athlete to practice or compete without praise or encouragement, to follow through in high-stress situations, and to continue participating after setbacks and temporary failures. An athlete's mental toughness allows him or her to continue working toward success when goals seem unreachable and when other athletes are dropping out of the program.

6. Self-sufficiency. This trait indicates the ability to rely on oneself for motivation and coaching when necessary and to rely on one's own skills for success. It includes a high degree of confidence in one's decisions and in one's ability to succeed without the help of others.

7. Dominance and leadership. Because of his skills, confidence, ability, and knowledge, an athlete with a success-type personality is able to take charge of the situation and of the people around him. Other athletes will begin to rely on the dominant athlete and look to him or her for leadership and support.

8. Intelligence and openmindedness. A success-type athlete has a broad knowledge of his or her sport(s) and a willingness to acquire more. He is not intimidated by new ideas and new information. He is intelligent enough to evaluate this information wisely and to know how to apply it to his situation.

9. Extroversion and sociability. Successful athletes are usually more outgoing than their nonathletic peers and respond positively to public attention. They enjoy being around others, are usually gregarious, and generally take part in activities outside of athletics. They are socially aggressive and are confident in social situations. (The negative side of this trait is represented by the typical "jock" who is suffering from an inflated ego and who is often self-centered, obnoxious, and a general pain to those around him.)

10. Adventurousness. Adventurousness, or risk taking, is a product of confidence, observation, aggressiveness, and experience. This trait develops over time as athletes see that they can make breaks for their teams by exploiting situations to their advantage. Playmakers are usually the most adventurous athletes; they play all-out, doing everything possible to reach their goals. Adventurousness does not mean taking wild gambles or playing recklessly. Instead, it means following the action of the game and meeting personal assignments, while also looking for opportunities to make things happen. Adventurousness means taking calculated risks when the best opportunities present themselves. More often than not, these calculated risks will end in success.

The Self-Concept, Personality Roles, and Athletic Success

Sports psychology is the area of study in which athletics and personality are investigated to determine the mental factors that make athletic success possible. A large body of knowledge has been developed that describes the personality in terms of the self-concept and the behavior roles that individuals adopt during childhood. The self-concept is one of the most important elements of personality because individuals can learn to monitor and manipulate their self-concepts in such a way as to produce behavior roles that are conducive to the achievement of their goals and expectations.

Olympic gold medalist Phil Mahre has a strong success-type personality founded on self-confidence, desire, mental toughness, self-sufficiency, and adventurousness (courtesy of K2 Corporation).

A person's *self-concept* is a package of beliefs about himself or herself that includes self-image, self-interest, self-esteem, body-image, and ideal self-image. All of these beliefs work together to tell the individual what he is, how he will behave, and what he will become.

The term *self-interest* represents the psychological drive that keeps a person operating in a mental comfort zone. An individual will balance his interests and options with his other self views in order to determine what type of situations and activities he is comfortable pursuing.

The *body-image* is the perception an individual has about his body. It describes him physically. Is he athletic? Weak or strong? Fat or thin? An individual can improve his body-image through weight training and other conditioning programs. Athletes commonly use their body-images to determine what sports they will compete in and how aggressively they will play.

The *self-image* is the individual's conception of what kind of person he or she is. Is he a success or a failure, happy or unhappy, friendly or unfriendly, worthy or unworthy? Is he dependable, intelligent, responsible, coordinated, talented, honest, aggressive, sociable? The self-image dictates behavior because everyone acts out the type of behavior that is consistent with his view of himself. A child will develop his self-image from his experiences in his environment; he forms a picture of himself before he is a teenager and, more often, before he is seven or eight years old. If a child's self-image decisions remain unchanged after they are formed, they will control his behavior throughout his life.

The *ideal self-image* represents what kind of person the individual would *like to become* and reflects his conception of success. The ideal self-image pushes an individual toward success, happiness, or achievement in his or her primary areas of self-interest.

Self-esteem represents the way in which the individual judges himself in relation to what he is and what he would like to be or what he would like to accomplish. A person with high self-esteem is one who is satisfied with himself and with the things that he has accomplished or hopes someday to accomplish. A person with low self-esteem is one who experiences negative feelings about himself because he feels that he has fallen short and has not accomplished all that he should have.

All of these beliefs cause people to adopt specific *personality roles* that allow them to act in ways that are consistent with their self-concepts. If one person believes himself to be honest and dependable, then he will behave that way in every situation. If someone else believes he is a procrastinator and sloppy in his approach to life, then his behavior will automatically reflect that negative self-concept.

In much the same way, an individual's participation in athletics will be a direct reflection of his or her *athletic self-concept.* For example, if a person's self-image and body-image tell him that he is an excellent athlete, that he is in great shape, and that he puts out 100 percent, then that will be how he approaches athletics. If, however, his body-image is that of a weakling and his self-image is that of an average athlete, these views will be reflected in his sports participation. When an athlete views his potential as average, his goals and future will be just that. But when his *ideal athletic self-image* is one of great potential, with college, Olympic, or professional abilities, that view will help him set high goals and will encourage him to pursue them.

Chapters 1 and 2 provide examples of how top athletes like Joe Montana, Ann Meyers, and others have succeeded in athletics because of their self-concepts. They have a keen interest in their sports, they believe that they can control their own future, and they have high ideals for themselves. Their success is self-made; they planned to succeed, set their goals, and reached them.

The following six steps explain in detail how to realign your self-concept and adopt the personality roles that will lead you toward your full athletic potential. Developing a successful athletic self-concept does not mean that you will become a slave to athletics and be consumed in the quest for sports excellence. Instead, the whole process will streamline your efforts by zeroing in on the most productive aspects of career building. Your school work, your relations with family and friends, your free time, and your sports participation will work together, enabling you to move toward greater accomplishment and all-out success.

Six Steps to an Athletic Personality and Sports Success

The development of a successful athletic self-concept is not an overnight project. The total amount of desire and motivation you begin with will determine how quickly you can adopt this success-type behavior. If you are already moving toward your full potential, you can use this section to organize that effort. Other athletes may need a complete self-concept overhaul. In either case, you should read this section several times, complete the exercises, and refer back to them often. You can use what you learn here as a guide to success in any area both in and out of athletics.

STEP 1: REPROGRAM YOUR THINKING

Every individual develops a mental image that describes what kind of person he or she is. This image is normally developed as a result of the individual's experiences during childhood and is based on childhood perceptions of how other people acted toward him or her. Consider these statements:

"You sure are coordinated."
"Good catch. You never miss."
"You're a natural."
"Look how good you are."

And these:

"You're always falling down."
"You're always the slowest one."
"Don't waste your time with sports."
"You run like a duck."

Several other comments often heard by children are: "You're the greatest kid in the world." "You're a darn nuisance." "You're always good." "Can't you do anything right?" "You're pretty smart." "You're dumb."

Each of these statements combines with others to form a positive or negative pattern. As a certain type of statement is repeatedly directed toward the same child, he or she will begin to believe the statements are true. Consequently, a child will shape his self views around what his parents and other people tell him, and his self-concept will develop accordingly (smart/dumb, happy/sad, worthy/unworthy) and will shape his behavior.

A good example of parent-programmed thinking is childhood fears. No child is born afraid of the dark, of heights, of water, or of bugs. These fears are learned reactions. Being shy is a learned behavior as well. Often a child is perfectly happy not saying a word to strangers. He is not afraid; he simply has nothing to say. But a nervous mother or father will quickly offer an excuse for the child: "Little Johnny is so shy. It takes him a long time to warm up to people." If the child hears this kind of statement often enough—about any type of behavior—he will gradually accept that type of behavior as part of his self-concept.

An athlete can realign his athletic self-concept through the same kind of programming, but now it is self-programming. The usual list of success traits includes: aggressiveness, leadership, confidence, extroversion, dominance, and sociability. Like all other personality traits, these are learned behavior patterns. Reprogramming allows an athlete to adopt a success-type personality and benefit from the staying power it generates; he can then act out the personality roles that will help him achieve his full potential.

It is important to realize that reprogramming is not a simple matter of thinking more positively about your sports participation. Thinking you can—as did the little engine that could, huffing and puffing its way up the mountain—is not enough to change your long-term behavior patterns. The only way to change your behavior is to change your self-concept. You become a full-potential athlete by reprogramming the negative beliefs that warp your self-concept, which in turn will allow you to become the kind of person and the kind of athlete you really want to be.

The first phase in reprogramming is to realize and accept the fact that you control your future. Your success depends on you, not on heredity, on other people's opinions, or on good luck. You cannot let any negative decisions which you made as a child control your future. Often people blame their parents for their behavior without making any efforts at change: "Well, you made me the way I am. If I'm lazy (dumb, slow, selfish, shy, irresponsible, or whatever), I learned it from you." An individual should realize that his negative beliefs about himself are rarely true; everyone has a great deal of untapped potential. If, as a child, an athlete was discouraged from sports participation, he can make up for that disadvantage now. If he feels he is not worthy of success, he can take a new look at that belief. If he has a low opinion of his ability, he can make a new assessment based on his true ability and potential. Reprogramming allows you to be free from negative beliefs and to take control of your lifestyle and your future.

The second phase in reprogramming is to begin and maintain an internal dialogue about the feelings you have about yourself and your future. As you read the rest of this book, you will probably hit a few snags of pedestalitis, fear of failure, or the old wait-and-see attitude. When you consider a sports option, your mind may react with a knee-jerk thought, such as, "I can't do that" or "I'm not that good." If this reaction occurs, explore those feelings by establishing an inner dialogue. Ask yourself, "Why am I not that good?" or "Why can't I do that?" Never give in to an old idea that you should behave in a certain way unless that behavior is consistent with your goals.

Use your internal dialogue to reestablish your self-concept along the actual dimensions of your real abilities and potential. Realize that it *is possible* for you to have success-type personality traits as part of your self-concept and that you can succeed in athletics and reach your full athletic potential. Use the facts that you discover about yourself today and in the future to keep your self-concept up to date. The purpose of the first two chapters is to destroy the myths and mysteries of athletic success. Heredity, for example, only sets the upper limits of your ability. Reprogramming allows you to determine what those limits are and to work toward them. As you complete the next five steps, keep an open mind about yourself, your self-concept, and your potential as an athlete; continue your internal dialogue with your basic feelings, and realize that you are in control of your lifestyle and your future.

STEP 2: CONSIDER YOUR SPORTS OPTIONS

An athlete's success depends on his knowing exactly what he intends to accomplish and how he intends to accomplish it. Success has to be planned. The problem with a typical wait-and-see approach is that the athlete has no idea where he is going or what he hopes to accomplish. He is like a vacationer with no destinations and no expectations.

You can begin considering your sports options through a form of career planning called constructive daydreaming. *Constructive daydreaming* is a productive way of visualizing your future and determining what you want to accomplish in life. It is the process of imagining what you want to become and exploring ways in which you can construct that sort of lifestyle. When most people slip into a daydream, they do it without the intention of accomplishing anything or learning something new about themselves. But constructive daydreaming lets you examine what you really want to do in life and helps you to get started.

All-America Susan Shurr. It takes a championship self-concept to accomplish championship feats (photo by Susan Camp, courtesy of Women's Athletics, University of Texas).

To consider your sports options, you will need some free time during the day when you can be alone to explore your wants and needs and to determine what you hope to accomplish in life. About thirty minutes per session is plenty of time to develop several ideas and explore the pros and cons of each. Begin each session where you ended the previous one, and use some of your free time between sessions to organize the ideas you develop.

Start by imagining where you want to be in your life and what you want to have accomplished five and ten years into the future. Consider everything in and out of athletics. Do you want to play pro football or soccer or basketball? What about a coaching job? What kind of college degree do you want? Examine your sports career from high school through college and beyond. Fill in the details, such as weight-training and summer-conditioning programs. You may want a shot at the Olympics or a career as a professional tennis player or golfer. Imagine all of the details, such as the "crack" of a baseball flying off a bat or the sound of helmets popping on the football field. Imagine how much harder you can work out in a summer conditioning program or how you can learn more about your sport. Imagine improving at your position each year and playing at higher and higher levels of competition.

Everything has a beginning, a middle, and an end, and your constructive daydreams should contain all three phases. It is not enough to imagine that you are a professional tennis player without having imagined how you got there. The three phases do not have to come in their exact chronological order, but all three must be considered. As you examine each phase, you should work out the details of your future *as you would like it to be;* do not be concerned with what seems possible right now. You are dealing with the questions of *how* you would *like* your future to be. You are not wishing or hoping, but *actually planning what you want to become and what you want to accomplish.*

As you reach your conclusions, regardless of what they are, write them down and keep the list handy so that you can make additions and changes as necessary. Writing your ideas down will make them real and meaningful and will allow you to examine them in detail. In looking at your options, try to become more specific and include more aspects about your long-range future. Consider what will happen after your sports days are over. What do you want to have accomplished fifteen to twenty years from now? Or even twenty-five to thirty years? Consider everything that comes to your mind and add to your list all the accomplishments you would like to have to your name. The list should be both general and specific and should include as many possibilities as you can develop. Remember to refer back to Step 1 now and again and to continue your internal dialogue about your feelings.

STEP 3: DEVELOP A BURNING DESIRE FOR SELF-IMPROVEMENT

A burning desire for self-improvement is an integral part of an ideal athletic self-concept. It is not enough to believe that a particular accomplishment is possible and then make only a halfhearted attempt to achieve it. Holding back in order to say, "I could have made it if. . ." is a 100-percent failure technique. To succeed in athletics, you will have to develop a sincere, unwavering desire to bring about the positive changes and self-improvements that will allow you to reach your goals.

Anticipation is one of the most powerful forces in people's lives, but many individuals never realize its full impact. The excitement of life grows largely out of the anticipation of better things to come. You can develop a burning desire for a better future by linking your imagination with your expectations for the future. To do this, imagine what the rewards will be for achieving the things that you have listed as possible accomplishments. Imagine the pride, the satisfaction, and the material rewards that will return to you once you are successful. What will be the benefits to you and your family if you succeed? A college scholarship? Perhaps a professional sports career? A coaching job in a major program? A new home? New car? New freedoms and responsibilities? A college education would be a solid benefit. A variety of job options would be another. There are also gains to be received from peer approval and in the respect of your coaches and family. As soon as your anticipation of these benefits and rewards grows and as soon as you *expect* to receive them, you will be fueling your desire to succeed in athletics. Make a list of these benefits and keep the list handy for changes and additions. The more you focus on the rewards of your athletic career, the better will be your chances of attaining them and of achieving your best in sports.

STEP 4: SET YOUR GOALS

The lack of specific, well-planned goals is the most common reason people live unfulfilled lives. They never reach their full potential because they have failed to consider their options, evaluate their capabilities, and then establish any forward thinking goals. This pattern of behavior most often results from letting other people make the decisions. Many students are in school because that is where they are supposed to be. Their classes are planned for them, and they graduate because it is expected of them; they are simply going with the flow. They have resigned themselves to being participants in the process rather than the architects of their future.

One of the loneliest feelings for some students is hearing the school door slam and realizing that they are out in the real world. Even the most popular, most athletic, and most intelligent students can hear the door slam. Their lives in school have been rosy enough and filled with many successes. They have been channeled from one accomplishment to another by following the best consensus of opinions. Usually, these students have kept their noses clean, have made good grades, and have gotten a degree, but somehow things have not turned out as they might have expected or wanted. If they had any goals, they were not connected with any well thought out destinations.

An individual should begin to establish his specific goals after he has listed the accomplishments that are most important to him, and he can see the benefits he will receive from those successes. The following information will help you to begin outlining some specific goals.

1. Never establish a goal lightly. Often individuals get in the habit of setting goals with no intention of reaching them. The problem with this habit is that these nonserious goals get in the way of reasonable, obtainable goals; they also establish the behavior pattern of abandoning goals. You should use your imagination to consider all your goal-options plus the necessary work required to reach each goal. Then, you should establish your goals with the full intention of reaching each goal and a full knowledge of the benefits to be gained. Finally, you should form the habit of following through to reach each goal by developing a strong desire for its accomplishment.

2. Arrange your goals in the proper order. Outrageous goals are often the result of goals having been established in a backwards order. Any accomplishment is a step-by-step project. A baby cannot run until he or she has first crawled and then walked. Placing major goals before preliminary goals only sets the individual up for failure. This result can be avoided by following the next guideline.

3. Establish both short- and long-range goals. The nature of athletics requires that an athlete learn to defer his rewards because many years of practice are usually required to perfect one's athletic skills. But no one can function without any immediate rewards; there have to be minor accomplishments along the way. If you want to be a professional tennis player, start by winning the city title and then the regional tournaments. After that you can work up to the state and national level. A similar step-by-step procedure is needed in football, baseball, basketball, and every other sport. Earn a spot on the first-string, and go from there.

Roger Bannister was the first man in history to run a mile in less than four minutes. Bannister was a medical student at Oxford University in England when he began competing in the mile run. After running a mile under 4:30 as a freshman in 1947, Bannister set his sights on breaking the so-called four-minute barrier. The record in the mile run had been slowly dropping. In 1864, the world record was 4:56; by 1900 it stood at 4:15.6. In 1934, Glenn Cunningham, an American, set a new record of 4:06.8. Bannister broke 4:11 in 1950 and cut his time to 4:02 in the spring of 1953. Almost a full year later, on May 6, 1954, he shaved the last 2 seconds at a meet in Oxford, England. Bannister broke the "barrier" with a 3:59.4. The new mark was seen as the greatest accomplishment in sports history: he had done the "impossible."

Roger Bannister's goal of a sub-four-minute mile might have seemed outrageous to many, but he was dead serious about reaching it. He cut one second at a time and tried to peak higher at each meet. Bannister blazed the way in a seven-year quest by meeting short- and long-range goals that led him to the "impossible." Your future should contain both short- and long-range goals that will help you reach your full potential. The next guideline will help you keep moving forward toward your goals.

4. Make your goals known to others. One of the hardest things for many people to do is to announce their goals to others. This is usually a holdover from a fear of being laughed at or a fear of public failure. There will always be victims of pedestalitis who will scoff at anyone who attempts to better himself. An athlete simply has to side-step that kind of negative feedback.

If you do not set your goals lightly, you will find it easier to reveal them to other people. Revealing your goals will help you reach them in two ways. First, it puts a certain amount of pressure on you to succeed. This pressure will keep the goals in your mind. People will ask how you are coming along and also encourage you to succeed. Other people have no way of knowing what is important to an athlete until he tells them what he plans to accomplish. When an athlete's family and friends become aware of his goals and of how important those goals are to him, they can rally to his support and encourage him toward success.

The second reason for revealing your goals is to allow you to hear yourself discuss them. Your goals will come to life as you explain your reasons for making your decisions and announce the benefits you expect in return. The more you discuss your goals, the more real they will become and the more you will believe that you can reach them.

5. Remember that progress is success. Athletes sometimes become discouraged because they are not making gains as fast as they think they should. If you are doing everything you can to reach your goals, you should not become discouraged by your progress. It took Roger Bannister six years to clock a 4:02 in the mile run and a full year to cut the last two seconds. You should make a point of enjoying all of your progress. As long as you are not loafing or cutting corners in your program, all improvements, no matter how small, should be seen as successes building toward larger successes.

6. Change your goals carefully. There is no disgrace in changing goals and moving in an opposite direction as long as the changes are made with the same consideration that accompanied the setting of your original goals. Occasionally, two or three goals can be combined if that does not distract from your progress. The important point is to set well-planned goals; then few changes will have to be made.

WARNING: If anyone tells you that there is no need for you to start setting your goals now—that you should wait until you are a little bit older—that person is wrong. Absolutely wrong! Putting the decisions off will only make them harder. If you put off setting your sports goals, you will suddenly be too old to reach them when you finally decide to get started. When a counselor or coach tells a student it is okay to wait until he or she has a year or two of college before deciding what to major in, that person is only hurting the individual's chances of making a good decision. Career decisions can always be changed, but if no decision is made in the first place, the individual will lack the incentive to determine what he does want to do. The wrong career decision or the establishment of goals in the wrong area will force the individual to look for something he likes better. Having no goals provides a false sense of security and a tendency to take no action and engage in no planning at all.

Goals will not come to you like dreams in the night. They have to be encouraged and developed. If you have not established some specific athletic, academic, and vocational goals within three months of the first time you read this book, ask your school counselor or parents for some help. Write yourself a note that tells you to set your goals in three months, and tape the note to your bedroom wall. Then get busy! Start some constructive daydreaming and decide what it is that you want to do in sports and in other areas. If you cannot make a decision, ask for some help. Without any athletic goals, you will probably have a sad-to-average sports career. Without any academic and vocational goals, who knows what you will have?

Kyle Rote, Jr.: Set Your Own Challenges

In the *Complete Book of Soccer,* Kyle Rote, Jr., discusses how an athlete can turn short-term goals into personal challenges that will speed the development of sports skills and overall sports success. Rote believes an athlete's dedication and desire will set the stage for these self-improvements:

ROTE: I suppose the one outstanding trait common to all successful athletes is a fierce dedication to their chosen sport. A desire for self-improvement is the most important element of this dedication and can best be exemplified by the endless hours top athletes devote to training on their own.

It is important when you're on your own to devise various challenges for yourself. For example, you might decide to head the ball consecutively twenty times without its touching any other part of your body or the ground. In this situation, if the ball hits the ground after the eighteenth header you would have to start all over again. The same approach would work if you are practicing shooting against a wall or a wooden kickboard. There are endless challenges (goals) you can set yourself, and all of them will help you to take your practice sessions seriously as well as make them more enjoyable.[1]

Academic All-America Ellen Mayer combined her academic goals and athletic goals and succeeded at both. Mayer was a co-captain of the Cornell women's gymnastics team and won the New York state title in vaulting. At the same time, she maintained a 4.0 average in her pre-medicine major (photo by Jon Crispin, courtesy of Cornell University Athletics).

Step 5: Make a Personal Inventory

There is no way to know what ingredients an individual will need until he decides whether he is baking a cake or making a fruit salad. But as soon as the decision is made, the cook can look in the cupboard or head for the store. The same logic applies in making career decisions. An individual has no need to deadlift 300 pounds if he is going to be a history teacher. Nor will his speed in the forty or his vertical jump matter if he has no plans to play football or basketball. Until an athlete has begun to determine his athletic goals, he cannot be sure of the full extent of his strengths and weaknesses and their impact on his success. But as soon as he has begun to establish his direction, he can take stock of his abilities.

If you have set your sports goals or have started to narrow them down, now is the time to begin a personal inventory of your athletic assets and liabilities. You will use this inventory to design your specific plan of action to reach your goals. The most exciting thing about a personal inventory is that, as you mature both in age and experience, you will be gaining more assets and decreasing your liabilities. Job placement counselors are well aware that an individual's interests are as important in determining job success as his abilities and experience. The same is true for athletic success because an athlete who truly wants to succeed can overcome many shortcomings through hard work in his training and conditioning programs. A personal inventory allows you to know where to begin the work that will make your successes possible.

Every aspect of your athletic performance and ability should be included in your inventory. Height, weight, speed, and strength are obvious listings. The mental aspects should be included as well. How much do you know about the theory, techniques, and fundamentals of your best sport? How much reading do you do about your sport? Do you talk to your coaches about strategy and other matters? Include your attitude toward practice and conditioning. Do you follow a summer conditioning program? How hard do you work at it? How hard do you plan to work in the future?

An athlete should talk to his coaches and ask them what they feel are his abilities and liabilities and where he should improve. These comments should be included in the inventory. In this discussion you should tell your coaches of your plans for college, the pros, the Olympics, or whatever other goals you have and get their evaluation of your strengths and weaknesses in relation to those achievements. If there is a college team in the area, you might talk to the coaches about "what it takes" to make it on their level. When you ask people for their advice and they have time to respond, they will usually be happy to help.

An athlete's inventory should contain everything that might influence his athletic career either positively or negatively. A sample inventory is listed below:

Positive

Speed — 4.9 forty
Strength — average; 220 bench and 260 deadlift
Sports knowledge — good
Grades — top 25 percent of class
Leadership — average team leader
Good sports perception
Knows football theory
Thinks well under pressure
Respected by coaches

First-team player
Set record in 400 meter relay

Negative

Weight—too thin
Self-confidence—needs boost, worries about commitments
Aggressiveness—loafs in practice, doesn't like full contact
  drills
Needs more upper body and leg strength and size
Needs to be a better team leader
Needs a better, more consistent diet
Needs skill improvements on pass-catching and blocking
Needs better use of free time
Needs to specialize in one sport
Has no long-term athletic goals
Has been a wait-and-seer
Smokes pot at parties
Lets some studies slide
Is nervous speaking before the team and public groups
Has weak vocabulary and poor typing skills
Has a poor knowledge of college sports programs

Listen to your gut feelings and be honest in your personal inventory. Include everything that might affect your participation. In the case of the above example, nervousness in public speaking can affect team leadership ability. Poor typing and low vocabulary skills can increase the time required to complete your homework and term papers in college. Talk to your coaches and get their opinions of your strengths and weaknesses. Throw out any unconstructive criticism, listen to their constructive criticism, evaluate it, and add it to your list. If you say you want to be an athlete and someone says that you are wasting your time, scratch that person off your list of advisors and move on. Hundreds of athletes were told they were "too small" or "too slow" or too something to play sports, but they went ahead anyway. They did so in an organized fashion that made up for their shortcomings. Complete a list of your assets and your liabilities, include an estimate of your desire to succeed, and keep the list handy to use in developing your plan of action.

STEP 6: DEVELOP YOUR PLAN OF ACTION

This step will help you set your sports dreams and sports goals into motion. Your plan of action is as important to your success as a blueprint is to the construction of a building. Without a well-planned program designed to outline your progress, there will be no way to insure that you are doing all you can to reach your goals. A good plan of action eliminates the wasted time and stop-and-go behavior that sends thousands of athletes' careers to the showers.

WARNING: Do not think that you are too good to complete an inventory and work out a plan of action. Regardless of your level of participation, a good plan will streamline your progress and help you reach your goals in less time. By writing your plan down, you will transform it into a tangible program that you can examine, improve on, and expand. You can be sure that your future competition is busy designing their programs and moving toward their goals.

When you start your plan, get your lists out and refer back to them. An athlete's list of goals might read as follows:

> Go to college
> Get a good job
> Play pro football (tennis, golf, basketball, etc.)
> Get married and have a family
> Own a BMW
> Own a ski boat
> Be a three-year starter in college
> Be an All-America athlete
> Run for politics
> Be happy
> Have lots of money
> Go to Europe
> Study political science and history

Organize your list by rewriting it and combining the main areas. Being rich might include owning a BMW or a ski boat. Add more items if needed, but try to organize the list into major categories. Also, list the items in their order of importance. There is no need to be overly concerned with the exact order; if several things are equally important, list them one after another and go on. The above list might look like this after being revised:

> Be happy
> Get married and have a family
> Earn a college scholarship
> Graduate from college
> Succeed in college and professional sports
> Own a home or a ranch (or both)
> Follow a political or business career
> Go to Europe
> Open my own business
> Enjoy my hobbies

After you have decided on your goals, take a second look at the inventory you completed in Step 5. Usually everything in an inventory can be classified under one of the main headings of sports, education, or personal habits. An inventory often looks like a dirty closet with everything on the floor. When it is rearranged, everything fits together. The previous inventory in Step 5 could be organized as follows:

Sports: Positive—has average upper body strength and speed; plays well under pressure; is an average team leader; has good sports knowledge; knows football theory; has good perception; is a first-team player; set 400 meter record. Negative—needs more size, strength, and weight; needs to specialize in one sport; needs more upper body and leg strength; needs more dedication in summer workouts; needs more aggressiveness in practice; needs skill improvement; needs long-term athletic goals; lacks knowledge of college sports programs; wait-and-seer.

Education: Positive—top 25 percent of class; knows sports theory; performs under pressure. Negative—is nervous speaking in public; has poor typing and vocabulary skills; lets some studies slide.

Personal habits: Positive—average team leader; thinks well under pressure; respected by coaches; can be dedicated. Negative—needs more confidence; lacks personal goals; needs better use of free time; smokes dope at parties; worries about commitments; needs a better diet; wait-and-seer.

After you have organized your inventory into these major categories, it will be easier to handle. When you compare your inventory with your list of goals, the picture is clear. In the case of the above athlete, it is obvious that he is not working hard enough to have much of a shot at a college scholarship or a pro career. He is more of a participant on the team than a full-time athlete. His goal planning and dedication are both poor; he is going with the flow rather than planning his career. He is a typical wait-and-seer. His off-season conditioning is poor, and he is behind in his overall weight training. Without a change, he will not be able to measure up in a tough college program or even an easy one. He should be considered a fair-weather athlete; he needs a major self-concept overhaul and a new training and conditioning program.

A plan of action always has to start with the personal category. Making school and sports changes are of no value if the individual does not change any negative personal habits first. For example, a good weight training and conditioning program will be useless if the athlete has always been a procrastinator and fails to change that habit. A good plan of action for the above athlete would be based on the previous inventory and his list of goals, and would be as follows:

PERSONAL: Remember that my future in and out of sports is my responsibility. Develop an ideal athletic self-image and accept the responsibility for reaching that ideal. Work on my fear of commitments through better planning and by understanding my decisions and the goals I set. Establish an organized set of specific athletic goals and stick to them. Use my free time more productively. Take charge of my sports career with better workout programs. Make a serious effort to earn a college scholarship instead of just hoping it will happen. Try to become a complete athlete rather than being just part of the team. Ask my family for some support and encouragement and let them know how important my goals are. Ask them to attend more of my games. Develop the desire to be a better athlete than I am today. Cut out the pot. Keep a notebook of my progress and record all of my workouts in it. Tell my coaches, parents, and friends that I intend to get a college scholarship and work toward a pro career. Take charge of my career.

SCHOOL: Do more outside reading. Improve my vocabulary. Enroll in public speaking class and an advanced typing class. Use my free time more productively. Take a trip to a college to meet the coaches and try to learn more about several area colleges and their programs. Plan my college major.

SPORTS: Follow a regular off-season and in-season conditioning program to improve my speed and strength. Learn more about college recruiting and recruiting rules. Talk more to my high school coaches about a college career. Get serious about sports and develop an image of myself as a top-notch athlete and one who is dedicated to reaching his full athletic potential. Drop the wait-and-see attitude about my future. Keep a notebook of all my workouts and my progress. Become a playmaker and make things happen on the field. Take control of my career.

After you have organized a broad sweeping plan of action similar to the one above, begin dividing the plan into daily, weekly, monthly, and yearly projects. Outline in as much detail as possible the things that you need to do now—today—as well as the things that you need to do this week, this month, this year, and so on. Weight lifting, endurance training, and algebra homework may be on Monday's list. Next week's list might include talking to your school counselor about your college major, improving your skill development efforts, and completing a term paper. Keep your overall plan and your lists of "things to do" handy, refer to them often, make changes when

With CATAPOLE™ in hand, Billy Olson prepares for the upcoming vault (photo courtesy of POR-TaPIT/CATA-POLE, Divisions of AM-PRO Corporation).

necessary, and maintain a notebook of your progress and improvement. Your plan of action will have to include a complete conditioning program similar to the one outlined in Appendix A.

Unlock Your Full Potential

Your success in sticking to a year-round plan of action and working toward your full athletic potential will depend on your perception of yourself as an athlete. To understand this fact, think about your conscious and unconscious levels of thought. For example, say you are in your bedroom thinking about the Super Bowl, the Olympics, Wimbledon, the Masters, or anything else, and you decide that you need a drink of water. At that moment your brain makes your body stand up, walk toward the kitchen, balance itself, and dodge all the furniture and your brother's and sister's toys. When you get to the kitchen, your mind tells you to turn on the light, get a glass, turn on the water, wait until it is cool, fill up the glass, and take a drink. Now remember that you performed all of those actions without thinking about them at all—you were thinking about the Olympics or Wimbledon. You did not have to worry about walking, balancing yourself, or dodging the cat; your brain did all of that for you.

In exactly the same way, if you believe you are a top-notch athlete, your mind will make you adopt that personality role and move you toward your goals. On the other hand, if you believe you are only an average athlete, then you will put out only an average effort to reach your average goals. Your perception of yourself stems from your personality which, in turn, is a reflection of your self-concept. When you *expect* to be a top athlete and when you *expect* to succeed in a sport, the adoption of the personality roles that will get you there becomes automatic. To do this, you have to believe that you control your own future, you have to develop your goals and the desire to reach them, and you have to develop a plan of action to make it all happen.

As soon as you complete all six steps, everything will seem streamlined and you will find that you are moving toward your full athletic potential. Just as your mind unconsciously directed you into the kitchen for a drink of water, it will begin to propel you toward your atheltic goals. As you develop a positive, ideal athletic self-concept, your goals will always be in your mind, and you will begin to look forward to the practices, the weight-training exercises, the conditioning programs, and the skill-development sessions because you will be looking beyond the work involved to the improvement and the progress you will be making. Your desire for success will be real, and like Pete Rose (see box below), you will work as hard as possible to make it happen.

Pete Rose: The Ideal Athlete

Pete Rose is a self-made success. The same fellow they called a "show-off" and a "hot dog" over twenty years ago is still playing baseball and still setting the example for thousands of athletes to follow. Rose has led the way with a career that has seen one record-breaking performance after another. A third of the way through the 1982 season, Rose passed Henry Aaron and moved into the Number Two spot on the all-time career hit list behind Ty Cobb. It was Rose's 3,772nd career hit that moved him to second place. As the 1985 season began, Rose needed just 95 hits to break Ty Cobb's "unbreakable" career hit record of 4,191.

After more than twenty years, Pete Rose is still going strong and is playing his way right into the National Baseball Hall of Fame. Rose first earned nationwide recognition in 1963 when he was voted the National League's Rookie of the Year. Ten years later, he won the National League's Most Valuable Player award. To date, Rose has appeared in sixteen All-Star Games and has won two Golden Glove Awards and seven National League batting titles.

Thirteen years into his career, in 1975, *Sports Illustrated* named him Sportsman of the Year.

Pete Rose has worked hard to excel, and his career is a textbook example of how to become a successful athlete. Rose has completed all six of the steps to athletic success. He knows he can control his future and has inventoried his assets and decreased his liabilities. He has explored his options, established his goals, and developed a plan of action to reach them. What brings it all together is Rose's burning desire to succeed—to be the best he can be at all times. He is a playmaker in every sense of the word: he has total confidence in his offensive and defensive skills, he knows he can contribute to his own success and the success of his team, and he plays 100 percent against everyone on every pitch. Rose is the master of his skills, who is always looking for ways to improve and to be more efficient. Over the years, he has played first, second, and third base, and left and right field.

Pete Rose is a talented athlete. But it is his personality more than his talent that has made him the great athlete he is today. He has a success-type personality that will keep him going for years: Self-confidence? Rose has plenty—enough for himself and almost everyone on his team. Leadership? Rose is an all-around team leader; his leadership is a cornerstone for success. Extroversion and sociability? Rose will talk to anyone at any time, offer advice to younger players, and sign autographs for as long as there are takers. Aggressiveness? He wrote the book on aggressive play. Mental toughness? Rose is a competitor from the word "go." The few setbacks and slumps he has had have hardly slowed him down. Between the 1970 and 1981 seasons, Rose missed less than ten games. Self-sufficiency and dominance? You bet. Rose figures he can play against anyone, anywhere, and come out a winner. He pushes himself to excel; his goals are as high as a kite in a hurricane (and he is reaching them).

Pete Rose plays baseball with the enthusiasm of a Little Leaguer, the proficiency of an All-Star, and the experience of an old-timer. Rose is an ideal athlete who has worked hard to build and maintain a phenomenal career. At the same time, he has shown that success is possible for those athletes willing to pay the price to make it happen.

Mary Lou Retton at age 14 (copyright © 1982 by Ray Reiss).

Chapter 4
A Flying Start: Junior High
and High School Sports

THE SPORTS OPPORTUNITIES AT THE JUNIOR HIGH AND HIGH SCHOOL levels are wide open and are limited by nothing more than an athlete's enthusiasm and by his or her desire to improve. Interscholastic programs are designed to turn promising beginners into well-trained athletes who often become local sports stars. At the junior high and high school levels, it is common for poorly-trained athletes to dedicate themselves to a comprehensive off-season program and emerge as first-team players at the start of the next season. The opportunity to excel is so great that well-trained athletes should be able to write their own tickets in their best sport, if not in several sports.

The route through junior high and high school athletics is filled with many unforeseen roadblocks such as inadequate skill development, poor physical conditioning habits, inferior opposition and competition, careless injuries, mistaken decisions, slow progress in the classroom, and a lack of sports knowledge. This chapter will help you avoid these roadblocks by showing you how to manage your junior high and high school sports participation, how to become a more coachable athlete, and even how to coach yourself when necessary.

Good Coaches Build Champions

Despite a national fascination with sports, good coaching is often poorly understood, and yet, it is one of the most important factors in athletic success. Because coaching is so important, athletes must be able to evaluate their coaches and the impact each coach will have on their sports careers. The best way to understand good coaching is to be able to recognize bad coaching.

The biggest downfall of a bad coach is his or her inability to teach. Whether this failing is due to poor communication skills, a poor attitude toward details, or a lack of specific knowledge, a bad coach's teaching has a hard time sticking with his athletes. This problem is usually compounded by the coach's lack of patience and his tendency to intimidate his athletes. If the athletes do not learn their assignments or if they make mistakes in practice or games, the coach will jump all over them, heaping the blame for the team's poor progress on them, instead of accepting it himself. When a mistake occurs, the coach may punish an athlete by making him run bleachers or laps instead of working with him and teaching him what he does not know or has not learned to do.

A second shortcoming of bad coaches is their inability to relate to all of their athletes; this can be seen in their tendency to have pets. A bad coach will always single out a few athletes he really likes and a few he really likes to hate. The pets tend to be several of the better athletes who, for one reason or another, cannot see the coach's faults; or if they can see his faults, they are getting so much attention that the poor coaching does not matter. The athletes the coach loves to hate may be one or more of the good players on the team or a less fortunate "fatso" whom the coach enjoys humilating. Good players lose the coach's favor when he realizes they are sharp enough to recognize his weaknesses. If he cannot bluff them (as he can the pets), he will tolerate them and their participation to help himself look better, but he will try to ostracize them as often as possible.

A third trait of bad coaches is their overemphasis on sports and sports participation. As long as their teams win, these coaches get along well with their top athletes and people who contribute to the sports program. Bad coaches oftentimes blow winning out of proportion and may encourage athletes to break the rules or injure opponents. They will spend extra time helping the top athletes excel, but they lack a genuine desire to help the below-average-to-average athletes and the rest of the student body. Their inability to teach carries over into the classroom, where again, they are intimidators rather than respected educators.

In comes cases, head coaches may not be the best coaches or the most helpful coaches at a school. Athletes can recognize a head coach's incompetence when his or her only contribution to practice is telling the assistant coaches how many laps or wind sprints the athletes should run. Oftentimes a mass exodus of assistant coaches will mean that something is not right with the head coach. Few assistants enjoy making a name and a living for an incompetent head coach.

Because coaches can control an athlete's future by letting him play or keeping him on the bench, the athletes themselves are usually the last group to speak out against a bad coach. Facing the coach at the next practice would be impossible. And, if an individual's parents speak up about a coach, that too can be athletic suicide. For the most part, an athlete's hands are tied when it comes to a choice of coaches. Most likely, he or she cannot change schools and has no desire to change sports. The best route to take with a bad coach is to be a top survivor: work hard, earn your position, and try to have the best year you can. It is best not to rock the boat. Of course, if the coach's practices are hazardous to the health of his or her athletes, the coach should be reported to the administration.

A bad coach and a good one are as different as night and day. A good coach's assistants enjoy working on his staff and his athletes are eager to play on his teams. This is so because the coach demonstrates a broad understanding of his sport(s) that includes knowledge of fundamentals which can help his athletes improve their individual performances and knowledge of overall strategies for different game situations which will help the team win. The athletes can sense that the coach may be able to lead them to their common goals, and as the season progresses, they gain confidence in the coach and come to respect his coaching style and philosophy. As a result, the athletes will work hard in both practices and games and will feel good about giving 100 percent to the team's success.

A personality profile of a good coach will usually include all of the success-type personality traits associated with champion athletes. Good coaches have strong leadership skills. They are effective communicators and have the ability to motivate athletes to perform their best in actual competition and to work toward perfection in practices and off-season programs. Good coaches are high achievers and are dedicated to their positions; they work hard, leave nothing to chance, and accept the responsibility for getting their athletes mentally and physically ready for each game or meet or match. Good coaches respond well to competition and adjust their game plan accordingly. A good coach is a confident decision maker. When the coach calls a down-and-out pass, a quarterback sneak, or a fake field goal, he knows why he selected the play and why he thinks the play will be effective. But regardless of the outcome of each play or an entire game, good coaches are not blinded by winning and losing. They tie all of their experiences together, learn from them, and become better coaches. They use each victory and each defeat as stepping stones to personal improvements and to team improvements that will lead to the accomplishment of long-term goals.

The most common ingredient of good coaching is the ability to teach. Mistakes, weak skills, and poor execution lead straight to defeat. Coaching a team or an individual athlete and avoiding the defeats is complicated, detailed work. Every single aspect has to be taught and retaught. A good coach not only teaches well; he knows if his athletes have really learned their assignments and if the lessons will carry over to actual competitions. Good coaches are usually good-to-excellent classroom teachers. They are fair minded in their teaching and can easily be respected for their even-handed attitude to all students. A good coach is a people person who can relate to all kinds of individuals and who has a genuine interest in the future of both his athletes and his students.

An athlete can rest a little easier if he has a good coach helping him get a scholarship. He knows the coach's personality or individual goals will not get in the way of his future. The coach will be effective when meeting college recruiters and discussing the athlete's strengths and weaknesses. A good coach will never oversell an athlete to a college recruiter, but will do his best to match the athlete with the right college program and give him all the help and selling he needs.

Learn to recognize both good and bad coaches and to estimate the impact their coaching styles will have on your athletic career. If you have an unhelpful head coach, you will need to make adjustments and depend on yourself and on help from the good assistant coaches in order to reach your goals. To have a realistic hope of any long-term athletic success, you must evaluate the actual contributions each one of your coaches can make toward your future and, then, adjust your total sports program so that you will benefit from each coach's knowledge and coaching style.

Lorraine Borman: It Takes Total Commitment[1]

Lorraine Borman has coached figure skating for almost two decades. Her most celebrated student is Rosalynn Sumners, the 1984 Olympic silver medalist and 1983 World Figure Skating Champion. In an interview after Rosalynn's victory in the world championships, Coach Borman spoke of the factors that contribute to athletic success and the importance of a good athlete-coach relationship.

COACH BORMAN: An athlete's success is the result of hard work and mental talent. Some physical talent is necessary, but mental talent is much more important. Mental talent includes control of emotions, mental toughness, self-drive, and dedication. Above all, an athlete has to make a total commitment. I've had lots of skaters who had complete physical talent but who didn't make the mental effort; they thought their physical talent would take them along—but it doesn't. I'd rather see athletes who are not so naturally talented physically, but who have very sharp minds—I like working with them as their coach. If they make the commitment and have the drive behind them, they can usually get their bodies to do what they need to do.

The home situation plays a big part in the kids making it. The

Coach Lorraine Borman and Rosalynn Sumners (copyright © by Howey Caufman.)

parents need to be involved and need to be encouraging. They have to be astute about selecting a coach and have to let the coach know that they want the best for the athlete. You shouldn't hire a coach on reputation alone. I think a trial period is good. It's important to observe a coach over a period of time to see how well he or she works with athletes. What you should look for is a good personality match.

I feel that total preparation both mentally and physically is really the answer, and the coach has to promote that, while giving the athlete time to develop to her real potential. The coach has to help the athlete work through the obstacles and maintain her commitment. Too many times kids see great athletes winning gold medals and never realize what the poor athletes went through to win the medals. They never see the hard work or the obstacles these athletes overcame. It's not a bowl of cherries; there is a sour side—athletes have to work hard and make sacrifices. A good coach is important because he or she can help the athletes through tough times and help them maintain a total commitment. In return, the athlete needs to trust the coach and listen to the coach. There has to be a good one-to-one relationship. The coach is there to help the athletes follow through and complete their commitment to success.

Get Your Parents Behind You

The parent's role in the life of an athlete is as vital as good coaching. A child's first exposures to sports should be fun and encouraging, and the more sports a child is introduced to, the more likely he or she will be to have a genuine, lasting interest in athletics. This section is written for parents as much as for athletes because the most lasting athletic successes are usually family efforts.

A parent's role in a child's athletic career should have several facets, none of which should be ignored because of the parent's sex. The chief role is that of a fan, a coach, and a counselor. There is more to sports than blocking and tackling or serves and volleys, and a parent can help an athlete understand his or her total participation in a sport. Even when an athlete is being coached by well-trained, experienced coaches, an effort by the parents to help him understand the fundamentals and the strategy of the game will go a long way in improving his performance. Not every parent is cut out to be an active coach of a Little League team, but they are all cut out for an active involvement in the athlete's sports programs. During the season, a 100-percent attendance by the parents is not necessary, but a 40- or 50-percent record is encouraging to an athlete. The reason for this is not so much for the parent to root for the athlete, but to allow the parent to talk to him or her after the contest is over. In both victory and defeat, the parent's analysis of the athlete's performance should be reasonable and accurate. The coach should never become an undeserving scapegoat, nor should the athlete be spared any deserving criticism. This type of involvement by one or both parents will help the athlete maintain a proper perspective on his sports participation and will encourage him to grow and improve in athletics.

A parent can be a tremendous help to an athlete by taking an interest in his or her off-season program. Coaches do their best to encourage each athlete to stick to a summer workout program, but the athlete's enthusiasm will usually fade as other activities come to seem more important. When the parents recognize the impact of a good conditioning program and understand its contributions to the athlete's overall health, his lessened risk of injury, and his improved performance, they can begin to encourage him to follow the program and reap the benefits. If they know the requirements of the program, they can notice when the athlete is not working out and encourage him or her to stay with the routine. This kind of encouragement will make a big difference in an athlete's self-concept. Anytime an individual sees that his participation brings positive recognition, he will think more highly of his program and of himself.

An athlete cannot sit back and expect his or her parents automatically to know what to do and how to do it. As the manager of your sports career, you should ask your parents to get involved, but at the same time, you should realize that the world does not revolve around you. Oftentimes, parents need to be invited to the athlete's sports events and given time to adjust the demands of supporting a family to the athlete's season schedule. In some cases, the athlete may have to open up the lines of communication on the subject and actually ask for the encouragement he or she needs. It is not at all out of the question for you to coach your parents in a sport until they are competent and knowledgeable enough to do the same for you. At the same time, you can get your brother or sister to play catch or shoot baskets with you. Family members are good practice partners and are often more loyal than anyone else in the neighborhood. With a little coaching, an athlete can get every member of his family into the act and have a whole stable of training mates and fans.

Most of all (and this cannot be overstressed), you should not make the mistake of approaching athletics without telling your family what your goals are and explaining how you plan to reach them. Let them know that you are serious about athletics. You cannot expect any support if you have not opened up and asked for their help. Once your family is aware of your ambitions, your goals will be more meaningful, and you will be surprised by the assistance and the encouragement you receive.

Sports Success Strategies

Every athlete asks the same questions as he or she looks toward the future. How can I be better? What do I need to do to excel in my sport? How can I get a scholarship? Regardless of an athlete's sport, these questions and many others run through his mind and occasionally leave him confused and wondering if he is really doing enough to reach his goals.

The following information will help you take control of your junior high and high school sports programs and make them work for you and your goals. The earlier you start making the most of your sports programs, the more success you will have; if you are already a senior in high school, then there is that much more work to do in a shorter amount of time.

MATCH YOUR DESIRE AND YOUR SPORT(S)

Athletes usually select their sports for a variety of reasons. Perhaps their mother or father played the sport, or it is the most popular sport at their school, or their friends are all playing it. These are usually the wrong reasons to participate in any sport. You should look at your future in athletics from the perspective of what *you* really want to play and what *you* really want to accomplish.

In the past, male and female athletes have had the tendency to judge their total athletic ability on their football or basketball skills. If a boy could not play both football and basketball and a girl could not play basketball, they usually assumed they were not very good athletes. This attitude was reinforced when athletes in other sports did not get the same support that football and basketball players received. Fortunately, today more people (athletes and coaches included) are beginning to realize the tremendous accomplishments of athletes in all sports. There are numerous opportunities in gymnastics, golf, tennis, volleyball, swimming, and many other sports. The amateur soccer program across the nation seems to be growing faster than any other sport in history. The popularity of these sports indicates that athletes are matching their interests and abilities to a wide variety of sports, rather than playing just the traditional sports of football, basketball, or baseball.

In approaching junior high and high school athletics, you should consider all the aspects of specialization discussed in Chapter 2. You have to match your desire to compete in any sport with your goals and expectations for your future. Just as it makes no sense studying to be a doctor if you want to be a carpenter, it makes no sense for an athlete to waste his time warming the bench in one sport if his heart and goals are in another. Instead of spending your time being an average athlete in two or three or more sports, consider doubling or tripling your efforts in your best sport and become a top athlete in that sport. Examine all of your options and begin making some decisions and commitments to the sport or sports that offer you the best opportunities to excel.

Study Your Sport(s)

For many athletes, the full extent of their sports education begins and ends with what their coaches have told them and what they have seen on television. As soon as these athletes leave the locker room, they forget everything until the next practice. They know their assignments and where they are supposed to be, but everything else seems to escape them.

When an athlete's knowledge of a sport and of athletics in general increases, his performances and overall career will be greatly enhanced. There are dozens of books available that you can read to become more familiar with the specifics of any sport. The serious athlete should go to the library or borrow a few books from his coaches and begin his sports education. The biographical and autobiographical books will be valuable if you will ask questions that begin with "what," "why,"

Approximately 925,000 athletes play high school football in the United States each year (photo by David Cheatham, courtesy of David Crockett High School, Austin, Texas).

and "how." There are several good magazines available that provide technical information as well as good, inside looks at different sports.

Your knowledge of a sport can make a difference in what positions you play and in the responsibilities you have during games. To become a team captain or a team leader, you will need to know more than the average go-with-the flow players. Your sports knowledge can also help you get a college scholarship. The more you know about a sport, the more apt you will be to make a good impression when the college recruiters interview you. If a decision is close, a recruiter will always go with the sharper athlete because he or she is more likely to be an asset to the team.

There is plenty to learn about athletics — from conditioning and strategy to diet and injury prevention. All too often athletes prepare for their sports career by doing nothing more than lifting weights and

Basketball is the second most popular high school sport when ranked according to the number of participants (courtesy of *Dalhart Texan*).

running wind sprints. You should become as involved in your sport as you can. Spend at least an hour or two a week learning more about your sport, and do a little extra studying in the off-season. If you will learn more than just what your coaches are telling you and what you are seeing on television, you will be surprised at how much both your performances and career outlook will benefit.

IMPROVE YOUR PHYSICAL CONDITIONING

Most high school and junior high athletes get in shape just as the season starts and try to glide through on the wind sprints and laps their coaches make them run. In college and professional sports, the top athletes take a more serious approach by following year-round programs that include weight training, flexibility exercises, and speed

A year-round strength-training program should include three weight-training sessions per week during the off-season and two weight-training sessions per week during the season (photo by Ken Litchfield, copyright © 1985).

and endurance training. It is not your coach's job to get you into shape; you are the one who is responsible for following a solid, productive conditioning program. An athlete's physical-conditioning habits form the foundation on which he will build his entire athletic career. You have to be able to look beyond the work involved to the progress you are making. The time that you spend maintaining and improving your strength, speed, endurance, and flexibility will be a direct reflection of your determination to excel in your sport(s). You can begin doing this by following a program your coach designs or the program outlined in Appendix A of this book.

Your Pre-Event Meal

Pregame and prepractice meals should be eaten three to four hours before competition. The meal should satisfy the athlete's hunger for the next several hours, provide his or her body with sixteen to twenty-four ounces of liquid, include several servings of carbohydrate-rich foods, and may include one four-ounce serving of high quality/low fat protein.

Try to relax during the meal, eat slowly, and be careful not to overeat. Naturally, you will need to avoid foods that upset your stomach or digestive system. During the season, make it a point to remember what foods give you the most energy and make you feel ready for competition, then stick to those foods as much as possible. Avoid candy bars and sugar-rich drinks one to two hours before your games or practices. Drink about sixteen ounces of plain water ten to twenty minutes before your competition begins. During the competition, drink as much water as you want, but try to spread your drinking out rather than gulping down large amounts at any one time.

DEVELOP YOUR SKILLS

No individual is born with any expert sports skills such as hitting a baseball, throwing a football, or sinking a jump shot. These are all learned, neuromuscular responses. Every sport skill from rolling a bowling ball and making a strike to sinking a sixty-foot putt has to be learned.

An athlete's level of skill development is a direct reflection of his dedication. A prime example of skill development is the basketball free throw. In the 1982 NCAA Championship Basketball Tournament, the Houston Cougars won their game against Boston College on the strength of their free-throw shooting. Actually, they owed their victory to the free-throw shooting of six-foot, six-inch freshman Reid Gettys. During the season Gettys had averaged less than eight minutes of playing time per game for the Cougars, but in the victory that put them into the final four games in New Orleans, Gettys played liked a seasoned senior. In the last eight minutes of the game, he sank 10 out of 10 free throws to lead Houston to a 99 to 92 win. The NCAA free throw percentage record holder is Rod Foster of UCLA. During the 1982 season, Foster sank 95 free throws out of 100 attempts.

Gettys and Foster do not shoot free throws better than other athletes because they were born expert shots. They shoot better because they worked harder at it than almost everyone else. The same is true for top athletes in other sports. Joe Montana is a top quarterback because he worked hard at learning the skills of the position. Garvey, Connors, Evert Lloyd, Lieberman, Nicklaus, Austin, and hundreds of others have succeeded because they developed their specific and general sports skills to perfection.

You cannot expect to improve your skills during your team's regular practice sessions. Skill improvement has to be done on your own. During your junior high and high school years, you will probably have few demands on your time and have plenty of opportunity to practice. Your long-term success hinges on how quickly you realize the control you have in developing your sports skills and how seriously you set out to improve them. Skill development is discussed in detail in Appendix A.

SECURE ADDITIONAL COACHING

Extra coaching is always available to an athlete if he or she makes the effort to arrange it. If an athlete has access to a YMCA or a Boy's Club or a Girl's Club, he or she should make use of their programs. These organizations offer special programs in many sports, as well as conditioning programs that apply to all sports. Other athletes may be able to get their parents to pay for the cost of membership in a health club or a sports camp, where they can get the benefits of such aids as special training, Nautilus equipment, videotape cameras, and expert coaches.

An athlete who does not have these clubs or facilities available can ask one of his school coaches to set up a special program designed to meet his specific needs. A tennis player might set up a special time each week during the off-season when she can play a match against her coach. A football player may need extra help with the fundamentals of his position or additional help in the weight room. Ask your coach for a specific evaluation of your skills and abilities and for additional coaching to improve your performances. When you seek a coach's advice, you will find that he or she is eager to help you improve.

MANAGE YOUR POSITION

How well you manage your position will determine how quickly you pull away from the "average" athletes and begin moving toward your full potential. Many athletes fail to recognize the control they have over the positions they play, and as a result, they start each new season with a wait-and-see attitude. The better athletes, however, are working to become skilled specialists with specific positions and definite goals in mind. During the season, these are the athletes who are off to a flying start because they are getting most of the playing time and gaining the most experience.

In all sports, positions are assigned according to the athlete's skills, speed, strength, endurance, performance, and intelligence. Coaches are looking for athletes who can not only benefit from the instructions they receive, but who can also coach themselves when necessary. A coach is encouraged when his athletes show up for the first practice of the season after having spent all summer or winter working on their own to develop their skills and improve themselves.

All-American Cheryl Miller was one of the most highly recruited high school basketball players in the nation. During her high school career, Miller scored over 3,500 points and made 1,604 rebounds. She scored a career high 105 points in a single game (courtesy of the University of Southern California Athletics).

To understand this from a coach's point of view, just look at the way a coach has to find his best players to fill out his team. If, for example, he is a tennis coach, he has to spend most of his time teaching beginners the proper grip and telling them not to foot fault. A gymnastics coach is often saddled with explaining the difference between the pommel horse, the parallel bars, and the balance beam to half-interested athletes who thought they wanted to become gymnasts. In the midst of all this mediocrity, if a coach can find a few athletes who are eager to improve, who will benefit from his coaching, and who can work on their own, he will recognize them as the better athletes on the team and the ones with the most potential. When you adopt a playmaker's attitude toward improvement and winning and set your goals to reflect a success attitude, you will gradually pull away from most of your teammates. You will find that your coach is depending on you for team leadership and that he is letting you compete at the better tournaments against the best competition.

In the team sports, such as football, soccer, and baseball, coaches are looking for athletes who can play certain positions better than anyone else on the team. Consider how positions are filled. For football, there is usually a footrace between all the possible players. The fastest athletes go to the backfield, and the slower ones go to the line. Within a few minutes, all the fast guys are throwing passes. Usually the three best passers become quarterbacks; the good pass catchers become ends and running backs. The slower players crash into each other for awhile, and the first and second-string offensive and defensive linemen are sorted out. In baseball and basketball, the positions are first filled according to the levels of the athletes' skills. After a few minutes of flies and grounders, the most highly skilled fielders are positioned in the infield and everyone else battles for an outfield position. In basketball, the most highly skilled ball handlers become forwards and guards, while the tallest athlete with the best skills is put in as the center. The others practice on the second team or head for the bench. Obviously, if an athlete has spent his summer throwing passes or popping the net from ten to fifteen feet, he will be the best bet to hold down a starting position.

At the junior high and high school levels, the opportunity is tremendous because most of the athletes are trying to make the team on raw ability with no specialization. If you will determine where the bulk of your ability lies and develop both it and the specific skills needed to play a certain position, you can begin to write your own ticket. If an athlete is not happy with the position he is playing, it is up to him to assess his general abilities (speed, strength, coordination, agility) and match these with specific skill development in order to qualify for the position he would rather play. At the start of the next season, if he can demonstrate that he is the best player at that position, he will probably get the starting nod.

At the same time, you have to look at position changes from the coach's point of view. A split-end cannot expect to be moved to quarterback in the middle of the season; the best offensive lineman will not end up in the backfield just because he wants to switch. The needs of a team will always overshadow the desires of an individual athlete. Many coaches also have an unwritten "senior security rule." This means that, if an underclassman wants to beat out a senior, he had better beat him consistently and not leave any doubt about being a better player.

There are no secrets to the success of today's top athletes. In professional sports, for example, the best athletes got to the top as a result of well-planned conditioning programs and skill-development sessions. The quicker you get started on a similar, organized approach to your sport, the better your chances will be of playing the position you want to play and having a thoroughly satisfying athletic career.

Avoid the Drug Scene

Young people are constantly bombarded with warnings and demands that they avoid the use of *alcohol (including beer), tobacco (both cigarettes and snuff), marijuana, cocaine, heroin, amphetamines, and other drugs. There are good reasons for such warnings because new research about all of these drugs continues to uphold the harmful effects of their use.*

For athletes, there are numerous detrimental effects of drug use that will directly reduce their ability to compete both mentally and physically. *All of these drugs* produce reductions in overall energy levels, in strength, and in speed for periods of time up to and in excess of twenty-four hours. *All of these drugs* impair reaction time, coordination, inhibitions, and judgments and increase the likelihood of accidents. *All of these drugs* produce irritations to the nervous system, increase the risk of serious health problems with their long-term use, are physically or mentally addictive, and decrease the body's ability to fight infections. Both tobacco (nicotine) and marijuana reduce breathing capacity and the body's ability to absorb oxygen, and each drug must be considered a carcinogenic factor in lung and mouth cancer.

Despite inept and uneducated arguments to the contrary, these drugs can do nothing but hurt your performance in sports by decreasing your ability to compete and to put out a 100-percent effort to succeed. Because all sports are games of inches, of hundredths of seconds, of calculated risks, and of seized opportunities, it is ridiculous to believe that the use of these and other drugs will not zap your strength, slow your speed, and warp your judgments just enough to cause you to be, at best, several inches short or a few seconds too slow to come out a winner.

It may be true that most of the people who experiment with drugs end up relatively unaffected, leave the drugs behind, and go on with the rest of their lives. But the effects of drug use vary widely from person to person and are largely unpredictable. Accidents, problems, and addictions don't always happen to just the other guy. You will have so much to lose if you happen to be the one student in several hundred who gets arrested for DWI, becomes psychologically addicted to marijuana, finds himself hooked on cocaine, or worst of all, kills himself or a couple of classmates in a drunk-driving spree that ends in a high-speed, head-on collision. There is no justification for sacrificing your long-term success in or out of athletics just to have "a good time" with alcohol or marijuana or any other drug.

You are responsible for yourself and your own success, and that responsibility extends beyond the weight room, the locker room, and the playing field. Everything you do today will influence the kind of person and the kind of athlete you become. Don't handicap yourself by building your own roadblocks with drug use.

Maintain a Good Relation with Your Coach

It is common for students to shuffle their schedules to avoid teachers they do not like or do not get along with in the classroom. In sports, athletes do not have this opportunity. If an athlete has a poor relationship with a coach, his whole season can suffer. The key to a good working relationship with a coach is to get off to a good start.

A coach cannot help but notice when an athlete reports to the team's first practice in top condition. And the first thing a new coach will do is pick out the athletes who look as if they are in good shape and ready to play. Coaches often form an early mental impression of their first and second teams and, once they have done this, the second-team players will have a harder time and less opportunity to earn a starting position. While an out-of-shape athlete is lagging in the early practices, those in top condition will be cementing themselves into their positions.

Not only can a coach quickly recognize positive and negative changes in physical conditioning, he can spot attitude changes just as quickly. When a coach is deciding between two athletes of about equal ability, he cannot help but remember which athlete ran all-out at the end of each wind sprint, who worked harder in the weight room, or which one is always ready and eager to compete. Coaches get excited when an athlete's attitude fires up the team in practices, games, and matches.

In addition, most coaches value courteous manners and behavior. There is not a coach coaching today who would not appreciate a "yes sir" or a "no sir" instead of a sloppy "yeah" or "naw." The common-sense rules about getting to practice on time and always being ready to play will go a long way towards creating a positive relationship. If athletes do not pay attention or if they clown around during practice, they can just about kiss themselves good-bye.

A coach might be compared to a person racing a clock while trying to put together a jigsaw puzzle. He wants all the pieces to be turned in the right direction and to fall into place without slowing him down. If you are a success-oriented athlete who can contribute to the total team effort, you will find that the coach will notice this and that your opportunities for a better season and career will be multiplied.

Balance Your Attitude Toward Practice and Games

An athlete needs a consistent mental attitude toward improvement. Any athlete can get up for the big games and even play over his or her head for a short time, but a consistent attitude toward improvement

Injuries can happen to the best athletes. Your first defensive against injuries is heads-up, aggressive play. Protect yourself at all times and never loaf in practices or games (photo by David Cheatham, courtesy of David Crockett High School, Austin, Texas).

comes from knowing why you are participating and what goals you are trying to reach. In practice, it means looking for the opportunity to improve.

Athletes enjoy practicing the things they can already do well. Tall basketball players like rebounding drills, while the shorter players would rather shoot baskets. The strongest individuals enjoy weight lifting, while their weaker teammates would often rather skip weight lifting altogether. Working on your strong points does not improve your weak areas. Most athletes have heard the statement that you play in games at the same level you practice. That statement is true only up to a point. In high-stress situations, athletes will often play just below their practice level, and the more tired they are, the more evident the drop in performance will become. Consequently, if athletes cut corners in their practices or drills, they will not suddenly improve for the big game.

You have to perform well in practice to be able to duplicate that effort in actual competition. Any time a day goes by and you have done nothing to improve, you will fall behind. If you cannot look forward to the practices, then look forward to the improvement. Look beyond the work involved to the goals you have set. Remember this: if any athlete consistently works harder and smarter than you do (or any team works harder and smarter than your team), you deserve to be beaten and probably will be beaten.

REDUCE YOUR CHANCE OF INJURY

Athletes can protect themselves against injuries in several ways: by maintaining total fitness, by not loafing, by warming up before practice, and by using their heads to avoid hazardous situations. Injuries occur quickly and usually appear unavoidable. But when the events that led up to an injury are reconstructed, one or more common factors usually appear: poor conditioning, loafing, and carelessness. Hard-nosed play is rarely the basic cause of injuries.

The largest injury category is early-season injuries. These usually occur when athletes of unequal condition compete against each other. For example, late in the practice session one athlete has plenty of energy and the other is dragging. Bang! The second athlete has a broken collar bone or a dislocation. This situation holds true for women athletes as well. Early in the season, the critics will claim that too many athletes are being hurt and that sports are too tough. But as the season progresses, the injury rate drops and the critics have little to bark about.

The fastest way to get injured is to loaf. Just as an athlete relaxes and starts to stand flat-footed, he will take an elbow to the face or a blow to one of his knees. The number of times football players have trotted leisurely down the field and had their "plow cleaned" must number in the thousands. Athletes have to have their heads in the game and be ready to play and protect themselves at all times.

Athletes are totally responsible for their own success. If you reduce your chances of injury both in and out of athletics, you will not be standing on the sidelines or lying in a hospital regretting your carelessness. Total responsibility means that you also have to eliminate the risks you take in automobiles and on motorcycles. Like everyone else, an athlete gets only one body, and replacement parts for it are either darn inferior or nonexistent.

Stay Away From Steroids

Many weight lifters, body builders, and other athletes advocate the use of anabolic steroids to produce fast and impressive gains in muscle strength, size, and weight. But regardless of their claims and occasional apparent success, you should know that the use of steroids is dangerous and can lead to serious, permanent damage. A list of the risks include liver, kidney, and prostate damage, changes in testicle size, sterilization, cessation of long bone growth, acne, hirsutism, cancer, and death.

The use of steroids is an invitation to long-term problems and dissatisfaction; there are no shortcuts to athletic success. The best advice is to stay away from steroids, work hard on your own, and let nature take care of your growth. In doing so, your improvements will be permanent, positive, and healthy.

CONTROL YOUR LIFESTYLE

An athlete does not have to be Boy Scout perfect to be a success, but he or she needs to consider that lifestyle. Respecting your parents (or helping them to be respectable), obeying the law, staying away from dope, working hard in your classes, and doing anything else that will help you be a better person will only make it easier for you to become a better athlete. You should not be influenced by your peers or by current trends. It is the long-term results you should be concerned with and work toward by controlling your immediate behavior in and out of athletics.

EXCEL IN YOUR CLASSWORK

Your classroom performance will directly influence the opportunities you have to compete in athletics. The reason for this is not only because the NCAA has specific academic eligibility requirements, but also because the coaches at both the college and professional levels are looking for smarter athletes.

The Dallas Cowboys and the San Francisco 49ers run the most complicated offensive and defensive sets in pro football. Consequently, when they are determining their draft choices, both teams rate intelligence just as high as physical ability. Dallas gives both intelligence tests and personality tests to possible draft choices and free agents. Similarly, 49er coach Bill Walsh has told his rookies that he can go out and find dozens of guys who want to hit people or find wild men who want to tear opponents' head off. But what he is interested in is whether his players can think on their feet, learn their assignments, react correctly, and contribute to the team's success.

College coaches share this same attitude; they are tired of recruiting athletes whose academic eligibility they have to worry about during the season. As a result, the National Collegiate Athletic Association adopted a new rule at its 1983 convention which sets new academic eligibility standards for athletes who compete in the NCAA's Division

I programs. The rule, which will take effect in 1986, requires that athletes entering a Division I program directly out of high school must have graduated from high school with a minimum grade-point average of 2.0 in a four-point system in a core curriculum of at least eleven academic full-year courses, including at least three in English, two in mathematics, two in social science, and two in natural or physical science (including at least one laboratory class, if offered by the high school). Also, the athlete must have a 700 combined score on the SAT verbal and math sections or a 15 composite score on the ACT exam.

This new rule will make the competition for scholarships tougher. Now, more than ever, your performance in the classroom will count just as much as your performance in your sport. To meet these standards and to score well on the college entrance examinations, there are several areas in which you must excel: reading, vocabulary, English, mathematics, and written and oral communications skills. Two courses you should definitely take are speech and typing because both will contribute immensely to your ability to perform your college work. Whether you are going to college, to the pros, or to work, your study in all of these courses will contribute to your success.

MAKE YOUR DECISIONS ABOUT COLLEGE

Selecting a college athletic program and a college academic program is a major process that should begin well before an athlete's senior year. The decisions that are made should revolve around the answers to two questions: "Can I make the team and get to play?" and "Can I get a usable degree?" At the very latest, you should begin making decisions about college during your junior year in high school. Pick three to five colleges that you think you would like to attend and begin studying the pros and cons of their programs. Before the start of your senior season, you should have a good idea of where you would like to go to college and what you are planning to study. Chapter 5 will help you make these decisions.

Linda Sharp: Women's Sports Opportunities Are Growing[2]

Coach Linda Sharp's University of Southern California basketball team completed the 1983-84 season with a record of 29-4. The Women of Troy ended the '84 season by winning their second straight NCAA Division I basketball championship with a nationally televised victory over Tennessee. Coach Sharp spoke in an interview of her recruiting and conditioning programs and of the growth and popularity of women's athletics.

QUESTION: What physical abilities

and personality traits do you look for in the athletes you recruit? How do you structure your recruiting program?

COACH SHARP: First of all, the total personality is very important in becoming a collegiate student-athlete. I think that that entails being a good student, having the personality to get along with people, having the energy and the willingness to work hard, and also having a good attitude that blends with the team and contributes to the team. Because of the demands that are put on athletes in college, they have to be very organized, very disciplined people, extremely responsible, and dedicated and committed to what they're doing. It's not an easy task to be a student-athlete; when you're going to school full-time, basketball is almost like a part-time job. So, I think those things are important. Physically, I think speed and quickness, jumping ability, and intelligence are very important in competing today in any particular type of athletics.

I try to scout as many games as I can and see the high school athletes play. But their season is the same time as our season, so my assistant coaches have to do a lot of scouting. I either see the athletes in basketball camps in the summertime or in an All-America game. It's difficult to see all the games. I have recruited a lot of young people whom I have never seen play in high school. I recruited them solely on the fact that they were good students, they were well thought of, and they were highly recruited.

I think that there are some advantages in recruiting with the NCAA rules. We can now go into the homes, we can talk to the parents, and we can talk to the student-athletes face-to-face off campus. Under the previous rules, we could only talk to the athletes on

Coach Linda Sharp (courtesy of University of Southern California Athletics).

campus. The opportunities to bring athletes to your campus for a visit, to go to their homes, and to go to their schools and watch them practice and compete in their environment are all advantages in getting to know the athletes.

QUESTION: Will you allow athletes to walk-on and try out for the team?

COACH SHARP: Yes. I have two walk-ons on the team right now. A walk-on has to go through our preseason conditioning program and then try out for the team. If I feel that a walk-on's personality will contribute to the chemistry of the team and that she will be able to help the team in some capacity, I'll keep her on the team. If she doesn't have a good attitude and doesn't blend with the team, I won't keep her. But if a walk-on works hard and beats someone else out, I'll give her a scholarship.

QUESTION: Do you maintain a study period for your athletes?

COACH SHARP: Yes we do. We have a mandatory study table for three to six hours a week for freshmen and anyone below a 2.5 grade-point average.

QUESTION: How do you think the academic requirements of Rule 48 will improve intercollegiate athletics?

COACH SHARP: The new rule will make the high school athletes, their school counselors, and the education systems in the high schools work harder. I think that the counseling in some of the high schools has not been that outstanding, and I think that some of the athletes have felt that they could wait until their junior or senior years to get their grades up and that they could still earn a scholarship and get into college. But now, maybe the athletes will work harder for four years in high school and will be better prepared for college. The rule will put the pressure back on the high schools to get the student-athletes ready for college. That's the way it should be. I think the rule will help men's athletics as well as women's.

QUESTION: Do your athletes follow a regular weight-lifting program?

COACH SHARP: Yes. We have a specific weight-training program designed to improve upper-body strength and leg strength, and to increase jumping ability. We start weight lifting in September and do it throughout the season. When we're playing a lot of games in January, we work out with weights twice a week, but prior to that, we lift three times a week. I think it has helped the girls and has been a real asset to the team. They feel stronger, it helps their cardiovascular systems, and they have more confidence.

QUESTION: What are your predictions regarding the growth and acceptance of women's basketball?

COACH SHARP: I think that it's going to continue to grow. I've seen it grow in the years that I've been involved since college. There was interest when I played but not anything close to the interest there is to-day. There are more women's games on television; there are weekly press conferences. The final four of the NCAA women's championship basketball tournament are sold-out without the home team being there—over 10,000 people at the game. When we've played on the road this year, we've broken almost every attendance record in the country. So, I think that it is going to continue to grow. I think also that the young girls and women are getting more opportunities to go to camps and are getting showcased in these camps so that they can have the opportunity to get an athletic scholarship and go to college.

QUESTION: What would you tell young athletes to work on as they look toward their future in high school or college basketball?

COACH SHARP: I think that younger girls, particularly when they are in junior high, should work on their fundamentals and skills. They should use a smaller ball and lower the hoops so that they can get the proper techniques down. When they get into high school, especially in their junior and senior years, they should start lifting weights. I don't think that they need to start weight training when they are younger because I don't think that they are fully developed physically until they are in their junior or senior year. They should work on their skills and on their academics.

The girls should try to go to camps and be showcased. I don't think a girl can do it all by herself. She should get her parents involved. Her coach and athletic director and even the press need to help and promote her. We hear about talented kids because people are doing things to promote them. The more people who know about an athlete, the more opportunities she'll have to play.

Keep an Athletic Diary

It is easy for an athlete to think he is doing everything he can to get ready for a sport season and later realize that he was not doing enough. The best way for you to make sure you are doing all you can is to keep an actual record of what you do every day to become a better athlete. Go to a bookstore or a sporting goods store and buy a workout diary that has plenty of room to record all of your training. *The Sports Success Workout Book* is designed especially for this type of record keeping; it has enough space to keep track of your team practices, your weight training sessions, and your speed, skill and endurance training, as well as other aspects of your sports career.

Keeping a record is simple. You should get in the habit of taking the book out each night before you go to bed. Spend a few minutes writing down everything you did that day to improve yourself. If you worked out with weights, write it down. If you participated in a team practice, write it down. Keep track of your running schedule and how much time you spend on the skills of your sport. There are additional items that can be included on a monthly basis, such as your height and weight, the size of your biceps and other measurements, how much weight you can lift on different exercises, your time in the 40 or 100-yard sprints, and a record of how much reading you do about your sport. You should also include your coach's comments and your own feelings about your program.

Make a sincere effort to write in the book every day. A workout record like this can be fun. After a while, it becomes really personal, and looking back is like looking at an old scrapbook of your baby pictures. If you get your name in the newspaper, cut out the article and glue it in the book. Include other items such as your team's scores, game highlights, and personal accomplishments.

By keeping an athletic diary, you can avoid fooling yourself; you will know exactly how hard you are working. Your workout record will take the guesswork out of whether you are doing all you can to reach your goals. If the pages are blank and your progress looks bad, you can always take charge of your career, change your program, and get going in the right direction.

A complete conditioning program will include three or more flexibility workouts per week. Each session should last twenty minutes or longer and stretch the major muscles and muscle groups of the body. An athlete should keep a sports diary to record his or her daily workouts.

Texas upsets #1 ranked USC (photo by Susan Camp, courtesy of Women's Athletics, University of Texas).

Chapter 5
Earning Your Scholarship

HERSCHEL WALKER IS LIVING A FOOTBALL PLAYER'S DREAM. HE PLAYED
the game so well in college that sportswriters had a hard time finding
enough high-powered adjectives to describe his ability. When he was
in high school, one of his biggest compliments came from the Montreal Alouetts of the Canadian Football League. The Alouetts wanted
him to skip his college career and play pro football in Canada as soon
as he graduated. At the same time, several pro coaches in the United
States felt that he was good enough to play in the National Football
League. Walker considered the Alouetts' offer, but ended the specula-
tion that he would join the CFL when he announced that his immediate goals included college football and a degree in criminology.

What made Walker the most sought-after athlete in the 1980 high
school crop? Well, the six-foot, two-inch, 220-pounder could run a
hundred yards in 9.5 seconds. In high school he had rushed for more
than 6,100 yards, scored eighty-six touchdowns, and led his team to
the Georgia state championship. He was an all-around trackman and
won the finals in the state shot put. On top of his athletic achievements,
his classwork was excellent.

During the recruiting period, Walker was contacted by almost every
major college coach in the nation, and his home town of Wrightsville,
Georgia, was visited again and again by eager coaches hoping to influence his decision. After several months of hectic recruiting and
close NCAA observation, Walker signed on to play football for the
Georgia Bulldogs. There he wasted no time living up to his earlier
reputation. During his freshman season, he rushed for 1,616 yards
and led the Bulldogs to the national championship. As a sophomore,
he rushed for 1,752 yards. One year later, he was the sixth junior in
history to win the Heisman Trophy. In three seasons with the Bulldogs, Walker became the NCAA's third-leading rusher and, in the
process, was voted a three-time consensus All-America running back.
His total of 5,259 yards was just 823 yards short of Tony Dorsett's
four-year rushing record. Walker ended his college football career one

year early when he decided to turn pro and join the New Jersey Generals of the USFL.

Whether an athlete is highly recruited like Walker was or recruited by only one college, the complexities of the recruiting process are the same. For most athletes the recruiting experience is a time of high anxiety. The right decision is often hidden by a thick fog of questions, answers, and more questions. It makes little difference if an athlete is a high school All-America, a blue-chipper, or just a darn good prospect; accepting a scholarship leads to a four- or five-year commitment to one college where getting to play and getting a degree may seem light-years away. This chapter is designed to help athletes understand the recruiting process, to help them distinguish between what is legal and illegal, and to help them make the best decisions possible.

The ABCs of the NCAA, NAIA, and NJCAA

At the turn of the century, college football was marked with disorganization and violence. The rules of the game varied from place to place, and there were no uniform recruiting guidelines to determine what was legal and illegal. The game was becoming more and more violent, and the number of injuries and deaths was on the rise. After numerous complaints, President Theodore Roosevelt threatened to ban college football if it was not reformed.

In 1905, a number of colleges and universities met to organize a nationwide college football program. Their success was widespread, and more and more institutions joined their association. In 1910, the group changed its name from the Intercollegiate Athletic Association to the National Collegiate Athletic Association. Over the years, the NCAA has undergone a variety of changes to enable it to supervise all phases of college athletics. The NCAA's current membership includes more than 750 colleges and universities, with 140 affiliated organizations.

The membership of the NCAA is divided into three divisions. The Division I-A and I-AA schools are usually the major colleges and universities with the most powerful programs in the nation. The Division II and III colleges offer smaller programs on a less competitive level. National championships are awarded by the NCAA in men's athletics in baseball, basketball, cross country, crew, fencing, football, golf, gymnastics, ice hockey, lacrosse, rifle, skiing, soccer, swimming and diving, tennis, indoor and outdoor track, volleyball, water polo, and wrestling. Women's championships are awarded in basketball, cross country, fencing, field hockey, golf, gynmastics, lacrosse, soccer, softball, swimming and diving, tennis, indoor and outdoor track, and volleyball.

In 1940, the National Association of Intercollegiate Basketball was organized, and in 1952, the name was changed to the National Association of Intercollegiate Athletics. The scope of the NAIA has broadened over the years to include colleges and universities that compete just below the major level. Today, the NAIA has over 500 member institutions across the nation and sponsors championships in both men's and women's sports. Men's championships are awarded in baseball, basketball, cross country, football, golf, gymnastics, ice hockey, soccer, swimming, tennis, indoor and outdoor track, and wrestling. Women's championships are awarded in basketball, cross country, golf, gymnastics, swimming, tennis, indoor and outdoor track, softball, and volleyball.

The second oldest intercollegiate governing body is the National Junior College Athletic Association, which was formed in 1937. The NJCAA provides national championship programs for more than 550 of the nation's junior colleges. Men's championships are awarded in 19 sports: baseball, basketball, bowling, cross country, fencing, football, golf, gymnastics, ice hockey, judo, lacrosse, rifle, skiing, soccer, swimming and diving, tennis, indoor and outdoor track, volleyball, and wrestling. Women's championships are awarded in 13 sports: basketball, bowling, cross country, fencing, field hockey, golf, gymnastics, skiing, softball, swimming and diving, tennis, indoor and outdoor track, and volleyball. Junior college programs offer athletes two years of competition and experience that otherwise might be spent on the bench at a four-year college. After graduating from a junior college, an athlete can transfer to a four-year program with two years of remaining athletic eligibility.

Two other governing bodies have been formed to meet the needs of particular colleges. The National Little College Athletic Association serves colleges with a male enrollment below 500. The National Christian College Athletic Association sponsors competitions between Christian and Bible colleges across the nation. Both of these organizations sponsor national championships for their members in a variety of sports.

The Scholarship Picture

While the national intercollegiate governing bodies share similar goals, they do not share the same rules and regulations. Variations can be seen in recruiting, eligibility, and financial aid. While a few of the variations among the different associations will be mentioned over the next few pages, the following information is based on NCAA Division

All-America Eddie Banach is the University of Iowa's all-time winningest (141) and pinningest (73) wrestler. Banach won three individual NCAA national championships and helped lead Iowa to four NCAA national team championships. Banach won a gold medal in freestyle wrestling at the Los Angeles Olympic Games (courtesy of University of Iowa Athletics).

I-A regulations and will provide a general view of the college scholarship picture. The chart titled "Division I Scholarship Totals" lists the number of scholarships that may be in effect at any one time in each sport at a Division I college. The Division II schools offer slightly fewer scholarships in each sport. The Division III schools compete in nonscholarship sports.

In order to balance the competition in men's athletics, the NCAA limits to seventy the total equivalent number of scholarships that a Division I college may have in effect in all of its sports, excluding football and basketball. The word "equivalent" is used because in all sports except football and basketball a college can divide a single scholarship between two or more male athletes. For example, in men's golf the Division I scholarship limit is five. To stay within that limit, a college may offer two full scholarships to two athletes and, at the same time, take the remaining three scholarships, divide them in half, and offer half-scholarships to six athletes. The school will then have eight athletes on golf scholarships, but it will be within the NCAA equivalent limit of five.

At the Division I-A level, football and basketball scholarships cannot be divided between athletes. A Division I college can have fifteen male and fifteen female basketball players on scholarship each year. In football, the total number of scholarships that can be in effect each year is ninety-five, but only thirty new scholarships can be offered per year—provided the number of new awards does not push the total number above ninety-five. The thirty-limit rule has helped to spread the high school football talent among more teams because colleges can no longer load up their football programs with more athletes than they could ever play.

In women's sports, the NCAA has established individual scholarship totals for each of the eleven female sports it sanctions, but it has not set a limit on the total number of women athletes a member institution may have on scholarship at any one time. Each scholarship may also be divided between two or more female athletes in all sports except basketball, tennis, volleyball, and gymnastics. The athletic department of each college or university is free to compete in any or all of the eleven sports sanctioned by the NCAA for women and can offer as many scholarships as its athletic budget and the individual scholarship limits allow.

The member institutions in the NAIA and the NJCAA are allowed to determine on their own the number of scholarships offered in each sport according to the emphasis each college places on various sports and the amount of money the school has to spend on each sport. This is necessary because these institutions rarely allocate large amounts of money to their athletic departments and the flexibility lets them field the strongest possible teams in the sports in which they can best afford to compete.

NCAA Division I Scholarship Totals

Sport	Men	Women	Sport	Men	Women
Baseball	13	—	Rifle	4	—
Basketball	15	15	Skiing	7	—
Cross country/			Soccer	11	—
Track	14	16	Softball	—	11
Fencing	5	5	Swimming	11	14
Field Hockey	—	11	Tennis	5	8
Football	95	—	Volleyball	5	12
Golf	5	6	Water Polo	5	—
Gymnastics	7	10	Wrestling	11	—
Ice Hockey	20	—			
Lacrosse	14	11			

A Summary of Eligibility, Recruiting, and Scholarship Rules

The following information provides a brief summary of the general rules that apply to high school and college student-athletes regarding eligibility, recruiting, and scholarships. *The reader is cautioned that the information given here is not complete and that the actual rules are always subject to revision. At the same time, many individual colleges and sports conferences have stricter rules that are enforced in the place of the NCAA or NAIA rules.* An athlete should contact the associations that govern the colleges that he or she might attend and also contact the colleges themselves to ask for a copy of their academic requirements and their recruiting and eligibility rules. It is the athlete's own responsibility to know the current rules and to protect his eligibility at all times.

ELIGIBILITY—AMATEUR STATUS
1. Amateur status is determined on a sport-by-sport basis. An individual may receive or may have received pay for participation in one sport without altering his amateur status in another sport. For example, receiving money in a rodeo event will not make an athlete ineligible for any NCAA or NAIA sports, but playing semipro basketball will make an athlete ineligible for intercollegiate basketball.
2. An individual *will not be eligible* for competition in a particular sport if the individual agrees verbally or in writing to be represented in that sport by an agent, an attorney, or an organization for the marketing of the individual's athletic ability or if the individual has made an agreement or signed a contract to compete professionally in that sport.
3. An individual *will not be eligible* for any sport if his or her name or picture is used in the advertisement of a commercial product or service.
4. An individual *will not be eligible* for a sport if the individual requests that his name be placed in the draft of the professional league of that sport.

ELIGIBILITY—ACADEMIC
1. Until July 31, 1986, a student entering a Division I NCAA member institution directly out of high school must have graduated from high school with a minimum grade-point average of 2.0 in a four-point system. Effective August 1, 1986, a student entering an NCAA Division I college or university

directly out of high school must have graduated from high school with a minimum grade-point average of 2.0 in a four-point system in a core curriculum of at least eleven academic full-year courses, including at least three in English, two in mathematics, two in social science, and two in natural or physical science (including at least one laboratory class, if offered by the high school), and the student must have a combined score of 700 on the Scholastic Aptitude Test verbal and math sections or a composite score of 15 on the American College Testing exam. Athletes who fail to meet these minimum standards may be recruited by a Division I college; however, they may not compete or practice during their freshman year and may not receive an athletic scholarship that year.

2. The academic eligibility rules for freshmen entering college directly out of high school for all NCAA Division II and III colleges and for all NAIA member colleges require that an individual meet all of the regular admission standards and eligibility requirements of the colleges that are recruiting them and that the student must enroll as a full-time student in good standing as defined by the college's own guidelines.

3. To be eligible for an athletic scholarship to an NCAA or NAIA program, a junior college athlete must meet all of the rules of the NCAA or NAIA and must have either graduated from high school with the necessary grade-point average and curriculum, or must have completed a specific number of transferable junior-college credits with an acceptable grade-point average while in residence at a junior college, or the athlete must have graduated from junior college.

NCAA RECRUITING RULES

1. In-person, off-campus contacts by an institution's representatives are limited to certain times in the high school athlete's senior year and a junior college athlete's school year.

2. During the legal recruiting periods, the recruiting institution's representatives may make three in-person contacts with an athlete and his or her family at the athlete's home and three in-person contacts at the athlete's high school or junior college.

3. The athlete or his or her family may contact a college as often as they wish.

4. An athlete may receive five expense-paid visits to NCAA member institutions, with each visit lasting forty-eight hours or less.

5. As soon as an athlete has signed a National Letter of Intent,

there is no limit on the number of in-person contacts that can be made by the recruiting college.

6. It is *not* permissible for a college or university's alumni or boosters to make any off-campus contacts with athletes for the purpose of recruiting them or influencing their scholarship decisions. These individuals or organizations may not spend any funds to recruit prospects or offer any inducements to influence their decisions.

FINANCIAL AID

1. An institution may offer a student-athlete the following forms of financial aid: tuition, room, board, books, and college fees.
2. Athletically related financial aid may be offered for periods of only one year, but may be renewed for additional one-year periods as long as the athlete remains eligible for NCAA competition.
3. No special arrangements for extra compensation may be offered in any other forms, such as gifts, cars, cash, special loans, gifts to family members or friends, or arrangements for employment of family members or high school coaches.
4. During the time classes are in session, athletes are not allowed to receive any income that, including their scholarship award, will exceed the actual cost of tuition, room, board, books, and fees. In other words, NCAA athletes on a full scholarship cannot receive money from employment except during the summer or official school breaks.
5. It is not permissible for an athlete to sell (or for the college to sell for him) complimentary tickets at any price to any group or individual.

Why the Rules are Broken

A winning program means much more to a college or university than getting its name in the paper and having something for its students to cheer about. A winning program means money and lots of it. Winning not only affects ticket sales and television revenues, it affects the attitudes of state legislators and benevolent alumni who supply the millions of dollars that are the lifeblood of an entire institution.

In order to produce a championship quality team, a coach needs a fair number of the nation's best athletes. A coach's ability to get the best athletes depends on one of two things: how good a recruiter he is or how much "help" he gets from illegal inducements. The pressure to get the best athletes often leads to a few bent rules that snowball into

Jackie Campbell (5) and Kim Larson (6). Volleyball is the third most popular women's intercollegiate sport when ranked according to number of participants (photo by Susan Camp, courtesy of Women's Athletics, University of Texas).

major violations; finally, the whole program becomes riddled with cheating, with athletes who want more than the rules allow, and with alumni who are happy to give that extra "help."

Many college observers feel that, when cheating is discovered, it only represents the tip of the iceberg. Allegations and violations range from ticket scalping and grade fixing to cash payments of thousands of dollars. Cars, clothes, apartments, phony summer jobs, and airplane tickets are often provided illegally for college superstars. Many athletes feel that they are being paid to play their sport, and that a few extra dollars here and there are no big deal. This attitude often spreads to the alumni, who feel they are just helping the school. Alumni contributions for books, buildings, and equipment do make a difference in the school's success, and they are necessary. But their illegal "help" can lead to probations, suspensions, and firings that may destroy the careers of both the coaches and the athletes they are so eager to assist.

Cheating can occur only when two or more cheaters get together. When an honest coach finds an athlete with his hand out, he will pass him by for someone else. When an honest athlete is approached with illegal offers, he will run the other way. But when a coach who cheats meets an athlete who wants to cheat, the desire for money or power or status forges an illegal bond that further warps their characters.

For the individual who has taken the time to develop his or her athletic goals, cheating and other illegal activities are roadblocks in the way of a complete career and can even lead to an athlete's premature exit from his sports program. If an athlete loses his eligibility, is booted out of his scholarship, and blows his chance to earn a college degree and show the pro scouts what he can do, he has lost more than he will ever gain from cheating.

Your High School Coach

An athlete's high school head coach is the one individual who should know his or her ability and potential, and who is in the best position to help the athlete get a college athletic scholarship. For this reason, college coaches place a lot of stock in what a high school coach says about an athlete, and the arrangement usually works well. Most high school coaches are happy to help their athletes during the recruiting process. They enjoy talking to recruiters and often contact different colleges on the athletes' behalf. In most cases, the coaches will make honest evaluations of their athletes' abilities and potential and will see that the recruiters get the athletes' best game films. The coaches will usually do everything possible to help their athletes find the right colleges or universities where they will be most likely to have successful careers.

There are exceptions, however, where the recruiting process does not proceed this smoothly and athletes have a hard time getting the help and support they need from their coaches. This situation can develop when a coach has a large number of athletes assigned to his program, and as a result, he or she may not know the athletes' goals and career plans. A second situation that can produce recruiting snags occurs when, for a number of reasons, the coach may be too busy, may not be interested, or may not want to take the time to help an athlete deal with recruiters and select a college athletic scholarship.

Because the high school coach's role in the recruiting process is so important, you must be careful to avoid these negative situations by making sure that your coach knows your goals and career plans and by determining whether or not the coach is interested in helping you receive a scholarship. To do this, you will need to list the coaches at your high school whom you would like to have making recommendations for you and helping you to meet the recruiters and to evaluate their offers and athletic programs. As you make your list, arrange the

All-America Ron Galimore, three-time NCAA vaulting champion (courtesy of Iowa State University Athletics).

names on a first, second, and third choice basis. The next step is to plan a meeting with the coach at the top of the list. Ideally, you should have this meeting during your junior year in high school. But this may not be possible, especially if your coach leaves your school and you have a new coach your senior year. Therefore, as early as possible, you should complete your list and make an appointment with one of your coaches to have a talk about your future. Asking the coach for help in the halls of the school or on the practice field is not good enough. Schedule a definite time to meet with the coach in the privacy of his office.

The meeting should start with you telling the coach that you want to participate in a college athletic program. Ask him or her for an evaluation of your potential and what size college you should try to attend. After you have done this, listen carefully to the coach's evaluation of your ability and potential. What you want is an honest appraisal. If you find that the coach makes such an evaluation and is happy to help you during the recruiting process, that is great and you may be off to a positive start. But, if it appears that the coach is going to downplay your ability and does not seem too interested in helping you, then you need to be aware of this fact. Every coach is not a model coach. Some coaches will not help any athletes but their pets.

If you conclude from the conversation that the coach is not interested, does not think that you would be much of a college athlete, or truly does not have enough time to help you, you should tell him or her that you will contact one of the other coaches at the school or the school counselor to get the help you need. Coaches are human and naturally get more excited about helping some athletes over others, and there is no need to worry about the coach's decision or feel sorry for yourself because of it. Simply check your list and set a new appointment with the next coach.

After you have found a coach who is genuinely interested in helping you, all of the other coaches at the school and even the high school principal should be told to direct all of your recruiters to that coach. Then, you and the coach should work together in coordinating your presentation of your ability and potential. Both of you should know the answers to the questions the recruiters might ask (these are listed later in this chapter). You should both know which game films best reflect your ability. Finally, you should both be aware of your goals and expectations with regard to a college career.

Once the recruiting starts, you will need to participate in the recruiting process and pay attention to what is happening around you. Too many times athletes let their coaches make the decisions. This is so because they usually respect the coach and have learned a great deal from him or her during the season. But, regardless of what your coach knows, it is your future that is being discussed, and you need to try to understand everything so that you can make the best decision.

During the recruiting period, it is a good idea to be aware of your coach's attitude toward each recruiter and the recruiter's college. When you take the time to notice the coach's attitude, you may find that the coach is trying to steer you to a certain college — maybe to his alma mater or to a school where he might like to coach in the future. He may also be pushing you toward a college that cannot offer you the academic programs that you hope to study. For whatever reason, the coach may want you to do what he thinks is best rather than doing what you think is best. It is important for you to recognize the pressure the coach is putting on you. It may be that the coach is absolutely right and does know what is best for you. Or his ideas may be off the mark and somewhere out in left field. The important thing is for you to evaluate everything that you are seeing and hearing from the recruiter, from your coach, from your parents, and from anywhere else, so that you have the greatest amount of knowledge and information available to make the most sensible decision possible about where you attend college. The final decision has to be your decision, and you have to believe that it is the right decision in order for you to be able to attend the college and make a full effort to succeed there in both your athletic program and your academic program. The following sections will help you to better understand the recruiting process and with your coach's advice help you to make the best decisions possible.

A Look at College Recruiting

Letters addressed to the high school superstars start coming early. A six-foot-six-inch basketball player may get several letters a week complimenting him on his season. The best running backs and linemen will be on several dozen mailing lists and will get letters from college coaches throughout their state and other parts of the nation. The top hockey players and baseball players will have pro scouts and college recruiters biding their time until their first chance to make a personal contact. Because recruiters are restricted to a certain number of visits and to specific dates when high school seniors and junior college prospects can be contracted, the U.S. Postal Service and the telephone become the hotlines to the best talent. Athletes receive information about different colleges from interested coaches and are asked to fill out and return questionnaires that describe their interests in sports and their athletic ability. Most college coaches are skilled recruiters and are as congenial and contagious as the best salesman. When they make their personal visits, they can be in and out of a high school and into an athlete's heart in thirty to forty minutes. Recruiting is as much of a challenge to the coaches as is beating their rivals on Saturday afternoon.

Athletes, however, need to keep the recruiting process in perspective. They are really being hired to do a job and will be paid with a "free" education. When the nation's top coaches are calling or coming to a prospect's school or home, the athlete needs to retain his common sense and play through to a good decision. All of the glorious attention of recruiting will be forgotten when the hard work of making the team is staring him straight in the face. An athlete should look at the recruiting process as a business deal (which it is) and try to make all of his decisions with both feet on the ground and his head down out of the clouds.

Each Division I college is allowed ten full-time football coaches including the head coach. In basketball, a Division I program may have three full-time coaches. The other sports, such as golf, tennis, or swimming, each have one coach and occasionally an assistant. All of these coaches have an eye and an ear open to find high school and junior college talent. Their eyes and ears extend to an unlimited number of alumni, professors, administrators, and friends, who are all on the lookout for hot prospects that the coaches might want to contact. In football, the major colleges will have one coach who is dubbed the recruiting coordinator. It is his job to work with the sports information director and as many secretaries as they can enlist to keep tract of each year's large crop of prospects. The tracking process includes letters, phone calls, questionnaires, public relations releases, and general news items about the colleges.

The first thing a coach will do as his recruiting season nears is look at his team's needs. He determines who is graduating or playing out his last year of eligibility. He also considers which players appear weak and may not be back the next season. He examines his teams's injury situation and his list of healthy athletes. A coach has to recruit for two, three, or four seasons into the future. A basketball coach may need several rebounders. The baseball team may need a boost from a couple of good pitchers or a power hitter or two. A football coach may need defenders and split ends. Whatever his or her specific needs, every college coach needs athletes who can play their positions and make solid contributions to the team. To find these athletes, the coach will look down his list of prospects and examine the questionnaires the athletes returned. The questionnaires seek a variety of information ranging from the athlete's height, weight, speed, and vertical jump to his or her hobbies and church preference.

During several hours of meetings, the coaches will match their needs with the qualifications of the best available athletes. They will compare notes from their scouting trips with the recommendations they have received on each athlete. The football lists are narrowed down to the top seventy-five to one-hundred-fifty prospects. A basketball coach may have ten to twenty top prospects, while a tennis coach may have only a half-dozen or so. In football and basketball, the prospects are divided among the coaches, and plans are laid to make the first contacts. In the other sports, one coach usually has to do all the recruiting by himself, and he will adjust his schedule to be able to contact as many athletes as possible.

The recruiting efforts of the colleges that compete below the major level are every bit as aggressive as those of the national powers. These lower-level colleges have to work harder to get the best athletes because they lack the prestige of the big universities. For example,

Missouri vs. Arkansas (photo by Scott Takushi, courtesy of University of Missouri Athletics).

Panhandle State University in Goodwell, Oklahoma, completed its 1981 football season ranked seventh in the nation in NAIA Division II football. To keep up with the bigger colleges, the coaches at Panhandle State contact over 500 high school coaches each year and then contact over 1,000 athletes by mail. That number is narrowed down to about 300, and finally the top 100 to 150 athletes are recruited in person. The smaller colleges are hurt in their efforts because they do not have as many coaches to do the recruiting or as much money to spend. Also, while the major colleges offer only full scholarships, many of the colleges below the major level offer partial scholarships and work grants. Despite these disadvantages, however, the small and medium-sized colleges get their share of the talent and produce quality teams.

Whether a coach is from a national powerhouse or a small college, the actual recruiting follows the same pattern. When a coach arrives at an athlete's high school, his first stop is usually the principal's office, where he has to determine whether the athlete is eligible to be recruited and offered a scholarship. The NCAA rules require that an athlete graduate from high school with a 2.0 GPA, complete a specific core curriculum, and score 700 or 15 respectively on the SAT or the ACT college entrance exam.* Once it is determined that the athlete is eligible, the college coach will contact the athlete's head coach. In some cases the recruiter will have an appointment, and in others he will simply drop in on the school.

During the first meeting with the high school coach, the recruiter tries to get a detailed rundown on the athlete in order to verify the information he has collected. The recruiter's intention is to evaluate the athlete's personality, his desire to compete, his dedication to his sport, and his competence as an athlete. Each of the high school coach's remarks will influence the recruiter one way or the other.

As soon as the recruiter understands the coach's feelings about the prospect, the athlete is called into the meeting. Here is where first impressions make a real impact. Usually, the college coach has not seen the athlete unless he scouted one or more of the school's games. After the introductions have been made, the recruiter gets down to business. He will ask the athlete a dozen or so questions as he tries to size up his intelligence, desire, interests, and goals. A recruiter's interest will grow or fade as he begins to get a feeling for the athlete's intelligence and personality. The questions the athlete asks the recruiter will indicate how much interest he has in competing at the college. Both parties should come away from the first meeting with at least a basic understanding of what kind of relationship might be possible if the athlete elects to attend the coach's college.

At the close of the meeting the recruiter will usually ask for one or two of the athlete's game films to take with him and view later. Most high schools film their football games, and these films become an excellent recruiting tool. If an athlete has a good chance of getting a scholarship in basketball or in any other sport, he should ask his coach to make arrangements to have at least one of his games or matches filmed. This will make the recruiting process much easier; moreover, if the athlete can have one of his best performances on film, it will greatly improve his changes of getting a scholarship.

A college coach may or may not make a firm scholarship offer at the end of the first meeting. Most high school prospects are told that several athletes are being considered for each scholarship and that the athletes who best fit the college's needs will be offered scholarships first. However, the top athletes or blue-chippers, those that make up

*Effective August 1, 1986 for NCAA Division I schools.

the college's list of "hot prospects," are usually offered a scholarship at the end of the first meeting and are also invited to the college campus for an expense-paid visit. In addition to visiting with the athlete at school, the recruiters like to meet the athlete's parents and will often make an appointment to stop by his or her house later in the day. A meeting in the athlete's home gives the recruiter a better chance to get to know the athlete and to make sure that he or she will fit into college's sports program.

The expense-paid visits to the college campus are important for both the recruiters and the athletes. Just as the college is still inspecting the athletes, the athletes should give the college a careful examination. The Division I colleges of the NCAA may bring ninety-five football and eighteen basketball players to the campus for expense-paid visits. The coaches know that many of the athletes will go to other colleges, so they bring in a large number and hope to sign on the best athletes among those who visit the campus.

Every minute of the athlete's time at the college is usually planned. The prospects are paired with athletes already on scholarship or with the college's cheerleaders and given a guided tour of the campus. Occasionally, a professional athlete who competed for the college may meet with the prospects on campus and encourage them to attend. The weekend is filled with meetings and introductions. The athletes may tour the city, attend a campus concert and frat party, or watch a basketball game and swim meet. The weekend may be wildly elaborate or quite simple, with the athletes hearing and seeing dozens of reasons why they should attend the college.

While the prospects are visiting the college campus, the coaches have to balance several solid scholarship offers with a number of first-come-first-serve offers. Each of the top athletes is told that a scholarship will be held for him until he decides where he wants to play. Many other athletes are given first-come-first-serve type offers in which they are told that they will be awarded a scholarship if they agree to attend the college.

As the weeks of the recruiting season go by, more athletes troop in and out of the college for their visits. Athletes are soon giving verbal commitments to different colleges or at least narrowing their choices down to two or three schools. As the National Letter Day approaches, the pressure on the athletes grows. Coaches are calling every night, quizzing the athletes, and throwing in a little more sales pitch. Occasionally, an athlete will get a call from the governor of a state or from a professional athlete who played for one of the colleges recruiting him.

By National Letter Day, most of the athletes will have committed to a college and will sign the official Letter of Intent that binds them to a

NCAA indoor pole vault champion Doug Lytle (courtesy of Kansas State University Athletics).

particular program. As soon as the big colleges fill their limits, the remaining athletes will start looking toward the smaller colleges. Some athletes will take partial scholarships in the hopes of earning a full scholarship before they start off their sophomore seasons. A few colleges will hold back one or two scholarships and encourage athletes to walk-on and try to win a full scholarship during the pre-season practices. By doing that a coach can have more athletes out for the start of the season and may discover a talented athlete who deserves a scholarship.

Fred Akers: We Want Champions[1]

Each year, Coach Fred Akers' University of Texas Longhorns prove to be one of the nation's strongest teams. During Coach Akers' first seven seasons as head coach, Texas has played in seven bowl games and, at season's end, has been ranked among the Top 20 teams six times. In an interview, Coach Akers discussed his recruiting philosophy, walking-on, and the making of athletic success and excellence.

QUESTION: What qualities and abilities do you look for in the athletes you recruit?

COACH AKERS: Obviously, an athlete has to have physical ability. He has to have displayed the fact that he can play football, that he has the speed, the reactions, and the natural instincts—as far as we can tell—to play at the major college level.

Beyond that—and probably as much as anything else and equal to his physical ability—will be how well he has performed in the classroom. That's getting to be more and more of a standard, and each year it goes up. Usually, you'll find a pretty fair correlation between doing well in the classroom and doing well everywhere—especially in leadership positions like at quarterback. You don't find too many good quarterbacks who aren't good students. And it's not only at quarterback; that's just one example. It wouldn't make sense, if you want to have a championship football team, to have a quarterback who has great physical ability but isn't smart. It doesn't make sense; I don't care how good you are, you won't win. One of the facts is that you have to be able to think — especially in positions of leadership.

Also, you want a young guy to be able to obtain a degree in anything that he chooses. I feel strongly that the more limited a person is in intelligence, the easier it is for him to be led astray and the tougher it is for him to see the overall picture of things. People like that have a limited, restricted view. I want people who can think; I want people who can think on their feet; I want people who can think off the football field. We go pretty heavy on how a player has reacted in school. There are different ways to gauge that. I think that his class rank— how well he has competed in high

Coach Fred Akers (courtesy of Men's Athletics, University of Texas).

school—will indicate more than any other way how he'll react on our campus, because usually if an athlete competes at a high level in one place, he will in another. I also like it when I see an athlete involved in other activities that require leadership and participation around the school. And I like the type of individual who gets high praise from those in the community. These are the qualities that we look for: leadership, involvement, intelligence, and physical ability.

QUESTION: Is it important for an athlete to be willing to change positions to have a better chance of making a college team?

Coach Akers: Not when he's just starting. What we tell individuals is that we are going to recruit them as football players, as athletes. Now, obviously, what they've played in high school is what they've had the most experience with, and that should be their best opportunity. So that's where we start them off. If they continue to improve at that position and if they can make it in college at that position, we'll leave them there. But if we think that they can be better at another position, we'll talk with them about changing—but not until they've proven themselves on our campus.

Question: When an athlete has not had a great deal of high school publicity and his team has not done well, but he is an exceptional player, will you make an effort to scout him or see his films if he and his coach contact you?

Coach Akers: Without question. We investigate all the leads that we have. Ken Sims was a Number 1 draft choice of the NFL. He was Lombardi Award winner and a two-time All-American who was pretty obscure in high school. We just had a tip about him—"Have you seen that young kid over at Groesbeck?" We had not, but we followed the lead and recruited him.

Question: As you approach your thirty limit, do you encourage walk-ons and save a scholarship or two for them?

Coach Akers: Yes, we do. We generally have a couple of scholarships we reserve for walk-ons.

Question: Can an athlete who is not considered a "natural" come into the program as a walk-on, spend a year or more working hard, and become a starter for Texas?

Coach Akers: Of course he can! That's what happens. I think the biggest obstacle in the way of a walk-on making it is placed there by the walk-on himself. He expects it

all to happen in the first six weeks, and if he doesn't make the second team by the middle of the first year, he feels that he's a failure—which is ridiculous. Being tenacious is a quality we look for, too. Those scholarships are for one year only. You've got to be a tenacious person to obtain a scholarship and to keep one. No one has a corner on the tenacity market. A walk-on can have it, and those that do walk-on and get a scholarship from us have it. Over the last three years we've given nine scholarships to walk-ons.

Question: Do you evaluate your walk-ons before they come out and perhaps direct them to another program?

Coach Akers: Each athlete has to make a decision whether he wants to play at a major college or somewhere below that. It's not important what I feel. It's important what *he* feels. If I were an athlete, I would not want a coach putting a ceiling on my ability, because he does not know what makes me tick. It might mean more to me than that coach is able to recognize.

We have some people who are not starting for us who have more physical ability than some of those who are starting for us. It's not only ability that makes a starter. Some have more heart; to some it's more important. They may not be as big or as fast as someone who's not playing, but they concentrate so well that they eliminate mistakes, and they take advantage of the good things they can do. They have that tenacity that I was talking about. They have fight; they'll never give up. And those qualities will win for you more than anything else.

Now, one of the things we do is not take a walk-on unless he has the recommendation of his high school coach. So we discourage a lot of guys. We get guys who want to play but who have not played football since seventh grade, some have never played at all or they may have played touch. We discourage those. And if we think a guy has a strong chance of being injured, we won't let him come out.

QUESTION: Should an athlete who hopes to play professional football be concerned about playing second or third team early in his career at a major college, when he could be starting somewhere else?

COACH AKERS: An athlete will have to make that decision whether he'd rather play second team with the top level of competition or start with a college that's at a lower level. That is a personal decision. There are different levels of ambition. Some guys are satisfied just to be in the team picture. Others are not satisfied until they're recognized as the best anywhere in the country. In their minds, they want to compete with the best and against the best, and those are the kind we're looking for. If anyone has the ability to be a pro, we'll find a spot for him on the team. That ability does not escape our eyes. If he's good enough, we're not going to have him stacked in behind several athletes. There are twenty-two positions he can play as a starter.

QUESTION: In the long run, what determines if an athlete can make it at a major college such as Texas?

COACH AKERS: I'm very strong on a person making a commitment. I'm not interested in promises; you don't obtain things by talking and making promises. You make a personal commitment which is deep down inside you, and the way that is communicated to other people is by what you do. I'll take a guy that is long on fight and heart and effort and consistency, and more times than you can imagine that guy will beat people who have more ability but whose consistency isn't as high and whose commitment isn't as deep. We've built this university with people like that. Our football players have a lot of ability, but the strongest thing we have is that deep-down commitment. People who come here *expect to* succeed; they *expect* to improve; they *expect* to complete against the best and to succeed against the best. Those expectations are not common. They're not an everyday thing. Too many guys have doubts about whether they can cut it at this level, so they don't come here. We try to get the type of individual who will make that commitment so that we can count on him. Being able to count on someone doesn't mean just on the football field, because you don't walk on the field and become a champion. You've got to be that type of person everywhere.

Decision Time: What Do You Want From A College?

According to the federal government's National Center for Educational Statistics, approximately three million seniors graduate from high school each year, and roughly 60 percent of those graduates attend college the following year. Across the nation, each new freshman class averages between 2.5 and 2.8 million full-time and part-time college students. The total college population is about 11,500,000. This seems like a huge number, but there is plenty of room for all of them in the nation's 3,152 two-year and four-year colleges and universities.

North Dakota vs. Michigan Tech. Approximately 4,500 athletes competed in NCAA and NAIA ice hockey each year (courtesy of University of North Dakota Athletics).

One reason there is room for such a large freshman class is that only about one-half of all the freshmen who enroll in college will stick it out to get a degree four or more years later.

The question of which college to attend is not always a black and white issue, and the 50-percent dropout rate stresses the importance of making the right decision and being able to fit into the college's overall environment. Just because a particular college is offering you a scholarship does not automatically mean that you should go there. Every year hundreds of athletes end up in sports programs in which they cannot compete or otherwise cannot stand. If they can fight off the urge to quit and are not run off by their coaches, thcy may survive the year warming the bench. For dozens of reasons, well-meaning, dedicated athletes wind up at the wrong colleges and in the wrong athletic programs.

Getting your education and being awarded a degree at any college or university, large or small, is really no problem. The catch comes for athletes when they try to produce a successful athletic career at the same time. Before top coaches like Barry Switzer, John Thompson, or Digger Phelps come knocking at your door, you should consider the following guidelines.

1. Pick the right powerhouse. Two of the most important questions you should ask yourself, your high school coaches, and your potential college coaches are: "How much can I play?" and "How soon can I play?" These questions are difficult to answer, and actually, you are the only one who knows how hard you will work to make the team. But because the bench is a lonely place to spend four years, the questions have to be answered.

How much can you play? That depends on many factors: how hard you will work; how good your competition is; how high your levels of ability and skills are when you start the program; how much strength, speed, and endurance you have; and how much desire you can muster to succeed. All of these factors have to be considered before a good decision can be made. If you overestimate your ability and enroll in a program above your competitive level, you may stand a good chance of becoming a talented blocking dummy or bat boy for an All-America. You will also be in a weak position because back-up players have no guarantee that their scholarships will be renewed or that the coach will not try to run them off.

The positive aspects, however, of a major college sports program are always attractive, and if you can avoid being lost in the shuffle of a big program, you may be better off competing against the best athletes in the nation. Often, the fastest way to improve is to get into a first-class program where you can be truly tested and are forced to work as hard as you can. The most sensible reason for participating in one of the best athletic programs in the country is that they usually have the best coaches, the best competition, the best equipment, the best weight-training facilities, and the best overall facilities.

A top athlete should never shy away from the challenge of a major program. If you are a blue-chipper, a high school All-America, or just a kid with all kinds of potential, you probably need to be playing at the major level to be able to develop faster. If a talented athlete chooses to play at a level lower than his ability, he is setting himself up for boredom and a slower maturing process; he will not have to work hard because he will have lower standards to meet. At the same time, a blue-chipper has to be selective. There is not much playing time behind a Herschel Walker or a Pat Ewing. If you are the best high school tight end in the state and a college team has half-a-dozen ends equal to you in ability, you should look around before you settle on a team.

An additional bonus of a major college sports program is that the competition between the top college teams is usually closer to the level of competition in professional sports than is the competition between the nation's small colleges. As a result, for those athletes who have hopes of a professional sports career, the transition from a major college to the pros is not as drastic as the same transition from a small college.

In the long run, however, the quality of an athletic program makes more difference in how quickly an athlete will improve than the competitive level of the program. There is no shame in playing for a middle-sized college or a small college. The shame is not getting to play at all or getting to play only when the team is safely forty points ahead. The junior college programs should be considered by athletes who need a couple of years in a good program where they can get experience before moving on to a major college. O. J. Simpson came up this route and did quite well, to say the least. Dozens of other pros came out of small, almost unknown colleges. Cliff Harris, one of the best defensive backs to play pro football, signed as a free agent with the Dallas Cowboys after having played college football at Ouachita Baptist University in Arkadelphia, Arkansas. The enrollment there is about 1,600. When the Cowboys signed Harris, he had never played on national television, was only six feet tall, and weighed less than 200 pounds. But the Cowboys found him, just the way hundreds of other athletes have been found, playing their hearts out at smaller colleges and moving toward their full potential. You have to determine the ability and potential you have for your sport and the extent of your desire to succeed in college athletics and then pick the college program that is best suited for you and your goals.

2. Consider your education too. When a recruiter asks you what you want to study in college, it will help if you have given the subject some thought. All colleges do not offer the same programs. For example, if you decide as a junior that you want to be an engineer and your college does not have an engineering department, you will not be able to earn the appropriate degree without changing colleges. The same thing applies to sports. If you want to be a coach and the only offense the head coach runs is the single wing or the four-corners, you may not learn much in his program.

By making the bulk of your educational decisions before you get to college, you will have the direction and purpose you need to earn a degree. You may change your mind later, and that is fine, but you will at least have set the habit of moving toward specific goals. People who advise you to wait to make any educational and career decisions are giving you bad advice. The decisions only get harder to make. Understanding the recruiting process includes knowing what you want from your educational program and having a good idea where you can get it.

3. Check out the amenities. Not everyone will want to be close to a beautiful beach where the temperature is hot and the air is dry and it rarely rains. For others, being able to snow ski four or five months of the year may be no big deal. And having to worry about hurricanes, tornadoes, or earthquakes may not make much difference to a lot of people. But if any or all of these things matter to you, then you should think twice about where you decide to go to college. There is more to a college than books and buildings, basketball drills, and blocking and batting practice.

Consider these things: How far is it from home? Can your parents watch your games? Where will you be living? Is there a church you can attend and enjoy? Can you afford the cost of living and dating there? Can you feel at home there for four years?

A major college usually offers more amenities than a small college and a small college town. But each has its own advantages. An athlete should not be turned off by such statements as "You'll be just another number at a big university," or "At a small college, you'll be so far back in the sticks your mail will come by pony express." The main factor is not the size of the school, but what each college has to offer you. Being able to do well in athletics every day has a lot to do with how happy you are with your total college program. Nobody is going to be completely happy with any program for four or five years, but if you will pay attention to the pros and cons of a school and not just its win/loss record, you will have a much better chance of completing a successful college career.

Recruiting: Maintain Control

1. Control how you are recruited. A high school athlete's attitude towards both himself and the recruiting process will set the tone for the way college coaches approach him and will also determine whether they will approach him at all. Throughout the entire recruiting process, an athlete is "selling" himself and his ability to the recruiter. A college coach may see a half-a-dozen high school prospects in one day; you will have to make a good impression on the recruiter just to keep him interested in visiting with you a second time.

A good example of the importance of first impressions is a frequently told recruiting story about John Thompson, the head basketball coach at Georgetown University. Georgetown won the 1984 NCAA Division I basketball championship with an 84-75 victory over the Houston Cougars. Coach Thompson is one of the nation's top basketball recruiters. Several years ago, he was in the home of one of the country's hottest basketball prospects, when the athlete started being disrespectful to his parents. Thompson politely ended the meeting and later said the prospect was "just not my kind of athlete."

You can enhance your chances of making a good impression in many ways. The three surest ways to do this are: one, establish your academic and athletic goals to assure the coach that he can count on you in all phases of your college program; two, be mindful of your appearance and behavior so that the coach knows that he is getting a sharp athlete who will help round out his program; and three, relax, be honest and sincere with the coach, and let him know that you are eager to compete in his program.

2. Remember what a recruiter tells you. It is easy for an athlete to be overwhelmed in a recruiting situation. It is not every day that one of the nation's top college coaches will travel hundreds of miles to visit a high school athlete. In these situations, an athlete has to control his reactions. When a college coach leaves the first meeting, it is common for the athlete to have trouble remembering what was discussed. A top athlete may be visited by half-a-dozen or more coaches in a week's time. The result is that he may have trouble remembering the various coaches' names, faces, and colleges. You should not be too embarrassed to take notes and write down the recruiter's main comments. An athlete may need a month or more to make his final decision, and it will be hard to remember all that happens as the days and meetings go by. A sharp athlete will keep a file on each college that contacts him. Their letters, a record of their visits, and the athlete's notes should be kept in a file.

In your meetings with recruiters, you will be more comfortable if you have an idea of what a recruiter might ask you and already have your answers in mind. You should not memorize your answers to the following questions, but you should have a good response prepared in advance. Review the list of questions below. In your answers, stick to the facts, get to the point, and be as informative as possible without being long-winded and boring.

> What is your forty time?
> How high is your vertical jump?
> How much weight can you lift in various exercises?
> What positions have you played?
> What is your best position?
> What kind of season did your team have?
> What kind of season did you have?
> Would you be willing to change positions on a college team?
> What other sports have you played, and how well did you do?
> In the past, how hard have you worked in the off-season?
> What type of off-season program are you following now?
> What were your best games this season?
> Who was the toughest athlete you played against? How well did you compete against him?
> Who is the best player on your team? Why?
> What will your major be in college? Why?

The first half of a Golden Gopher double play (photo by Wendell Vandersluis, courtesy of University of Minnesota Athletics.)

What are your goals and plans for the future?
What colleges are you the most interested in attending?
    Why?
Do you plan to get married anytime soon? If so, how will
    that affect your college life?
How excited is your family about you playing a college sport?
Will they come to your games?
What are your hobbies and interests?
Do you want to play for my college?
Do you think you can play for my college?

3. Be ready with your own questions. Too many times a recruiter leaves the first meeting before the athlete really knows for sure how he will fit into the college's program. This is the fault not of the college coach, but of the athlete. You should be ready with two sets of questions for each recruiter who contacts you. You need two sets because the coach may not be sure how he plans to use you until he gets back to the college and reviews your films and sees who else is being recruited. The first set of questions is general, while the second is more specific. At the first meeting you should ask the following questions, and the recruiter should be able to give you at least a general answer:

What style of offense or defense do you coach?
How many athletes do you have at the position(s) I can play?

> Are there any positions where I might have a better chance of making the team?
>
> How would I be used during my freshman and sophomore seasons?
>
> Do you have a junior varsity? Who plays on it and how many games do they have each season?
>
> How often do you redshirt athletes, and who gets redshirted?

You should follow the coach's lead in asking other questions. Most of the following questions are usually best saved for the later meetings after the coach has a better idea of your potential. You should feel comfortable asking these questions because the answers will help you decide how well you will fit into the coach's program.

> Now that you have seen my films, how do you plan to use me on the team?
>
> What positions could I play and what are the starting opportunities at those positions?
>
> Who else is being recruited at my position?
>
> Does it look as if I might be redshirted? (Remember a redshirt year can give an athlete extra time to mature.)
>
> What is the head coach's coaching style?
>
> What type of weight-training equipment do you have? Do you have a full-time weight-training and conditioning coach?
>
> Do you have a full-time academic advisor or "brain coach"?
>
> Do you have mandatory study halls?
>
> What is the percentage of athletes who graduate from the program?
>
> What if I have to take a lab that conflicts with practice during an off-season semester?
>
> Are there any NCAA (or NAIA) investigations or probations pending or in effect now?

An athlete should realize that, if he just sits there like the laces on a football without asking any questions, the recruiter will either think that he is not too interested in going to his college or that he is not too smart. If you do not participate in the meeting, there is no way he can judge whether he should continue trying to recruit you. Do not worry about being nervous. Every recruiter knows an athlete is going to be nervous, and he will not let that affect his decision as long as the athlete shows an interest in the meeting and seems eager to be recruited.

4. Control your college visit. The college visit provides the athlete with the opportunity to evaluate what the coaches have been telling him and to carry out his own research on the college. The NCAA allows an athlete five expense-paid, forty-eight-hour visits to member institutions. An athlete should be concerned with meeting the coaches and checking out the college rather than just taking a trip for the fun of it.

Before your visit, you should try to contact the head of the department you intend to major in and set up an interview. This may not be possible if you visit the college on a weekend, but it is worth a try. During the visit, you should try to talk to students outside of the athletic department to get a better flavor of the campus. Pick up a copy or two of the campus newspaper to read later. While touring the campus, you should ask yourself what you have not seen. Some college's weight rooms look like dungeons. If possible, visit the college on a class day to get a better idea of the campus and the students.

5. Consider the head coach's style. Your particular position and career goals should cause you to check out the head coach's coaching style and philosophy. During your campus visit, ask several athletes about the head coach's reputation. How does the coach conduct his practice sessions? How does he motivate his athletes? Once you have a good understanding of what the coach is really like, try to decide whether or not you will fit into his program. A coach is not going to change his style or philosophy to accommodate one player.

An athlete should also be careful about participating in a program just because of one coach. While you visit the campus, make sure you want to play for the college and not just the coach who is recruiting you. Coaches are often fired or jump to different schools with little warning. If you decide to overlook several negative factors just to play for a certain coach, you may end up regretting your decision if that coach is given his walking papers. A coach can certainly make a program more pleasant, but you should be sure you can survive at the college with or without the coaching staff that is recruiting you.

6. Know what you are being offered. Coaches and athletes may commit verbally to each other, but until the athlete signs and returns the college's official scholarship offer sheet, there is no binding agreement. If an athlete mistakenly believes he is being offered one thing and turns down other schools' offers in that belief, he may have an unpleasant surprise. You should ask the coach to explain carefully what the college is offering and how long you have to accept.

After you commit to a college, you should get an official scholarship statement or offer sheet telling you exactly what is being offered and a Letter of Intent. You will sign these on or after the National Letter of Intent Day for your sport and will return them to the college. As soon as you have made a decision to attend a particular college, are certain of the type scholarship offer you have, and have told that recruiter of your decision, you should contact all of the other coaches who have made you offers in order to tell them of your decision.

7. Handle the recruiting pressure. Until an athlete finally signs a Letter of Intent, all of the coaches will continue to try to sway him or her toward their respective teams. As National Letter Day approaches, the coaches will increase the pressure to get the top athletes to commit. A top athlete may get several calls a night. The coaches will be telling the athletes that the scholarships are going like hotcakes on the training table, and they may be. If a college wants you badly enough, they will save you a scholarship, but — if you have only one or two offers — you should make your decision as quickly as possible. First-come-first-serve offers usually do not last long.

After you make your decision, you should realize that it is natural to have a feeling of buyer's remorse. You may wonder if you should have selected a different college. When this happens you need to put the decision behind you and get on with the business of getting ready for your first intercollegiate season. If you make the decision after considering all of the aspects listed here, you will most likely have made the right decision. In the end, it will be like jumping into a cold swimming pool; once you are in, you will be glad you took the plunge.

Selling Yourself

Despite the all-out scouting programs which college recruiters conduct to find the best high school prospects, talented athletes occasionally have to sell themselves to the recruiters. There are many reasons that might cause an athlete to be overlooked: poor newspaper coverage of the team and its athletes, extremely weak competition, a small and out-of-the-way school, a terrible team record, or injuries that hurt an athlete's senior season play. In such cases, what you need to do is to start your own publicity campaign. The key to a good campaign is timing. If you feel you are not going to get enough publicity during your senior season, you should start your campaign during the spring or summer before your senior year. Structure your program in the following manner.

1. Evaluate your level of competition. With your high school coach, evaluate your level of play today and adjust it by the amount of improvement you expect to make after a good off-season program and your last season of play. Set that level of play as your goal and begin (or hopefully, continue) an all-out conditioning and skill-development program to reach or surpass that level.

2. Start your scouting program. With your coaches, school counselor, and parents, begin looking for several colleges that compete at

We won! Susan Shurr and Juliet Cuthbert after the 400-meter relay (photo by Susan Camp, courtesy of Women's Athletics, University of Texas.)

your projected level of play. The junior colleges and smaller four-year colleges are an excellent place to start. If you look closer to your home, you may find that coaches are more eager to scout your games, but all of the colleges you are interested in attending should be considered. Narrow the list to your top half-dozen or so choices.

3. Write your letters. During the spring or summer before your senior season, you and your coach should each write a letter to every college on your list. The coach's letter should describe as honestly as possible your ability, strengths, athletic desires, experience, and athletic goals. Your letter should express your desire to be considered for a scholarship in a particular sport and describe your sports experience and the conditioning program you are following. Both letters should get quickly to the point, with the coach's letter containing more "sales pitch" than the athlete's. Include a schedule of your senior season and circle the dates when the team is playing close to the college campus. The anticipated best match of the season should also be circled and described as a good game to scout. The letters must be well written, typed, and mailed in the same envelope. Probably one or more of the college coaches contacted will respond in some fashion to your high school coach.

4. Put it on film. If you complete a good off-season program and follow it up with a top-notch senior season, you may find that several other coaches are recruiting you in addition to those you contacted yourself. In any case, make sure that at least some, if not all, of your games or matches are filmed so that you have a record of your performances to use as a selling tool.

5. Post-season selling. In the event that you have a good season and still have no recruiters, all is not lost. Ask your coach to contact several college coaches by phone and try to drum up some interest. You might consider making an appointment with a coach and traveling to his or her college with a couple of your best films to make your sales pitch in person.

6. Walk-on. Most top schools and almost all small college programs will be glad to have athletes walk-on and try to win a position on their teams. Often these colleges will save a scholarship or two for the best walk-ons. After an athlete has visited with a college recruiter and has not received a scholarship offer, he should ask if he may have permission to walk-on. In football, most coaches are glad to have walk-ons because they like having more athletes to work with in practice. In the sports where fewer participants are required, like tennis, golf, gymnastics, or even basketball, too many walk-ons will often get in the way. But regardless of the sport, an athlete should ask permission to walk-on. If you have scouted the colleges well and matched your ability with the right colleges, you should find that coaches are willing to give you a tryout during the next season's practices.

7. Investigate other forms of financial aid. There are many types of financial aid available to college students, with most of it based on need. Corporations, businesses, city governments, and civic clubs offer full or partial scholarship awards to students. The federal govern-

Jill Sterkel (courtesy of Women's Athletics, University of Texas).

ment has several programs to help students get their college education. The key to these programs is to start looking early and to not give up until you find several that offer you a fair chance of getting an award. You will have to work closely with your school counselor and the financial aid office at the college of your choice. The search may be frustrating, but the benefits can make the different in getting where you want to go. As soon as you are a college student, you can always walk-on and begin earning a place on the team and a full athletic scholarship.

All-America Wayman Tisdale (photo by Ric Moore, courtesy of University of Oklahoma Athletics).

Chapter 6
Succeeding in College

EVERY SPRING THE STORIES ARE THE SAME; ONLY THE NAMES OF THE ATH-letes change. There are athletes who have had five years of college—ten full semesters—but who will not graduate in the spring. Others have attended college for four years and have completed all of their athletic eligibility, but they lack a few necessary credits to graduate with their class. Still other senior athletes lack one, two, three, or more full semesters of the classwork required for their degrees. In a survey of twenty-one senior All-Americas who were the top prospects for the National Football League's 1982 draft, the *New York Daily News* determined that 70 percent, fifteen of the twenty-one athletes, would not graduate on schedule.

Other stories report additional problems in intercollegiate athletics. The University of San Francisco decided to drop its men's inter-collegiate basketball program after continued reports of NCAA rule violations. The University of Southern California was found guilty of running a ticket-scalping operation that funneled cash to football team members. After winning the 1981 national championship, the Clemson University football program was placed on a two-year pro-bation for recruiting violations. Additional investigations led to pro-bations of other programs including the basketball teams at Wichita State and Oregon State and the football team at the University of Florida. College athletics was rocked by more bad news in March of 1985 with the arrest of three Tulane University basketball players who were accused of shaving points in two games during the 1984-85 season.

The critics are quick to seize all of the bad news and use it to discredit the nation's college athletic programs. There will probably always be some coaches, some athletic department directors, and numerous alumni who will break the rules to get that extra edge in order to help their team win. But the majority of the people in inter-

All-America Karen
Andrews' pitching
helped lead UCLA
to the NCAA
national softball
championship (photo
by Stewart Wright,
courtesy of UCLA
Athletics).

collegiate athletics are running honest shops, and today more than
ever before, the NCAA seems determined to root out the undesirables.
Two rule changes adopted at the 1983 NCAA convention reflect this
new attitude. Off-campus contacts with recruits by alumni and boosters
were made illegal. And coaches' contracts now carry a provision that
they can lose their jobs if they violate any NCAA regulations. The
NCAA's Presidents Commission has also proposed major changes in the
way college athletics is administrered that are intended bring tighter controls and squeeze out cheaters.

The critics' charges that the nation's college athletic departments
have a misplaced emphasis on sports and that they fail to educate their
athletes are easier to refute on both an individual and a general basis.
Despite the specific cases of individual athletes who never graduate,

the overall graduation rates are encouraging and indicate that most critics fail to do their homework. There are, in fact, many positive examples. Coaches John Thompson and Joe Paterno have individual graduation rates for senior athletes that hover around 90 percent or better. Earl Campbell's Class of 1978 at the University of Texas boasts an 88 percent graduation rate of senior football players. The University of Oklahoma graduates about 80 percent of all of its athletes who stay at the University for four or five years.

Moreover, the graduation rates for women athletes are generally higher than those of their male counterparts. The reason for this difference may be the women's more realistic emphasis on the college degree as a means to future employment. Because there are few professional sports opportunities for women athletes, most of these athletes view their sports participation primarily as an avenue to a degree. In contrast, more males view their sports participation as a route to the pros, a fact which may be evidenced in the National Football League Players Association study which indicates that only 36 percent of the NFL players have college degrees. The critics are quick to point out that this figure looks extremely low. What they fail to realize, however, is that that percentage is similar to the graduation rates of all four-year college students.

A recent study by the NCAA is more specific and, in fact, quite positive. In 1975, the NCAA and the American College Testing Program began a five-year survey of NCAA member institutions to determine how the graduation rates of athletes who win varsity letters compare to the graduation rates of nonathletes. Data from 46 member colleges and universities were carefully monitored, and the records of 36,365 men were maintained for the five-year study. The overall five-year graduation rate for all of the men in the study was 42.4 percent. The graduation rate for the athletes alone was 49.9 percent; for the nonathletes alone, it was 41.5 percent. The general conclusions of the study were that the male athletes graduated at a rate equal to or higher than the rate for males who were not athletes. It might be noted that the two lowest groups of graduating athletes were football and basketball players, who had a five-year graduation rate of approximately 42.5 percent. Track athletes had the highest overall graduation rate of approximately 51 percent.[1]

An examination of why students fail to get degrees should begin with their individual reasons for attending college. Some students attend college to avoid going directly into the work force; others attend simply to have a place to go after high school; a third group is working towards a degree; while others are participating in the Great American Husband or Wife Safari. Similarly, there are athletes who attend college primarily to play sports or to have a place to go after high school.

Florida State's Jeff Ledbetter set NCAA records for single season home runs (43) and career home runs (97). Ledbetter is congratulated here after a three-run homer (courtesy of Florida State University Athletics).

A college cannot be faulted for failing to educate the students or athletes who have enrolled with no intention of getting a degree. An institution might be questioned for failing to change a student's outlook while he or she is there, but not for losing a student or an athlete who gets all he or she wants and then leaves.

The athletic department's first responsibility is to offer its student-athletes a complete opportunity to earn a useful college degree. If an athlete is given the opportunity and time to pursue his or her education and fails to do so, the institution is not at fault. On the other hand, if athletes are required to miss an exceptionally large number of classes in order to participate in a sport or if the athletes are not allowed to attend afternoon labs or other classes because they conflict with their athletic program, then the institution is at fault. As long as the athlete has a fair opportunity to be both a student and an athlete, the responsibility for getting a degree is his or hers.

Succeeding as a College Athlete

1. Re-examine your goals. One of the hardest things for a freshman athlete to do is to adjust to the lack of attention and the rougher treatment he or she will receive in the first season of college athletics. Suddenly, he has to take a big step down from being a top-dog in high school to being a nobody in college. He is no one's hero and nobody knows who he is. College coaches have to find out as quickly as possible who wants to play and in the process do not bother to spare anyone's feelings. Preseason college workouts are designed to separate the playmakers from the participants. In the process of teaching their systems to their athletes, the coaches push them to their limits and still ask for more. After the less-serious athletes drop out, the coaches are left with the athletes who are prepared to play and will put out a full effort.

If an athlete does not re-examine his athletic self-image, his reasons for playing a sport, and his goals, he will have a high potential for becoming a dropout. The coaches might baby their juniors and seniors who they know can play; they will put up with their moods and take the time to personally encourage them along. But freshmen do not receive that pampering. If an athlete in college is not sure of his role in the program and fails to provide his own motivation for following through, he will usually be out of the program in no time. You have to know what sort of athlete you are, believe totally in yourself, and then act out the personality role that will lead you to your goals.

2. Adopt a year-round conditioning program. To succeed in college athletics, an athlete has to devote himself to an all-round, year-round conditioning program. It is not enough to work really hard a month or two before the season starts. Conditioning has to be a full-time project. An athlete should follow his coach's year-round program or the one outlined in Appendix A of this book.

3. Learn the system and the people. An athlete needs to know the coaches and to make sure that they know him or her in a personal way. As soon as you can get past an employer-emloyee setup, you will be in a better position to survive the long run of four or five seasons. You should communicate well with your coaches, earn their respect, and develop a mutual friendship. The most common occurrence is for an athlete to be thoroughly intimidated by his coaches and avoid any unnecessary contacts. If an athlete can move past these initial barriers and work toward a friendship both in and out of sports, he will improve his chances of a satisfying career.

4. Showcase your ability and skills. When freshmen move in to a college program, they often take a subordinate role and play less aggressively because they are intimidated by the upper classmen and do

All-America Dana Smith (4) played on two Southern Cal national championship volleyball teams. Smith is an Academic All-America and the 1984 USC Scholar Athlete of the Year (courtesy of University of Southern California Athletics).

not want to be singled out as hotshots. An athlete, however, has to showcase his talent at all times. Both in practice and in games, you have to make the situation work for you by being a playmaker. Mistakes will not count against you as much as a poor effort. Nothing turns a college coach's head more than aggressive, intelligent, and opportunistic play from a freshman.

5. Consider changing your position. If you are not getting to play in a college program, you may need to consider a position change. It is probably better for a third-string quarterback with little chance of playing that position for the next three or four years to become a receiver or a defensive secondary man and thus get a chance to play instead of warming the bench all those years. Similarly, a back-up third baseman might make a great outfielder and thereby get a lot more playing time. Cris Collinsworth was an All-America high school quarterback who changed positions in college to become an All-America wide receiver; after the 1981 NFL draft, he helped lead the Cincinnati Bengals to the Super Bowl. Collinsworth probably would have had a tough time making it in the pros as a quarterback, but as a wide receiver his future is unlimited. Similarly, if your chances of playing can be improved with a position change, make the suggestion to your coach. A change may open up a whole world of opportunities for you.

6. Reduce your chance of injury. The main causes of injuries remain the same in college as in high school: poor conditioning, loafing, and carelessness. An injury during the preseason practices can make a bench warmer out of a good player even after he recovers from the injury because, while he is recuperating, someone else will be earning his position. Protect yourself at all times both in and out of athletics.

7. Avoid being run off. Getting a scholarship is easy compared to keeping it for four years. Look at the numbers. In Division I football, a team can give out thirty scholarships per year as long as the total number of scholarships does not exceed ninety-five. In basketball, the total number is fifteen for both men and women athletes. In all sports, new scholarships can only be offered as the athletes on scholarships graduate or drop out of the program. Usually, colleges have a sufficient turnover through graduation or because the weaker athletes eliminate themselves when they see they cannot compete with the other players; however, this is not always the case. If an athlete wants to continue playing but the coach does not think he is improving or performing as well as he should, the coach may turn up the pressure on him to improve dramatically or get out of the program. The way to avoid being run off is never to take your scholarship or position for granted and never to let your conditioning and skills fall below your true ability.

Ray Meyer: It's Your Will to Play That Counts[2]

At the end of the 1983-84 season, Coach Ray Meyer retired after his forty-second year as the head basketball coach at DePaul University. During those years, Coach Meyer ran one of the most respected college basketball programs in the nation and led the Blue Demons to the NCAA championship tournament twelve times and to the National Invitation Tournament eight times. In an interview before he retired Coach Meyer spoke of a few of his best athletes and the route to athletic success.

QUESTION: What does it take for an individual to succeed in sports? Can an athlete who is not an outstanding high school player come into a program and develop and compete at the top levels of the NCAA?

COACH MEYER: Yes. We've had lots of them do that. One boy in particular was Bill Robinzine. He played for DePaul and then played in the NBA, but he never played high school basketball. Neither did George Mikan, but that's going way back. What's important is the boy's attitude. If he's lazy or has an I-don't-care attitude, we don't want

him. We want a player that has ambition, that wants to be good. Let's put
it this way: the real difference
between a successful athlete and one
who does not make it is not the talent
or the knowledge of the game alone,
but his will to play. What he wants to
do with his talent is what matters; it's
not the quantity of practice, but the
quality.

A great example is Terry Cummings
(the 1983 NBA Rookie of the Year).
In his freshman year he started out
playing on the second team. He had
such a strong desire that he worked
hard in the off-season. He had a
average sophomore year. Then, all
summer long he worked as well and
as hard as any man we've ever had.
In his junior year he was an All-
American and a first-round draft
choice. It's how you work and what
you do with your talent that makes
the difference.

Ray Meyer (courtesy of DePaul Athletics).

Get Your Degree

Making it in the classroom requires a fair amount of planning. The
following tips may seem quite simple, but if an athlete will follow
through with them, he or she will have a much better chance of getting
a degree in four years.

1. Declare a major or specific area of study. Before you enroll in a
college, decide what you want to major in or what general area you are
interested in pursuing. Even a wrong decision is helpful because it will
force you to find something you like better. Do not make the mistake
of selecting a physical education major just because it is easy or
because you figure that you will play pro sports, and you do not need
to major in anything else. Major in something only because you have a
reason for studying it and have a specific use for the degree.

2. Get a course adviser outside the athletic department. Many
athletic departments have excellent programs that offer athletes
course advisers and tutors. If your college provides you with a good
brain coach, you should work with him or her as often as you need the
extra help. But a brain coach should not take the place of an adviser in
your specific major. Talk to the director of your academic department

and arrange for a specific individual to act as your academic adviser. This adviser will be much more aware of the requirements for your degree and can help arrange your schedule to fit in with the demands of your sport. Make a point of explaining to the adviser that you intend to complete your course work and get your degree. As you talk to him or her, you will be able to determine if the individual feels any prejudice against athletes. Most professors do not, but there are a few who think all jocks are dumb. Get to know your adviser and let him or her help you earn your degree.

During your academic career, you should avoid the tendency to stack a bunch of easy courses in the semester when you participate most heavily in your sport. Put your hardest courses in the off-semester, but do not go overboard with this strategy and blow off one semester while loading up the other. You might also examine the option of taking a course or two during the summer.

3. Attend class. Many teams have a rule that athletes have to eat breakfast during the season, but as soon as the season ends, the breakfast checks end, too, and the athletes start to sleep in. You will miss plenty of classes without adding a few extra cuts for your own reasons. Make the commitment to attend classes and follow through on it; the habit will go a long way in helping you get your degree.

Avoid These Stumbling Blocks to Success

1. Living expenses. The NCAA rules do not allow an athlete on a full scholarship to have a job while his college is in session. An athlete on a partial scholarship cannot earn more money (including the value of the scholarship) than the actual cost of tuition, room, board, books, and fees. The NAIA rules allow athletes to work only as long as their jobs are not provided as a result of their sports participation, and they do not receive any preferential treatment on the job. What this boils down to for most athletes is that money for dating and other living expenses must be provided through a summer job or by the athlete's parents. With the cost of living as high as it is, athletes who have not planned for their college expenses can wind up in a poor situation in a hurry. Being short of cash often leads them to fall into the following traps.

2. Ticket scalping. In some states selling a ticket for more than its face value is perfectly legal; in others it is against the law. But these laws make no difference when it comes to the NCAA or NAIA rules that forbid scalping. Athletes are usually given tickets to their games that are to be used by their family or friends. The NCAA and NAIA rules state flatly that athletes cannot sell (or that the school in their place cannot sell) these tickets to anyone at any price. The University of Southern California football program paid a heavy penalty for breaking this NCAA rule. In April of 1982, the NCAA Infractions Committee handed out a probation that barred the Trojans from bowl games following the 1982–83 and 1983–84 seasons and prohibited television appearances during 1983 and 1984. Regardless of an athlete's cash-flow situation, he should avoid the risk of putting himself and his college in this situation.

3. Agents. The NCAA rules state clearly that an athlete may not enter into a written or verbal agreement with any agent, individual, or organization for the marketing of his athletic ability. This rule is really for the athlete's own good. As soon as an athlete looks as if he has the potential to become a pro ballplayer, the hangers-on appear and try to get him to agree to let them represent him in any future negotiations. Most of these people who ask an athlete to break the rules in the first place are interested in nothing but helping themselves. Basketball players and baseball players have a special problem in this area because they do not have to complete their eligibility to be drafted. There are plenty of people around who will be glad to talk an athlete out of a year or more of eligibility for the privilege of representing him after the draft. Whether an athlete is ready for the draft makes no difference to an unscrupulous individual who wants only to get a piece of the athlete's contract.

You will have plenty of time to decide on an agent or attorney (see Chapter 9) to represent you should you turn pro. If anyone comes along offering money, gifts, or free advice, steer clear of the individual and his gifts or cash. If you sign a contract with an agent, you can be certain that the agent has taken the time to make sure it will be binding in the eyes of the law. When this happens, you will be locked in with the agent for better or worse, you will lose your eligibility, and you may subject your college to the wrath of the NCAA. Avoid such people at all cost until the time is right and you have considered the full picture of whom to hire.

4. Other gift givers. Rick Kuhn is a former Boston College basketball player who was sentenced to ten years in prison after being found guilty of conspiracy to conduct racketeering, conspiracy to commit sports bribery, and using interstate travel to further a crime. Kuhn was convicted with four other individuals for agreeing to fix the point spread of six games during the Boston College 1978–79 season. In March of 1985, three Tulane University basketball players were arrested after being accused of shaving points in two games. Officials in the case indicated that cocaine was the motivating factor in the point shaving scheme.

The chance is small that you will have to worry about the people

Two-time Big 8
long-jump champ
Veryl Switzer, Jr.
(courtesy of Kansas
State University
Athletics).

who bring gifts and cash with big smiles and pats on the back, while asking for only a few favors. However, the possibility is always there, and when there are a million-and-one ways to make money both legally and illegally, an athlete has no way of knowing what some people may want. The first contacts are generally innocent enough and are often made by a student or a fan, or a businessman or woman. In fact, agreements and deals are often so unobtrusive that an athlete may be locked into some guy's con before he knows it. Then after the first payment has been made and the threats start, he may feel he has nowhere to turn. In every case, look at the long run, always keep your goals in mind, and be aware of what you are doing.

Looking Toward the Pros

An athlete with hopes of a pro career is in luck because the pro teams are looking for him. Throughout the year, scouts of the major sports leagues are following every lead they have to find the best professional prospects. The catch is that each athlete has to attract their attention with superior performances during his college or, in some cases, high school career.

The scouting programs for all four of the professional leagues work in much the same fashion. The NFL, NBA, and major league baseball have the most complete national scouting programs. The hockey scouts concentrate on the northern part of the nation. Most pro teams belong to a league scouting agency or to a smaller group-scouting organization that shares information among its members. At the same time, a team will employ from two or three to as many as eight or nine team scouts. The nation is divided into zones, regions, or states, and the same scouts usually work the same areas and schools year after year.

If you have any professional sports ambitions, it is crucial for you to tell your coach about those goals. The pro scouts generally know the coaches in their regions and trust their judgment about the type of talent the coaches have on their teams. Several times a year, each scout will call the coaches and ask them if they have any athletes who appear qualified to play pro ball. If your coach knows your goals and if you have demonstrated the actual ability needed, he will usually do his best to get the scouts to watch your films or to scout a couple of your games or practices. Of course, if you want your coach to do these favors for you, you need to have a good personal relationship with him and with the other coaches on the staff. Selling an athlete to one or more pro scouts and to the coaches of a professional team is often more demanding than getting a college scholarship for a high school athlete.

In the NFL and USFL, the scouts are looking first for height, weight, speed, ability, and intelligence. Some teams have strict standards: linemen must be six foot three or taller; running backs must be clocked in the forty at 4.8 or less; and linebackers must be six foot one or taller and weigh at least 200 pounds. Other teams may not be as strict and will overlook a shorter player or a slower player if he seems to have special ability. All of the teams want athletes with quick feet and agility. The college players are graded on a variety of qualities — from coordination, quickness, and acceleration to their personality and their history of injuries. The footballers who probably will be drafted in the first four rounds are checked over by three or four doctors and are tested and timed by several scouts and coaches. There are several minicamps prior to the draft, and the athletes are examined and reexamined before the teams make up their minds about who gets drafted first, second, and third. The professional football scouts usually recommend 800 to 900 athletes from colleges all over the nation. About half of these athletes are drafted, and the others usually sign as free agents.

Much the same kind of system exists in professional baseball. The scouts call the high school and college coaches and get the scoop on the best ballplayers. Unlike the pro football and basketball teams, however, the major league baseball, soccer, and hockey teams are not usually made or broken by athletes drafted in the previous draft. In baseball, athletes who are drafted are almost always sent to a minor league team to develop and wait for their turn to make it at the major league level. This practice is followed because few college and high school players are ready to step into the big leagues and compete against the likes of Mike Schmidt, Darryl Strawberry, and George Brett.

Potential baseball draft choices are graded on the strength of their throwing arm, their running speed and lateral speed, their fielding ability, and the speed and quickness of their bat swing. The scouts are looking for quick hands and quick feet. As many as 750 to 900 athletes will be drafted in the summer draft, and 250 to 350 will be drafted in the winter. In the past few years, the pro clubs have been relying on the college teams for most of their draft choices. Today, about 80 percent of the athletes drafted are college players.

Scouting in the National Basketball Association works in much the same way that it does in the NFL. The NBA has a scouting service that provides information to the teams, and each team has one or two or more individuals who scout the best teams and players in the nation. Coach Bob Bass[3] of the San Antonio Spurs indicates that most of the teams will try to draft athletes to fill specific needs and will hope the individuals drafted can work into the positions within a few years. According to Coach Bass, the pro scouts in the NBA first look at an athlete's general skills: running, jumping, speed, agility, and quickness. Next they look at his basketball skills: passing, shooting, rebounding, defensive play, and his ability to perceive the flow of the action of the game. After that, they check the athlete's personality: his attitude toward himself, his teammates, and his coaches; how he responds to winning and losing, how coachable he is; and his attitude toward work, practices, and games. If all these qualities compare well with the demands of a professional career, the scouts will consider the size of the athlete in relation to the demands of his position. Playing in the NBA is extremely demanding, and if an athlete lacks the size at a position, he usually cannot compete.

The Major Indoor Soccer League has the most loosely structured scouting program of all the professional sports leagues. The reason for this, according to Al Miller,[4] the former head coach of the Dallas Tornado professional soccer club, is because the soccer teams do not rely on the previous draft for immediate players. The draft is an insignificant part of a team's short-term success because there are not many players, if any, who come out of college ready to walk right in and play professional level soccer. Miller believes that, like baseball, soccer needs a development system. Soccer is an international sport; about 134 other countries play the sport and produce talent. Because America is behind other countries in its emphasis on soccer, an American college player will not have developed as much of his talent as a professional athlete from any other soccer country. At the same time, Coach Miller sees this situation slowly changing now that there is more emphasis on building good soccer programs throughout the nation: "The junior program across the country is becoming very organized. The better coaches are in charge of picking the future Olympians and bringing them to the Olympic Training Center in Colorado Springs, where they train under good coaching and excellent conditions." Consequently, Miller sees a bright future for soccer in the United States: "I would say that, right now in America, our twelve-and-unders, from age six to twelve, are comparable to kids anywhere in the world, except for their lack of total exposure to soccer. Over here, soccer is just not in the air." As better programs and coaching become available and as more emphasis is placed on soccer at the junior high and high school level, Miller feels that the better soccer players will continue to play soccer in high school and college instead of gravitating to other sports.

Moses Malone on Turning Pro[5]

Moses Malone played almost flawlessly during the 1982–83 season and led the Philadelphia 76ers to the NBA championship. The six-foot-nine superstar was voted the league's 1983 Most Valuable Player and the MVP of the Championship Series. When interviewed about the opportunities in the NBA, Malone offered this advice for athletes thinking of turning pro:

MALONE: It's hard. You've got to believe in yourself. I think if a person plays because he likes the game, the work will be easy. An athlete should set his goals for something else and play for the love of the game. The best thing to do is to go

Moses Malone (photo by Gary Fine).

to college and work to get an education; then put your hope on the line that you make pro ball. But don't count on making pro ball—it's a difficult thing. There are not too many athletes playing pro ball.

In the meantime, as interest and participation in soccer continue to grow across the country, the professional soccer clubs are becoming more interested in building their teams with American players. To do this, all of the pro teams have at least one individual who is in charge of keeping track of the college players. This scout maintains a record of the players on the All-America lists, scouts a few games, attends the playoffs and championship games, and scouts the College Senior Bowl. Some coaches may be looking for an athlete to work into a particular position like goalkeeper. Others may go for a particular quality or ability, such as speed, ball control, defense, or scoring ability. When scouting for the Tornado, Miller looked for three things: first, athletes who played in winning programs; second, athletes who had a good deal of athletic ability and who could develop in his program; and third, athletes with good character, able to avoid problems in personal conduct.

Scouting in the National Hockey League is extensive in all areas of the United States where the sport is played at both the high school and college levels. As in baseball, a fair number of athletes are drafted from high school and usually sent to a team in the Canadian junior leagues until they are ready to move into the drafting team's farm program or directly to the NHL team.

The hockey scouts are looking for skating speed, hockey sense and savvy, shooting skills, and a desire to get into action and mix it up. In the 1984 NHL draft, 55 United States high schoolers, 22 U. S. college players, and 2 U.S. junior-league players were drafted. Those numbers compare well with the 130 Canadians and 40 Europeans drafted. Size is not a big factor in the NHL if an athlete is a clever skater and has demonstrated enough durability to last throughout the long and hard NHL season. The National Hockey League has its own scouting service that shares information about all high school and college prospects with each of the NHL franchises. In addition, each team usually has a number of full-time or part-time scouts that beat the bushes for the best talent.

The scouting programs in the major professional leagues are so sophisticated that almost every athlete with any degree of potential is usually given at least a good look or two by one or more pro scouts. In a few cases, however, a coach and an athlete may have to make the first contact with a pro team or a scouting agency. Occasionally, there are sleepers whom the pro scouts just miss, and in these cases the athlete and his coach may have to sell the athlete's ability in the same way a high school coach would sell a prospect to a college coach. This is more common in soccer than the other sports because the soccer scouting network is not as extensive as those of other leagues.

There are a number of other opportunities in professional sports for athletes who may need a year or two more of experience before making it in the big-time professional leagues. Kurt Rambis is a good example. He played basketball in the European leagues in Greece before coming back to the United States and helping the Los Angeles Lakers win the NBA crown in 1982. Other athletes tighten up their skills in the New York or California Summer Basketball Leagues. The NBA uses the California League to test new rules and develop referees.

Football players can find a number of semipro teams across the nation. Of course, the pay is not too great, $5 to around $25 a game, but it is a chance to continue playing and maybe develop enough to earn a spot in the NFL, the Canadian Football League, or the United States Football League.

Soccer players can look to the Major Indoor Soccer League as an alternative to the NASL. During the 1983 season, the MISL achieved better attendance than the National Basketball Association in five of nine cities where the two leagues compete head-to-head for fans. The MISL consists of thirteen teams which compete in a forty-eight game season that leads to the MISL Championship Series.

Other professional opportunities can be discovered by the athlete's own imagination, drive, and desire. Kurt Thomas, one of America's greatest gymnasts, turned pro and began touring the country with a professional gymnastics exhibition. Nancy Lieberman organized a women's professional basketball tour that played exhibition games in a number of major cities. Lieberman has also written a book about basketball. Many other top athletes make the rounds as sports counselors and trainers at youth camps. Along with professional tennis and golf (which are discussed in Chapter 8) there are opportunities in professional softball, racquetball, rodeo, jai alai, horse racing, bowling, skiing, squash, ice skating, cycling, and running. For the more adventurous athletes, there is always boxing or professional wrestling.

The problem that many individuals have regarding the possibilities of having successful college sports careers or of becoming professional athletes is that they do not believe that they can reach those goals in the first place and therefore do not really try. They are loping along, hoping for miracles, while other individual are planning their careers and working to succeed.

No one knows how many talented athletes might have been good enough to make it in college athletics or in one or more of the professional sports leagues because so few athletes actually achieve their full athletic potential.

But that does not have to happen to you. There are plenty of opportunities for improvement and success at all of the levels of competition for individuals who will make a conscious effort to set their goals and work toward them. Success in athletics, as in any other endeavor, is possible for those who truly have the will to succeed and the confidence that they can make it happen.

Rosalynn Sumners (copyright © by Howey Caufman).

Chapter 7
The Olympics

MENTION THE OLYMPICS AND MEMORIES OF THE GREAT ATHLETES SPRING
to life in living color: Mark Spitz swimming to seven gold medals;
Bruce Jenner sweeping the decathlon in 1976; Dorothy Hamill, Sheila
Young, and Ann Henning skating to championships; Eric Heiden racing to five gold medals at Lake Placid; and the U.S. hockey team
beating the unbeatable Russians.

The Summer and Winter Olympic Games provide an individual
with an opportunity to showcase his or her athletic ability against the
best competition in the world. Taking advantage of this opportunity
requires tremendous doses of dedication and determination, but in
return it offers the satisfaction of reaching the greatest heights in
athletic competition. The variety of sports—from aquatics to yachting
and almost everything in between—provides a wide opportunity for
each athlete to become an Olympic gold medalist.

Qualifying for the Olympic Games

The United States Olympic Committee (USOC) is the coordinating
agency for all athletes who compete for the United States in the Olympics and in the Pan American Games. The USOC's responsibilities include operating the Olympic Training Centers in Colorado Springs
and Lake Placid; sponsoring the National Sports Festival; coordinating the efforts of the thirty-seven National Sports Governing bodies;
sponsoring an extensive sports medicine program; and organizing,
managing, and transporting the members of the U.S. Olympic Team.

The USOC coordinates the thirty-seven National Sports Governing
Bodies that have the authority to establish the rules and regulations
and organize the competitions that lead the athletes to the Olympic
Trials, where the final Olympic Team members are selected. The
National Sports Governing Bodies sanction hundreds of competitions

from the lowest local events to the national championship meets. The National Sports Governing Bodies are listed in Appendix B. In addition to these thirty-seven organizations, there are eleven National Multi-Sport Organizations that are members of the USOC. These organizations also offer training and hold competitions that can lead an athlete to national and international events. These multi-sport organizations are:

> Amateur Athletic Union of the United States
> American Alliance for Health, Physical Education, Recreation and Dance
> Catholic Youth Organization
> Jewish Welfare Board
> National Association of Intercollegiate Athletics
> National Collegiate Athletic Association
> National Council of the Young Men's Christian Association
> National Exploring Division, Boy Scouts of America
> National Federation of State High School Associations
> National Junior College Athletic Association
> United States Armed Forces

The USOC indicates that the United States is probably the only country in the world to use head-to-head competition for the selection of its Olympic Teams. The process of qualifying is simple on paper but demanding in competition. An athlete usually takes his or her first steps toward the Olympics in training and competitions at the local level on his or her school's sports teams, on a YMCA team, or on an individual basis. If an athlete competes successfully in the local and area competitions, he or she graduates to the state, regional, and national contests. After proving himself or herself there, the athlete's next step would be to compete in the international events and, finally, the Olympic Trials.

The route to the Olympics requires a sincere, personal commitment to self-improvement and sports excellence. All of the factors discussed in Chapter 2 regarding sports specialization must be considered if an athlete hopes to improve as quickly as possible and to move to higher levels of competition. World-class swimmers train for five and six hours a day, swimming mile after mile. Between the 1980 and 1984 Olympics, Kitty and Peter Carruthers, the 1984 silver medalists in pairs figure skating, trained almost every day for more than eight hours a day. The U.S. women's volleyball team follows an astonishing six-day-a-week training schedule that includes everything from weight training to computer analysis of their volleyball skills. The year-round training of the Russians, the East Germans, and the other athletes of the world requires that American athletes dedicate themselves thoroughly to the long hours and years of training if they are to have

Silver and gold medalists Steve and Phil Mahre (courtesy of K2 Corporation).

any chance of competing at the world-class level. As an athlete moves to the higher levels of competition and demonstrates the ability and potential to represent the United States team, the USOC can provide special training designed to help speed the individual's progress and to allow him or her to train more efficently for world-class competition.

Athletes who qualify for the Olympic Trials must meet all of the eligibility requirements of both the USOC and the International Olympic Committee, pass a medical exam, and sign an eligibility form. The eligibility requirements for the Olympic Games have always stressed that athletes be amateurs, but the definition of "amateur status" has been debated for years with many countries appearing to have different standards. Today, the rules are becoming more liberal. In early 1985, it was announced that certain professional athletes may be allowed to compete in future games. As the eligibility requirements change for Olympic competition, each athlete is responsible for maintaining his own eligibility and must understand the requirements for his sport. These requirements can be obtained by writing the National Sports Governing Body for the sport(s) in which an athlete hopes to compete.

The USOC will pay the expenses of athletes who compete in the Olympic Trials, including living and travel expenses to and from the competitions. Athletes who are selected for an Olympic Team will also receive additional expense money to cover some of the costs of training and representing the United States in the Olympics.

The Olympic Training Centers

The United States Olympic Committee operates two Olympic Training Centers, one in Colorado Springs and one in Lake Placid, New York, that are designed to provide athletes with ultra-modern training facilities, increased competition opportunities, and sophisticated sports medicine analysis. The Olympic Training Center in Colorado Springs has provided all-around sports training for more than 75,000 athletes since opening in 1977.

The Colorado Springs Olympic Training Center can house 650 athletes at one time and provides training in all of the Olympic sports for approximately 12,000 athletes each year. The center's all-weather 400 meter track is one of the finest in the world, with electronic testing and timing equipment and a Super-Turf infield for soccer, field hockey, and other sports training. A new $4.5 million multi-sport field house contains six separate gymnasiums. When construction is completed in the mid-1980s, the Colorado Springs Center will have a new swimming and diving complex, several ice skating and hockey rinks, and a cycling velodrome.

The Lake Placid Olympic Training Center opened in December of 1982. The center and the surrounding Lake Placid community offer almost every conceivable type of athletic facility for both summer and winter sports training. The facilities include several gyms, swimming pools, ice rinks, and a speed skating rink, as well as facilities for bobsledding, ski jumping, and cross-country and alpine skiing. The center can house 350 athletes.

Bob Mathias, a two-time Olympic decathlon record holder and the former director of the Colorado Springs Olympic Training Center, is enthusiastic about the opportunities the two centers offer. Speaking in *The Olympian*, Mathias commented that "America's successes at the Olympic and Pan American Games have been due, for the most part, to the stubborn dedication and drive of the athletes themselves. For most, getting prepared to compete for a position on the American team has involved great personal sacrifice, hardships, and significant personal expense." The majority of the athletes who train at the Olympic Training Centers are not considered world-class athletes, but they are invited to the center because they have been recognized as having Olympic potential. And although most of them will not qualify for the Olympic Team, the opportunity is there. Mathias emphasized this point: "Something really extraordinary happens to the kids who come here . . . a kind of mystique. I guess it's the same feeling each of us

Mary Decker Slaney leading the pack (courtesy of NIKE, Inc.).

gets when we've been singled out for something special. For most, training with us is as close as they'll ever come to the Olympic Games. But the important thing is that we're putting the Olympic dream within the reach of more and more of them every year."[1]

Athletes are selected for training at the Olympic centers by the National Sports Governing Body for each sport. In the same way in which an athlete works to qualify for the Olympic Team, he or she can qualify for a position at the training center. For example, an athlete can begin training and competition in gymnastics at his or her school or local YMCA. After competing successfully in local and regional meets, the athlete should contact the U.S. Gymnastics Federation and ask for a list of future national meets. If the gymnast can demonstrate an exceptional potential in all of his or her meets, an invitation to train at one of the centers may not be far behind. Acceptance to the Olympic Training Centers is based solely on an athlete's ability and potential. The training and knowledge acquired will provide an athlete with a tremendous boost toward reaching his or her full potential.

Why Not Break Some Records?

In his book *Sports and Psychology,*[2] Dr. Frank Ryan discusses the psychological limits or barriers that stand in the way of sports accomplishments. Ryan reviews how a sub-four-minute mile, a seven-foot high jump, and a sixty-foot shot put were thought to be impossible three decades ago, and how today all three "impossible" marks are broken routinely. While many coaches attribute today's records to new training and conditioning techniques, Ryan attributes the new records to the top athletes' ability to overcome their own psychological limitations. He feels that athletes share an unconscious inhibition based on the norms (that is the records and standards) of their day and that this inhibition impairs their performance more than any physical limitations. He suggests that no athlete may have truly achieved his or her complete athletic potential because he has been stopped short by his own psychological limits.

The connection between superior athletic performances and the surpassing of psychological limits is more convincing than attributing superior performances to training and conditioning alone. It is obvious that the mind has to believe an accomplishment to be possible before the body can perform the feat. For example, Dr. Ryan points out that within two months of the date that Roger Bannister broke the "impossible" four-minute barrier in the mile run, other athletes began bettering his time.

What Dr. Ryan stresses is that psychological limits are unconscious inhibitors that hold athletes back. Thinking more positively will not get an athlete past these inhibitions. What is needed is psychological reprogramming and the adoption of the belief that one is capable of improving his or her own performance and reaching higher and higher levels of accomplishment. Time and time again, athletes limit their success with expectations that are low and that lead to the establishment of equally low goals.

Whether you are working to qualify for the U.S. Olympic Team or just trying to beat your brother or sister in tennis, your success depends on your expectations about your performance, on your interpretation of your overall potential, and on your desire to reach that potential. If you accept a low expectation about your performance and a poor evaluation of your potential, you will be building the psychological boundaries that will limit your success. Don't let that happen. If you have a good chance of running a fifty-four-second quarter mile, then work toward and believe that you can hit a fifty- or fifty-one-second clocking. If you are going to be a first-team player, why not set your goal to become an All-City or All-State player? You can begin breaking records and meeting new accomplishments as soon as you make up your mind that you are capable of reaching those levels and believe that you are in charge of your ultimate success.

1984 Summer Olympic Sports

Archery	Rowing
Baseball	Shooting
Basketball	Soccer
Boxing	Swimming
Canoeing-Kayaking	Synchronized Swimming
Cycling	Team Handball
Diving	Tennis
Equestrian	Track and Field
Fencing	Volleyball
Field Hockey	Water Polo
Gymnastics	Weight Lifting
Judo	Wrestling
Modern Pentathlon	Yachting

1984 Winter Olympic Sports

Alpine Skiing	Ice Hockey
Biathlon	Luge
Bobsled	Nordic Skiing
Figure Skating	Speed Skating

The National Sports Festival

The USOC held the first National Sports Festival in 1978 in Colorado Springs with more than 1,900 of the nation's best athletes competing against each other in twenty-nine different sports. Today, with more than 2,500 athletes competing each year, the National Sports Festival is well on its way to becoming one of the nation's most exciting sporting events.

The athletes who compete in the National Sports Festival are chosen by the National Governing Body in each sport based on their potential as Olympic athletes and their record in past events. The 1980 United States hockey team, which defeated the Russians in the Winter Olympics at Lake Placid, was selected from the eighty athletes who competed in the sports festival just before the 1980 Olympics. The USOC pays the cost of transportation for the athletes who compete in the festival and also provides housing during the event.

Bob Mathias: It Takes Perseverance[3]

At age 17, Bob Mathias became the youngest man in history to win the Olympic decathlon. Four years later, when he won again, he became the first man to win the Olympic decathlon twice. Today, Mathias is still actively involved in sports and physical fitness; he was the Director of the Colorado Springs Olympic Training Center for over six years. In an interview before he resigned his post as director in January of 1984, Mathias spoke about the Training Center and the route to the Olympics.

QUESTION: How is an individual selected for training at the Olympic Training Center?

MATHIAS: The National Governing body for a particular sport will choose a group of athletes it feels has Olympic potential. We get all types of athletes. For example, we might get fifty junior hockey players who come in for training and competition. The elite swimmers will come here for extra training two weeks before they go to Europe to meet the East German swimmers. A few months ago, we had fifty to sixty of the best basketball players in the nation. We held a tournament, and the best fifteen girls were selected for the World Tournament Team. Those girls then trained together here at the center before going to Europe.

The training depends on the kind of camp we have. Usually the average stay is about two weeks, but it can be longer. Right now, we have over 100 permanent athletes here. These are the best weight lifters, cyclers, or boxers who are training for the Olympics. We have all kinds of training periods — one week, two months, and on up to two-and-one-half years. We have 650 beds for the athletes who train here.

QUESTION: Where should an individual start training for the Olympics?

MATHIAS: An athlete should start on the local level at the "Y" or wherever he or she can get the competition. The real competition starts in the schools, where there are organized meets and travel between schools. The next step is the college level where there is a higher level of competition, better coaching, and bigger meets. That leads an athlete to the national competitions. In the Olympic Trials, the first three places make the Olympic Team. For example, in track and field, the three best high jumpers or the three best 100-meter sprinters make the Olympic Team. The Olympic Trials are based strictly on ability.

QUESTION: What does it take for an athlete to be able to qualify for the U.S. Olympic Team?

MATHIAS: In today's sports world, an athlete has to have a lot of determination because there is so much competition today for young people growing up in sports. You have to stick to your basic training in whatever sports you choose. You have to be a person with perseverance who has dedicated himself to becoming good in a sport. This takes a lot of time and you have to give up a lot. What a person needs the most to make a national team or the Olympic Team is a lot of dedication and determination.

The Olympic Ideal

The opportunities for developing athletic excellence through any one of the United States Olympic Committee programs are an expression of the American dream that anyone can succeed if he or she really

**Davis Phinney
(copyright © 1983
by Geoffrey
Ohland).**

wants to make it happen. Selection to the Olympic Training Center, the National Sports Festival, and the United States Olympic Team is based on the athlete's ability and potential. With competition in over thirty sports, every athlete has a wide-open opportunity to match his athletic ability and interests with one or more sports and make progress toward his Olympic goals. This is the Olympic Ideal — that the opportunity for athletic excellence is open to everyone. The American sports system is unique in that it allows the athletes themselves to determine their own goals and, then, provides them with an opportunity to excel based on each individual's commitment to self-improvement and athletic excellence.

Calvin Peete (courtesy of the Professional Golfers Association).

Chapter 8
Professional Sports

VINCE PAPALE COULD BE EVERY ATHLETE'S HERO. NOT BECAUSE HE would want it that way, but because he did what other athletes think about, dream about, and never get around to doing. At age thirty, Vince Papale[1] became the oldest rookie to make it in the National Football League. He did in the pros what most athletes will not try in college: he walked-on and made it.

What is so unique about Papale's experience is that he never played college football. He played in high school and led his county in touchdown receptions, but he weighed only 145 pounds and stood barely five-and-a-half feet tall. By everyone's standards he was "too small" to play college football. So Papale took his 4.5 speed in the forty and a pole vault that was just three feet off the college record and accepted a track scholarship to St. Joseph's University in Philadelphia. "I would have loved to play college football," Papale said, "but St. Joe's didn't have a football program. I got the itch after I became a junior in college because I'd gotten bigger. I weighed 185 and had shot up to six-foot-one, and I could run like the wind."

Papale stayed at St. Joseph's and got his degree. He started teaching and coaching and continued working out. "The itch got me," he said, "and I started training for the decathlon. I had read in the paper about some world-class athletes having done certain things in the decathlon. I'm looking at it and saying, 'I used to do that when I was in college.' " He began an all-out training program and hoped to eventually compete in the Olympic Trials. But he found it hard to register for meets as an independent, and as he says, "That's when I started getting this football bug."

For three years, Papale wrote the Philadelphia Eagles football team asking for a tryout and each year he got a form letter turning him down because he lacked college football experience. But Papale knew he could play, and he jumped at the chance to try out for the Philadelphia Bell in the World Football League. Eight-hundred athletes showed up for the Bell's tryout and about half of them were sent home after being timed in the forty. Even though Papale was twenty-eight years old, he ran back-to-back 4.5's, survived three tryout camps, and started with the Bell from day one. He played in the WFL until the league folded two years later.

The WFL was like a shot in the arm. "I beat out guys who had played in the NFL. That's when I started to think about the National Football League. I had never had an opportunity to compare myself with anyone on the pro level until then. I had always looked out at guys on the field and thought that I could play as well or better than some of the guys I had seen, but I was never given the opportunity."

Paple's experience with the Bell earned him a tryout with his hometown Eagles, and he finally had the opportunity to compete against the cream of the crop in professional football. Papale remembers that it was not easy, to say the least, and that he had never worked so hard. "I was scared at first. In the back of my mind I was thinking, 'What am I doing? I'm thirty years old. Do I really think I can make this team?' " He relaxed as the camp started and ran stride-for-stride with the younger players. Papale had an excellent camp and led the wide receivers in preseason catches. During the season, he played on special teams and earned a reputation as a ferocious hitter. His attitude fired up the team, and the "old man" was an instant hit with the Eagles' fans. At an age when most NFL veterans are thinking about retiring, Papale was making tackles, causing turnovers, and catching passes. He played for three seasons with the Eagles, 1976 to 1978, and spent the 1979 season on the injured reserved list. Today, after having been turned down three times because he had no college experience, Vince Papale is a retired NFL veteran. He did what others only dream about and did it against some of the best athletes in the world.

A Pro Career: It's Not All Roses

Life as a professional athlete is not always as pleasant as it's cracked up to be. There will always be hundreds of athletes yapping at your heels trying to get your job, and then there is the chance of a career-ending injury. Whether an athlete begins as a draftee or as a free agent, he has to work hard both to earn a position and to keep it. While the prestige usually outweighs the disadvantages, an athlete should start-out with an understanding of some of the negative aspects of a professional sports career.

1. **Short-lived pro career.** The average length of most professional sports careers is short indeed: baseball, 4.7 years; basketball, 4.5 years; football, 4.2 years; and ice hockey, 4.8 years. Many factors contribute to the shortness of the career—injuries, loss of ability, old

age (say, age twenty-eight to age thirty-eight), loss of desire, stiff competition, and poor conditioning. The public is accustomed to seeing professional athletes lead long careers of twenty or more years. For example, when Gaylor Perry won his 300th game, he became the 15th pitcher to pass that milestone. He did it at age forty-three after twenty-one years in major league baseball. But most athletes do not last that long. One reason is because the veterans are so hard to beat out. A veteran may start at a position for eight or nine years, while every year, a half-a-dozen or more younger players are given the chance to win his position. Each of these newcomers who fails to take his place is cut, and the next season a new crop of youngsters is brought in to take their shot at the old pro. Consequently, at the start of training camp, most young athletes have no assurance that they will be around the next week, let alone the next season.

In the individual participant sports such as golf and tennis, the same names have been on top of the money-winner lists for years. Jack Nicklaus won the NCAA championship in 1961 and his first U.S. Open in 1962. Now, over twenty years later, he is still burning up the courses. Jimmy Connors won the NCAA tennis championship in 1971 and was ranked the Number 1 player in the world for six years from 1974 through 1979. Chris Evert has been at the top or not far from the top since she won her first two major tournaments, the French Open and Wimbledon, in 1974. And even Billie Jean King is still playing and made it to the semifinals of the 1982 and 1983 Wimbledon tournaments. In the Ladies Professional Golf Association, the three all-time top money winners, JoAnne Carner, Donna Caponi, and Kathy Whitworth, who have each won more than one million dollars, invariably beat their competition and finish at the top of the standings year after year.

While all of these seasoned professionals continue to win each year, the rookies begin their careers following a hard and uncertain route that can end at any time. Just as the team sport rookies have to beat out veterans, the new athletes on the pro tours have to earn their wings by beating the best professionals who have already won their place on the tour by beating the best athletes before them. Most professional athletes have short careers because few, if any, of the "old pros" are ready or willing to come down from the top of the mountain.

2. Loss of career freedom. The draft and pro contracts lock athletes into a system where they lose their freedom to pick their employer. After an athlete is drafted or signs as a free agent, his employer has full control of where he plays, when he plays, and whether he plays at all. This control has been limited somewhat by the collective bargaining agreements the players' associations have negotiated with the club owners, but a rookie athlete and others in the early years of their careers can be cut, traded, waived, or sold and sent off to a new team or out of the league in no time. If an athlete likes hot weather but is drafted by a team in Minnesota, that is tough. If he is a top player but has to spend most of his career with one of the worst teams in the league, he is simply out of luck.

3. Family inconveniences. Family problems are more obvious than some of the others. Everyone knows that professional athletes have to travel. Baseball and basketball players have long road trips that may keep them away from home for over a week at a time. All of the professional leagues have preseason camps that last for up to two months. There are also many demands made on an athlete's life and plenty of negative public attention. With no warning at all, an athlete may be traded and sent to another team in less than forty-eight hours; it does not matter if his kids like their school or his wife enjoys playing cards with her friends—a trade is a trade. The inconveniences may be as minor as missing Thanksgiving with the family or as major as causing a divorce and other related problems. It is part of the job, but being told that does not make it any easier.

4. Uncertain future income. Only a few athletes get guaranteed contracts, and despite the news of high salaries in professional sports, most athletes have the same money worries as everyone else. The minimum salary in the four major professional sports is approximately $30,000—not $100,000 as some might expect. When the average salary in a league is $120,000, there are plenty of low-paid athletes to average out the half-million-dollar contracts. If an athlete is injured, his earnings are immediately in doubt, but his house payments and other bills are still due. When an athlete does not make a team, he is usually cut and his contract canceled. Suddenly, he is out of both luck and an income at the same time. In golf, tennis, or professional bowling, it is not all roses either. A long slump can wipe out an athlete's earnings as well as his career. Travel expenses can cost an athlete more money than he wins if he finishes too far from first place. These aspects of a pro career put many professional athletes on a financial tightrope. Athletes can sometimes protect themselves through investments or contract insurance, but oftentimes the net is insufficient.

5. Second-career decisions. When an athlete's playing days are over, he has to start looking for a job just like anyone else. Finding a good job is not always an easy task, and finding a satisfying job is often harder. An athlete may gain several good contacts through his sports participation, but in the business world the bottom line is how well he can do the job—not how many yards he gained carrying the ball. The veterans eventually qualify for the league's pension, but they still have to find a way to spend their time. Not everyone can go into broadcasting, and most second careers do not offer the satisfactions of a pro sports career. Usually athletes handle their second careers well enough, but for many, changing to a satisfactory second career is an unsolvable dilemma.

You Might Be Drafted

Despite the drawbacks, a professional sports career offers an athlete a whole world of challenges and excitement that cannot be found in many eight-to-five jobs. Most athletes start their pro careers through the draft system.

In football and basketball, the draft is a major factor in a team's short-term and long-term success. The San Francisco 49ers picked several players who were instrumental as rookies in helping them win Super Bowl XVI. In basketball, one key player can change a team's entire season for several years to come. Before the 1982 NBA draft, the owner of the Los Angeles Lakers offered six million dollars to the San Diego Clippers for the first pick in the draft and the right to select seven-foot, four-inch center Ralph Sampson. L. A.'s offer shows how much a first-round draft choice can be worth to a team. Careless drafting can send an NFL team or NBA team to the bottom of the standings in a hurry.

In baseball, soccer, and hockey, the draft is not usually a critical factor in the team's immediate success because few college and high school athletes are ready to step into the pro leagues and play against some of the best athletes in the world. The farm systems in both baseball and hockey establish an almost automatic apprenticeship for all but the rare superstars who come along every few years. The draft is important in a team's long-term success, and if a club manages to have several years of poor drafting, it will be left with weak replacements for their aging players. The next few pages outline the procedure of the draft in the major professional leagues.

PROFESSIONAL FOOTBALL

The National Football League and the United States Football League hold their annual college drafts after the post-season bowl games are completed. Both drafts are similar in design. The NFL draft consists of twelve rounds in which 336 athletes are selected. The twenty-eight teams select in reverse order of the previous season standings; in other words, the previous year's last place team picks first. Each team has one pick per round unless it has traded away its selection or has traded for others.

In the past, a draftee was locked-in to his drafting team for an indefinite period, but now NFL draftees have special rights that require

Barry Redden (courtesy of the Los Angeles Rams).

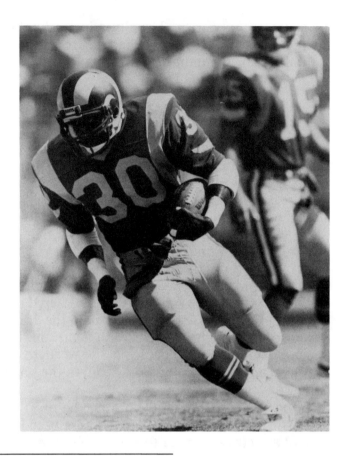

a team to negotiate in good faith toward a mutually acceptable contract. This change allows drafted athletes to sit out one full year and be drafted again if the player and the team that first drafted him cannot reach an acceptable contract. If an athlete is drafted again and still cannot agree upon a contract, he becomes a free agent after the next year's draft.

When an athlete is drafted, he has no guarantee of making a team—in fact, the odds in both the NFL and the USFL are against him. In the NFL, there are forty-five active players and four inactive players on each of the twenty-eight teams; this means that there are 1,372 jobs up for grabs each season. All of these positions, however, are held by experienced players who have no intention of being beaten out. A survey of the last several seasons reveals that, on the average, less than half of the NFL's 336 draftees will earn a position the next season on the opening-day rosters of the twenty-eight teams.

If an athlete is not drafted the first year he is eligible, he becomes a free agent immediately after the draft. Each year the NFL and USFL teams will sign as many as 1,200 athletes as free agents and bring them to their rookie camps for preseason practices, but most of these rookies are cut before the veterans get to camp. A free agent may contact any or all of these teams and sign with the team of his choice — if they are interested in having him. A free agent does not have an easy route to the pros, but as Vince Papale and many others have shown, free agents do make it and often make it in a big way.

MAJOR LEAGUE BASEBALL

The American and National Leagues and their minor league affiliates conduct two selection meetings for the purpose of drafting amateur baseball players who are residents of the United States. The drafts are conducted under the guidelines of professional baseball's "Rule 4." Each selection meeting is conducted in two phases. The first phase is called the Regular Phase, in which athletes who were not drafted at the previous meeting are eligible to be drafted. The Secondary Phase consists of the selection of athletes who were drafted at the previous meeting but who did not sign a contract after being drafted. Once an athlete is drafted, the club has exclusive rights to negotiate a contract with the draftee for approximately six months. The club is responsible for beginning negotiations with the draftee within fifteen days of the close of the selection meeting. If an athlete has not signed a contract within six months after the selection meeting, he is eligible to have his name entered in the next draft.

The twenty-six major league teams choose athletes at each meeting in the reverse order in which they finished the previous season. That is, the team with the worst record will get the first pick unless it has traded its selection away. Each team normally has one draft pick in each round, but there is no limit on the number of rounds or the number of athletes who may be drafted by any of the teams. The major league baseball teams will draft about 200 to 300 high school athletes each year. The rules governing eligibility state that no high school student may be signed to a contract if he is eligible for participation in high school athletics. If a high school athlete's eligibility has expired, he may be signed to a contract as long as the contract does not require him to report to the team before his class graduates from high school.

A college baseball player will normally not be eligible for the pro draft until his class has graduated from college — unless he meets one or more of five special conditions: a) reached his twenty-first birthday; b) completed his junior year; c) flunked out of college; d) completed his full four years of college eligibility; or e) withdrawn from college and remained out of college for 120 days. Junior college players may sign a contract only after their regular season and post-

Matt Young (courtesy of the Seattle Mariners).

season play has ended.

High school and college athletes may try out under special conditions for a major or minor league team, but the team may not reimburse the athletes for their expenses. A representative from a pro club may talk to an athlete concerning the merits of a pro baseball career, but the representative may not encourage an athlete to drop out of any current program nor may he discuss specific contract details with the athlete until he has been drafted. It is permissible for a club representative to ask a ballplayer before he is drafted what terms he expects to receive when he signs a contract, but the representative cannot comment on the athlete's evaluation of himself and cannot make any counteroffers.

When a student-athlete still has eligibility remaining, he must remember that he is subject to the rules of the governing body for his sport. For example, the National Collegiate Athletic Association has several rules stating that an athlete will lose his eligibility if he hires an agent to represent him in any contract negotiations, if he enters into an agreement to play a professional sport, or if he requests that his name be placed on a list of athletes to be drafted.

Athletes who are drafted have a choice of entering the professional leagues or participating in college play. The National Association of Professional Baseball Leagues estimates that a ballplayer takes an average of four years to work his way up to a major league team. For athletes who do not make a major league team, the average career length is only three years. An athlete good enough to be drafted after his high school career is good enough to earn a scholarship on any college team in the nation. Considering that it takes an average of four years to make the majors, an athlete should decide whether the experience he will gain in college and the degree he can earn at the same time make that option more attractive than going straight to the pros. The average salary on a Class AA minor league team is about $1,100 per month and about $850 per month on a Class A team.

THE NATIONAL BASKETBALL ASSOCIATION

The NBA holds its annual draft in late June or early July. The twenty-three teams conduct a ten-round draft, and as many as 230 players may be drafted. As in all the leagues, the clubs may trade away their draft picks for established players or cash. The drafting teams have exclusive rights to negotiate contracts with their draftees. If a player remains unsigned, he can request to have his name entered in the next draft.

To be eligible for the NBA draft the rules require that an athlete either complete his college eligibility or ask that his name be added to the draft pool. As soon as an athlete notifies the Commissioner's Office that he wants to be included in the NBA draft, he forfeits his remaining college eligibility. Even for the best college athletes, the decision to turn pro early requires considerable thought.

In an amazing fashion, three NBA players skipped college completely and jumped from high school to the pros. Moses Malone, the NBA's 1982 and 1983 Most Valuable Player, headed for pro basketball and the Utah Stars in 1974. Malone was traded to several teams and finally settled in with the Houston Rockets. At the end of the 1982 season, Malone became a free agent and signed a multi-million-dollar deal with the Philadelphia 76ers. Darryl Dawkins was drafted by the 76ers after his high school senior season in 1974. Dawkins started as the 76ers' center and helped lead the team past the Boston Celtics and into the 1982 NBA finals. The third players to skip college and make it in the NBA is Bill Willoughby. Willoughby played for Atlanta, Buffalo, San Diego, Cleveland, Houston, and San Antonio. The astronomical odds against making it should prevent most athletes from taking this route. An athlete's experiences in college can smooth out many of the bumps in a pro career.

The NBA's roster limit of 12 makes room for 276 players on 23 teams. About one month before the draft each spring, the NBA scouting service holds an evaluation camp where the top 48 college prospects are evaluated by all of the teams' scouts and coaches. The record has shown that most of those top prospects and a handful of other players are the only athletes out of the 200 or so draftees who make it each year. In 1984, 51 rookies made the active roster on opening day; in both 1983 and 1982, 48 rookies survived the last cut; but in 1979, only 39 rookies suited up for the first game of the season.

MAJOR INDOOR SOCCER LEAGUE

The MISL holds an annual four-round draft each year with the thirteen teams drafting athletes in reverse order of their previous season's standings. High school and college athletes are eligible for the draft if they have completed their eligibility. College athletes can request that their names be placed in the draft pool, but in doing so they lose their remaining college eligibility. Athletes who are eligible for the draft but are not drafted become free agents and may sign with any team in the league. The roster limit in the MISL is twenty. Every team holds open tryouts for all comers, as well as separate tryouts for certain athletes. Since the quality of American athletes' play is improving steadily each season and better programs and coaching are made available for junior high, high school, and college athletes, the sport will become uniquely American as these athletes are drafted and begin playing in the MISL. At the same time, the acceptance and popularity of soccer will expand.

THE NATIONAL HOCKEY LEAGUE

The NHL holds its entry draft each year at its annual meeting in July. The teams select players according to the number of points scored in the previous season, with the lowest scoring team selecting first. There are ten rounds of drafting and any athlete aged eighteen, nineteen or twenty can be drafted. At the present time, any athlete over the age of eighteen who has not been drafted may sign with any club as a free agent. The drafting club retains exclusive negotiating rights to its draftees until forty-eight hours before the next draft. If a drafted player elects to attend college, the drafting team retains the right to negotiate with him for 180 days after his college participation has ended. The usual route for a draftee is to head for a Canadian junior league team or one of the club's minor league affiliates until he is ready to play in the NHL. A hockey player has to consider the gains of a minor league career versus the experience of a college career and the benefits of a college degree before making his decision to turn pro.

THE CANADIAN FOOTBALL LEAGUE

The Canadian Football League conducts a draft only for Canadian college athletes. Citizens of the United States are considered free agents. The Canadian football teams are required by the League rules to keep a "negotiating list" of the names of U.S. citizens they hope to sign. This means that, before a football player from the United States can negotiate with a Canadian team, he must find out if his name is on a team's negotiating list. If he is on a team's list, he must begin negotiating with that team. In other words, he is not really a free agent, but if he cannot reach terms with that team and they will release him from their list (or sell him to another club), he may have some discretion as to where he plays. The Canadian Football League limits each team's roster to fifteen American players. Training camps in the CFL are opened around May 30, and the season ends after the championship game in November.

Rookie Free Agents

All of the professional teams rely on free agents to fill out positions they cannot fill with drafted athletes or their own veterans. To have enough athletes to hold their preseason practices, each pro team needs to pick up at the very least one dozen to several dozen free agents. Athletes who are eligible for the draft but are not drafted become free agents and may sign with any team that wants them.

Many of the pro teams will hold one or two-day minicamps where recommended athletes and volunteers are allowed to try out. These tryouts include tests for speed, quickness, strength, and agility. Some teams give intelligence and personality tests to the best prospects. The athletes are usually required to demonstrate specific skills, such as catching passes, throwing and hitting a baseball, shooting baskets, or anything else the coaches feel might be related to the sport. During these camps, as many as 500 to 600 or more athletes may be tested. Of these, a half-dozen to a dozen may be given invitations to a second minicamp or may be offered a minimum-salary contract and invited to training camp. During the camp, if the athletes are cut, the contracts are simply terminated. In most cases everyone is happy even if an athlete is cut: he got his big chance, the team had somebody to help fill out the practice squads, and the veterans had someone else to run over instead of each other.

Because the scouting systems are so extensive, it is hard for football, baseball, basketball, or hockey players to be overlooked before the draft. The scouts are everywhere, looking at almost everyone in a uniform. In soccer there are not as many scouts, and a good athlete in a small program or on a losing team can be overlooked. But regardless of the sport, if an athlete and his head coach think he is good enough to be a professional athlete, they should not hesitate to contact the scouting service of the professional league or one of the teams in the league. What this contact requires is a few letters to several teams or scouting services and a great deal of patience. There is no secret to selling yourself except to back up your letters with impressive game films, excellent play, an all-out desire to succeed, and the persistence to earn a tryout. If an athlete needs a little more experience before going into one of the major professional leagues, he should not overlook the opportunities discussed at the end of Chapter 6. There are plenty of semipro teams and minor league teams where an athlete can gain extra experience and maybe get a pro scout or two looking his way.

The Players' Associations

One of the best things to happen for the benefit of professional team sports athletes has been the organization of the players' associations. Pro sports are big business, as evidenced by the two-billion-dollar television contract ABC, CBS, and NBC signed with the National Football League. Not too long ago, professional athletes had about as much control over their sports careers as cattle at a livestock auction. They were literally owned by the teams that drafted them and were considered nothing more than the property of the team. The players' associations have worked to make the careers of professional athletes more satisfying in a variety of ways.

The biggest task of the players' associations has been negotiating acceptable collective-bargaining agreements, but their work has not stopped there. These associations offer a variety of benefits that include: credit unions, investment counseling, insurance plans, retirement and pension plans, career counseling, legal counseling, youth programs, and special events. If an athlete is reaching the point where he might be drafted into a league or become a free agent, he should contact the players' association of his sport for additional guidance or advice. The addresses of these organizations are listed in Appendix B.

Individual Participant Professional Sports Opportunities

Just because an athlete cannot play football or is not a seven-foot-tall basketball player, he or she should not automatically think that the opportunities for a pro career are not there. Individual participant sports offer a wide range of opportunities to everyone regardless of size and sex. The "how do you get started" questions are answered in this section. In all of these sports, an athlete is truly limited more by his or her desire and determination to succeed than by the aspects of physical ability.

THE PROFESSIONAL GOLFERS ASSOCIATION

The PGA approved an All-Exempt tour that went into effect with the 1983 season. Under the new system, the top 125 money winners will be automatically eligible for the next year's forty major PGA tournaments. Players holding long-term exemptions for prior achievements will be added to the list of the 125 immediately eligible golfers. New golfers will be added to the list after a series of PGA Tour Qualifying Tournaments that begins late in September of each year, with approximately eighteen local qualifying tournaments across the nation. The top golfers in these events will advance to eight regional qualifying meets, and a final field of 200 golfers will be selected from the top regional golfers to compete in the final qualifying tournament in Ponte Vedra, Florida. The golfers finishing first through fiftieth in the final qualifying tournament will be issued new membership cards. Each year, there will be approximately 200 to 230 golfers who will be eligible to compete in the PGA's forty major tournaments.

What the All-Exempt tour means to aspiring golfers is that fifty openings will continue to be filled for each new season. (For established golfers, it means that fifty of them may be booted out.) An applicant for the PGA Qualifying Tournament must have a USGA handicap of two or less. Once an athlete starts playing in the local qualifying tournament, he will be on his own to prove himself and to earn his PGA card.

THE LADIES PROFESSIONAL GOLF ASSOCIATION

The LPGA was established by eleven professional women golfers in 1950. It is a non-profit association designed to publicize the professional side of women's golf and, like the PGA, is dedicated to fund raising for numerous charities. Today, the Association is divided into approximately 250 tournament players and 300 teaching members. In 1984, LPGA members competed for over eight million dollars in prize

Jan Stephenson
(courtesy of the
Ladies Professional
Golf Association).

money in thirty-nine tournaments in the United States, Canada, Japan, England, and Ireland. The average purse per tournament is about $200,000. The LPGA operates two Qualifying Schools each year. Applicants must by 18 years old or older, have a USGA handicap of three or better, and two letters of recommendation from qualified professionals. Each year approximately twenty-five to thirty-five golfers are added to the tour through the LPGA Qualifying Schools.

PROFESSIONAL TENNIS

As soon as a tennis player begins beating everyone in sight, he or she begins wondering if it is time to take on the world. But before anyone drops out of school and heads for Wimbledon, they should join the United States Tennis Association and try to get a national, sectional, or district ranking. Each year the USTA awards more than 15,000 rankings to amateur athletes in several age groups ranging from boys' and girls' twelve-and-under to men's eighty-and-over. The application process is simple enough. An athlete has to be a member of the USTA and play in a minimum number of tournaments during the ranking period. For juniors, this period is from October 1 to September 30; for other age groups, it is from January 1 to December 31. The athlete's record from all USTA sanctioned events and approved high school tournaments must be included in the application. The records of all the athletes in a particular age group are compared, and the rankings are issued. Each year, the USTA sponsors hundreds of tournaments that will lead an athlete from local events to the state, sectional, and national level. National championships are offered in the 12-, 14-, 16-, and 18-and-under age groups, as well as an open class.

Most tennis coaches feel that the route to the pros begins with the USTA junior program or an athlete's junior high and high school tennis program. In almost all cases, the next step is to compete in a top-notch college program. The NCAA tennis championship offers some of the best tennis in the nation. An important advantage of college tennis is that during the summer an athlete can compete as an amateur against the pros and still retain his scholarship. If an athlete heads for the pro circuit before he is ready for the competition, he may have to worry more about where his next meal is coming from than who his competition is.

The USTA offers a pro satellite circuit for men that includes fifty tournaments. Virginia Slims sponsors a similar professional tour for women. After athletes begin winning at these tournaments, their success rests on their ability to work their way up the computer ranking lists to qualify for the major tournaments.

The best consensus of opinion indicates that before an athlete seriously considers turning pro he or she should play four years of college tennis or win the NCAA or USTA national championship. In winning one of these tournaments, an athlete will have beaten the best amateur competition and should have a good chance of surviving as a professional player.

Chris Evert Lloyd: A New Role for Women

Practice. Practice. Practice. Chris Evert grew up in a tennis family. Her father won the national junior indoor championship in 1940 and became a captain of the Notre Dame tennis team. Chris started playing tennis at age six just to have something to do. But after a while, the fun of the game and the challenge to get better captivated her.

Chris played tennis every day; she practiced two hours each day after school, three to six hours on the weekends, and four to six hours a day throughout the summer. Gradually, she began to think like a tennis player, planning her shots and moving her oponents with pinpoint placements. Before long, she was controlling the court and making everyone else play her game. Her friends at the time could not understand her love for the game and her devotion to it. She would skip the parties and playtime and the dolls and dates, but she rarely would miss the practice sessions and tournaments. She passed up cheerleading and chumming for ground strokes, passing shots, and spin serves. Ten years later, as she settled into her tennis career, no one was questioning her motives and the result of her hard work and persistence.

For almost a decade, Chris Evert Lloyd has been the dominant personality in women's professional sports. She has won the U.S. Open six times, the French Open five times, and Wimbledon, the most prestigious, three times. When she won her first national recognition, she was just a bouncy, five-foot-four, 105-pound teenager who could play with the best women tennis players in the world and win. It was exciting to see her going head-to-head against Billie Jean King and others. Her nicknames review her evolution through tennis. She was the Cinderella of Tennis; America's Sweetheart who became Little Miss Cool, the Ball Machine, and the Ice Maiden. Her career has been both up and down and is a reflection of the rigors and hazards of competing at the top levels of professional sports.

But through it all, she has demonstrated that she is a champion in every way. She is determined and driven. She has a tremendous will to win, and she demands of herself that she excel, improve, and suc-

Chris Evert Lloyd (courtesy of Wilson Sporting Goods).

ceed. In truth, Chris was never a tennis Cinderella or an overnight success, but a determined, dedicated athlete who set her goals and worked toward them. Through her matches and tournaments, she quietly led the way and solidified the role of women in sports. Underneath the braids and ribbons and the mascara and blush, it was okay to be hard driving and unyielding in the pursuit of a goal. It was okay to be a woman and excel and succeed in athletics. It was all right to view a sport as more than a hobby and more than a way to kill a couple of hours on a summer afternoon. Over the years, she has shown that women can compete with killer instincts and with a passion for winning and yet be feminine at the same time. She has shown that women should strive for the same success and achievement in sports as men, and in return, receive the same respect for their hard work and accomplishments.

Throughout her career, Chris Evert Lloyd has been a dedicated, consistent competitor striving for her best and pushing herself to the limit. She is a true champion who quietly set the standards and direction for thousands of women athletes in all sports to work toward and surpass.

THE PROFESSIONAL BOWLERS ASSOCIATION

The first PBA tour began in 1959 with prize money totaling $49,500. Today, the PBA National Tour includes thirty-four major tournaments with more than 3.5 million dollars in prize money. In 1982, Earl Anthony became the first professional bowler to stretch his career earnings past the one-million-dollar milestone.

There are two classifications of memberships in the PBA: national and regional. A regional membership allows an individual to compete in top weekend tournaments without the expense and time required by a national membership. The regional competition does not offer the top prize money, but it does offer stiff competition and is the first step toward the top tournaments and prize money. A national membership allows a bowler to compete in the major tournaments with a shot at the big money.

An applicant for the PBA must be at least eighteen years old or a high school graduate and have maintained a minimum average of 190 pins for sixty-six or more games during the two most recent seasons prior to applying for membership. Within one year of membership, each member must successfully complete the PBA Members' School. The application process takes approximately six weeks, and the application blank is available through the PBA.

THE LADIES PRO BOWLERS TOUR

The LPBT was organized in January of 1981 and gained control of women's professional bowling when the Women's Professional Bowlers Association closed its operations. The LPBT has grown in stature and popularity as its seasons have expanded to include new tournaments and pro bowling opportunities.

Membership in the LPBT is open to all women bowlers. An applicant must meet several requirements, including an average of 175 pins in the previous two seasons or a show of just cause for being allowed to join the League. There are about 200 professional bowlers in the LPBT and no limit on the number of applicants who will be accepted. The opportunities are wide open for the best women bowlers who want to compete professionally.

Marshall Holman (courtesy of Professional Bowlers Association).

PROFESSIONAL RACQUETBALL

The Racquetball Manufacturers Association sponsors a number of men's professional racquetball tournaments. Women's racquetball is well organized and controlled by the Women's Professional Racquetball Association. The amateur side of the sport is also well managed by one governing body, the American Amateur Racquetball Association (AARA).

An athlete is usually on his or her own in working toward a career as a racquetball player because few schools offer racquetball as a competitive sport. The route to the top of the pro racquetball circuit requires as much determination as it does talent and practice because admission to many of the top tournaments is by invitation, with manufacturers allowing only athletes who are on contract to compete in the events.

As in all sports, an athlete has to work his way to the top. A player should contact the AARA or its state affiliate for a list of the current year's tournaments and the eligibility and application requirements. Once an athlete is winning most of the tournaments he or she enters and builds a reputation as a top state or regional player, he may be able to attract a sponsor and receive free equipment and expense money. At that time, the athlete can begin qualifying for the major open tournaments. Chuck Leve, the Editor of *National Racquetball* magazine, says that it takes about five years for an athlete to earn national recognition as one of the top players in the country. For those who do make it, the climb is worth it. Marty Hogan, for example, has been one of the best professional racquetball players in the nation since 1978; he earns approximately $500,000 per year in prize money and endorsements. Hogan's serve has been clocked at 142 miles per hour.

Jim Kelly (courtesy of the Houston Gamblers).

David Goodin (photo by Ken Litchfield, copyright © 1985).

Jim Beattie (courtesy of the Seattle Mariners).

Chapter 9
Selecting a Sports Agent

AN ATHLETE'S SELECTION OF A SPORTS AGENT OR ATTORNEY TO HELP manage the business side of his or her sports career is one of the most important decisions the athlete will face when it is time for him or her to turn pro. This is so because the representative's influence will usually extend beyond the contract talks to include everything from investment and tax advice to advertising opportunities and personal appearance agreements. The selection of a poorly qualified representative will set the stage for inferior contracts, missed opportunities, and considerable dissatisfaction.

At the professional level, sports are far too complicated to be considered "games." With contracts starting at about $30,000 and quickly going over a million dollars, there is little room for uninformed athletes trying to manage their business affairs without expert, outside advice. Because so much has to be considered and so many decisions have to be made, there is no doubt that an athlete should hire a qualified individual or group of individuals to help make the business decisions. The important word is *hire*. The athlete is the employer. Just as an athlete should shop around for the most qualified surgeon to perform an operation, he should also shop around for the most qualified sports agent or attorney to represent his interests. The best decision can come only after several individuals have been interviewed and the advantages of each are compared.

The most important considerations in hiring a sports representative are the individual's honesty and experience. An honest representative with no experience may not be an effective negotiator. A dishonest representative, regardless of his experience, is of no value at all. An athlete can get an idea of a representative's experience and honesty by talking to his current clients. Every potential representative should be able to provide an athlete with a list of clients and phone numbers where they can be reached. It is obvious that no one is going to give an athlete a list with several names of dissatisfied clients, but a list of "satisfied" clients will allow an athlete to get several opinions about the representative. In talking to a representative's clients, you should not be shy about asking questions that get right to the point. Did he (the representative) do a good job? Would you recommend him? Is he honest? Whom else has he represented, and were they happy with his work? Would you recommend someone else who might be better? With these questions (and the ones listed below), an athlete should be able to get a feeling for the representative's honesty, experience, and ability.

When hiring a representative, most athletes choose between a sports agent or an attorney. There are several differences in the way agents and attorneys operate their businesses. The first difference is the way they secure new clients. Attorneys are usually prohibited from advertising and do not normally solicit clients. Agents, on the other hand, are often attracted to top athletes like flies to a picnic. At some colleges it seems that there are as many new agents trying to get clients as there are athletes on the teams. The better-established agents will usually rely on their current clients to tell other athletes about their services; occasionally, they will contact a few top prospects.

A second difference between agents and attorneys can be seen in the fees that are charged for their services. Agents usually charge a flat percentage of the athlete's gross salary and bonus. This percentage may range from 3 percent to 10 percent or higher. Attorneys usually charge a flat legal fee based on the number of hours they work negotiating the contract. In many cases, when an athlete hires an agent, he may still need to hire an attorney to check the paperwork. The difference between an hourly rate and a percentage can be substantial. If an athlete signs a three-year, $40,000-a-year contract with a $40,000 singing bonus, his gross salary and bonus will be $160,000. If an agent charges him 10 percent to negotiate the contract, the athlete will owe $16,000. If the athlete had hired an attorney to represent him, he probably would have saved some money. Attorney's fees vary, but a rate of $100 per hour can be considered about average. A $40,000-a -year contract would be considered peanuts in today's professional leagues, and the contract could probably be negotiated without too much trouble. But assuming the negotiations required a full week's work (forty hours) at $100 per hour, the athlete would owe the attorney $4,000. If the negotiations took half a day, he would only owe the attorney $400. That fee is a great deal less than $16,000.

Along with the basic fee for negotiating the contract, most agents and attorneys require their clients to reimburse them for any expenses involved. The expenses an athlete may be responsible for include: accountants, tax work, a typist, copying, phone calls, transportation, hotels, and food. These charges will vary from representative to representative, and in some cases they can be negotiated out of the deal or at least reduced.

The question for the athlete is not "Where can I get the cheapest representative?" but "Where can I get the best?" Including his fees, a good attorney or a good agent can make an athlete more money in the long run than the athlete can negotiate for himself or more than some fly-by-night, bargain-basement-priced representative can negotiate for him. A good contract includes both a salary and a package of benefits, option, and incentives. A representative who is looking out for himself instead of the athlete will go after only the big salary and big bonus and not worry about any options that will not make *him* any money. An unscrupulous representative may even work both sides of the bargaining table or enter into a situation involving conflict of interest. For example, *Sports Illustrated* reported the story of an agent who had a financial interest in a professional sports franchise, yet was representing athletes who were drafted by his own team. Other agents may take under-the-table money and encourage their athletes to sign inferior contracts. A first-class representative will avoid all conflicts of interest, will bargain for each of his client's best interests, and will go for the benefits just as hard as he goes for the salary and bonus.

A good agent or attorney does not mind being questioned about his qualifications. Before hiring an agent or attorney, you should discuss each of the following areas with every representative you are considering:

1. Discuss his current clients and ask for their phone numbers.
2. Discuss the fees the representative will charge and the expenses that you will be expected to pay. Can these expenses be limited? If travel is involved, there is no need to pay for a $125-a-night room when a $75 room will be just as convenient.
3. What services does the representative offer? Some packages include a tax service, accountants, investment advice, money management, contract insurance, and overall career management for public appearances and endorsements. Some representatives claim to have these services; then they suddenly disappear after being paid the fee for negotiating the contract.
4. How much experience does the representative have negotiating professional sports contracts? What kinds of deals has he negotiated in the past?
5. How much time will the representative devote to getting the athlete a good contract? How busy will he be with other clients?
6. How will the payment be made? Some representatives expect to be paid all of their fees from the athlete's signing bonus. *Never agree to this.* The representative should only be paid as the athlete himself is paid. It should be agreed in writing that any overpayments to the representative will be immediately refund-

ed to the athlete.

7. Is there a chance that a conflict of interest exists between the athlete, the representative, the team, or any other athletes on the team?

8. How easily can the athlete contact the representative after the negotiations have ended?

9. How can the representative be fired? This procedure should be spelled out in writing. Some individuals try to get a lifetime hold on their client's income, binding the athlete so that they can never be fired. The procedure for terminating the business relationship between the athlete and representative should be well understood, written out, approved by an attorney, and signed by both.

In deciding whom to hire, an athlete should realize that there are no superstar agents or attorneys who can talk any professional sports team into paying a salary or bonus that is higher than what the athlete is actually worth. Some representatives are fast-talking touters who claim to be able to get an athlete more money than all of the other representatives combined. This is just not possible. All of the professional teams have a good idea of what they are going to pay an athlete long before they draft him or sign him as a free agent. The teams go by a rough, unwritten formula. The first-round draft choices get so much; the fifth-round choices get so much; and the free agents get so much. Of course, the teams will always sign an athlete for less than they thought they would have to pay him and be happy to do so. A good representative knows in advance how a team will negotiate and what they want to pay an athlete; he knows the value of his client, how much the bonus should be, and how the benefits and incentives should be packaged. A good agent will not get an athlete any more money than a good attorney and vice versa. A "great" representative will not do so much better than a good one. The secret to negotiating a good contract is knowing how to get the team to pay the athlete everything they intended to pay in the first place plus as much over that as possible. A good representative knows how high a figure to use to start the negotiating process, when not to come down, and most importantly, when and how to compromise.

One of the most important questions to ask a representative before deciding whom to hire is "How much am I worth to the team and why?" A good representative should be able to give you a solid idea of how much money he expects you to be able to sign for long before the negotiations start. If he knows his business, he should know the current "market value" of athletes with different levels of ability. Because the salary levels in all of the leagues are somewhat structured, each representative who estimates your value should do so in about the same salary range. If one of the representatives you are considering estimates your value at $100,000 more than everyone else, it probably means that he does not know his business too well. A representative should be able to explain to you why he estimated your salary at a particular figure. His answer might sound something like this: "Well, so-and-so is 'this good' and his salary is 'this much money.' And so-and-so is making 'this much' but he is not as good as you. The average salary for your team is 'this much' and they usually start negotiating for an athlete of your ability at about 'this much money.' So I figure that you are worth X-number of dollars."

After you compare each representative's estimate of your projected salary, the amount of money he will charge you to negotiate your contract, his expected expenses, and his honesty and experience, you will be able to make a good decision. Hiring an agent is serious business, and you should not hire anyone until you have shopped around and have an excellent idea of what you are getting.

Consider These Negotiating Points

The answers to the following questions provide an overview of several critical points that should be fully understood before an athlete's contract is negotiated. An athlete and his representative should discuss the answers in detail to be certain that each has a clear understanding of the athlete's expectations and an understanding of how those expectations compare to what might be possible once the negotiating process begins.

1. What is the actual ability and future potential of the athlete? What is that worth to a professional team? How much will that value go up in the future?
2. How are equally talented athletes compensated in both salary and benefits?
3. How should the salary and benefit package be balanced? How many years should the contract be in force? Should part of the salary be deferred? How much money should the athlete receive as a signing bonus?
4. How will the league's rules, the standard player contract, and the collective bargaining agreement affect the total package?
5. What are the renewal provisions of the contract? How will they affect the agreement?
6. What kind of offer will the team make? How does the team negotiate?
7. What are the laws that will apply to the contract?
8. What options and extras should be considered and included in the contract?
9. At what figure should the negotiations begin? When and how should compromises be made?

Know the Tricks of the Trade

After an athlete hires a representative to negotiate his contract, he should take a hint from Hollywood's toughest agents. One of the rules these agents have is that their actors and actresses never get involved in contract negotiations. When the agent or attorney does all of the negotiating, the client is spared all the stress connected with the negotiating process. This is why an athlete has to hire a top-notch negotiator because, once the wheeling and dealing starts, the athlete should disappear and let his representative do all the talking and worrying. If you take your time and hire a good negotiator, you will be able to trust his judgment and his honesty and have complete faith that he will get you the best deal possible.

As the negotiations start, you should realize that the professional sports teams are professionals at negotiating contracts. From the team's point of view there is nothing fun about contract talks because it is their money that is being discussed. There are many tricks of the trade that are designed to help them save every dollar they can. Even though an athlete should stay out of the negotiating process, he should know how to recognize these maneuvers and be ready for them if the negotiations do not proceed smoothly. There may be a dozen variations of these, but the four listed here should give an athlete a good idea of what he might expect.

1. Let's be friends. Many professional teams like to appear to be one big happy family. A pro club likes to look as if it has taken all of its athletes under its wing and is protecting them while it offers them a great opportunity to play the sport. If you find yourself falling for this line, just watch how nice the teams are when it is time to cut the athletes who do not measure up. Business is business, and everything a team does should be seen as an attempt to save money. The "let's be friends" tactic goes something like this: "There'll be more money after your prove yourself. You'll be on this team a long time and make plenty of money. This is a fair offer for everyone. Come on! Start thinking about making this team—we've got a championship to win, and you can help. So sign right here."

Friends? Don't believe it! The National Football League Players Association has provided draft choices and free agents with salary information and negotiating tips to help them get better contracts. The NFL Management Council did not like that and sued the Players Association for illegally counseling draft choices in their individual negotiations. How this suit is settled will be determined later, but it underscores the seriousness of the management in contract negotiations. Would a friend deny another friend valuable information that

would help him get a better contract? Do not let the 'let's be friends"
ploy keep you from listening to your representative. And during the
negotiations, do not worry about being a "loyal" team member or
making somebody angry at your for hiring an agent or an attorney
and for asking to be paid fairly for your contribution to the team.

2. Your agent must be crazy. When the negotiations are not going
well for the professional club, they will try to discredit the athlete's
representative. "That idiot," they'll say, "is trying to keep you out of
professional sports. You will never play for us if you let that jerk ruin
your career." These remarks can be both confusing and frightening.
But if you have hired a good representative, you can sidestep this type
of negative talk and go play some golf or drink another soda by the
side of the pool. All the team wants to do is to cause a split between
you and your agent and then jump in and sign you to a contract.
When the negotiations are going badly, you have to hang tough with
your representative and never show a lack of confidence. An athlete's
best reply if the team wants to negotiate with him personally is: "Talk
to my attorney. That's why I hired him."

3. That's our final offer—take it or leave it. This tactic usually
comes after the pro team senses a weakness on the part of the athlete.
All of a sudden the team makes a final offer and breaks off the contract talks, telling the athlete to forget it unless he is ready to sign the
contract under their conditions. In this situation, an athlete simply has
to wait and trust his representative. He should check with the players'
association to be sure his demands are in line with his ability. If worst
comes to worst, he can ask to be traded or, as a last resort, sit out the
season and ask to be drafted by another team the next year. Any sign
of a weakness or a lack of confidence will only cause the team to hold
on to its final offer and will keep them from negotiating.

4. Let's talk about it at training camp. The pro teams are happy to
let an athlete come to camp and negotiate his contract between practices. If the athlete decides to hold out and not come to camp until he
has a good contract, he will have to worry about losing his position to
someone else and getting cut from the team. There is not much an
athlete can do in this situation except follow his representative's
advice. Again, he should check with the players' association to be certain his demands are not out of line. An athlete might consider hiring
a second representative to try his hand at the negotiating table just to
give the team someone else to dicker against. Occasionally, a change
in personalities will get the talks going again; it is more expensive, but
if there is enough money on the table, it may be worth a try.

Negotiating a pro sports contract is no different than buying a car
or selling a house. It is a simple buyer-and-seller discussion with a little
give-and-take, and finally an agreement, a contract, and a handshake.

Once the athlete is signed up, he can get on with the business of making the team and reaching his goals. If you will consider several good representatives and hire the best available, your contract negotiations should be relatively simple.

Agents and the NCAA and NAIA

The NCAA and the NAIA rules restrict the relationships athletes can have with individuals or organizations for the marketing of the athlete's athletic ability or reputation. These rules are summarized below:

1. An athlete will forfeit his eligibility *in all sports* if he agrees or has agreed to be represented by an agent, an attorney, or an organization on a general basis for the marketing of his athletic ability or reputation.
2. An athlete will forfeit his eligibility *in a specific sport* if in that sport he: a) agrees or has agreed to be represented by an agent, an attorney, or an organization for the marketing of his athletic ability or reputation; b) negotiates or signs a professional contract regardless of the legality of the contract; c) receives directly or indirectly any pay; d) requests that his name be placed in the draft of the professional sports organization; or e) receives cash, checks, or gifts from anyone or an organization wanting to represent him at a later date.
3. An athlete may sign a professional sports contract with or without the advice of a representative and accept pay in any form *in a specific sport* without forfeiting his eligibility in other sports.
4. If an athlete is offered a contract by a professional sports organization, the athlete may hire an *attorney* to evaluate both the contract and offer without forfeiting his eligibility in that sport provided no negotiations take place, no counter offers are made in any form, and no contract is signed.

Keep in mind that this is only a summary of the rules and that the rules are always subject to change. To be on the safe side, an athlete should query the appropriate governing body before making any move toward professionalism. The best route for a high school or college athlete is to stay completely away from agents until the athlete and his or her parents and coaches agree that the time is right to turn pro.

Jimmy Connors (courtesy of Wilson Sporting Goods)

John Madden and Pat Summerall (courtesy of CBS Sports).

Chapter 10
Sports-Related Careers

AN ATHLETE'S SPORTS CAREER DOES NOT HAVE TO END AFTER HIS OR HER actual playing days are over. Nor is it important for you to become a professional athlete to have a world of sports-related opportunities open to you. Many of America's best known sports figures were good high school or college athletes yet never played professional sports. Paul "Bear" Bryant, Bobby Knight, Linda Sharp, Jody Conradt, Lorraine Borman, and Pete Rozelle are all former athletes who have excelled in sports-related careers without having competed professionally.

The keys to a successful, sports-related career are planning and preparation. Before your high school and college careers are over, you must take the time to make some decisions about your future and develop your plan of action. The opportunities are unlimited. People who are young today will eventually take over as the new athletic directors at Boston College, Stanford, and Wisconsin. Many individuals will pursue sports-related business careers and will become the new executive officers of NIKE, K2, CBS Sports, and *Sports Illustrated*. Others will stay close to the competition and will someday replace the nation's best coaches like Tom Landry, Tommy Lasorda, and Billy Cunningham. Your challenge is to recognize these opportunities, establish your goals, and make them a reality.

Interscholastic and Intercollegiate Sports-Related Opportunities

Careers in an interscholastic and intercollegiate sports program are connected with several areas of specialization: athletic administration, physical education, teaching, coaching, and athletic training. In all of these positions the bottom line is performance. Your success in working your way through the junior high and high school ranks or even the college and professional levels depends on what you know and how well you do. Can you coach? Can you teach? Can you manage the people, the pressure, and the responsibility?

To excel in these sports-related careers, an individual needs to complete a well-rounded college curriculum that combines a core of physical-education courses with a specific area of specilization, such as sports administration and management, coaching, or sports medicine. Because high school coaches are usually required to teach one or more classroom subjects, an individual can improve his or her chances of employment by minoring in a high-demand program, such as mathematics, English, natural science, computer science, or business. At the college level, a doctorate or masters degree in physical education or athletic administration will help open the doors to many opportunities.

Possible collegiate positions:
Administration: college of health, physical education, and recreation
Athletic director
Director of intramural sports
Health, physical education, or recreation instructor
Head coach/assistant coach
Business manager (tickets, concessions, etc.)
Sports information director
Director of facilities and equipment
Athletic/academic advisor
Training specialist

Possible school-system positions:
School athletic director
Coach/physical education instructor
Teacher
Training specialist

Professional Sports Opportunities

Professional sports opportunities in both team and league organizations are often open to athletes who have proven themselves in competition or to individuals who have established excellent reputations in college athletics or in the business world. For these careers, a degree in business administration, accounting, finance, management, marketing, communications, law, or other related fields will be helpful.

League positions:
League commissioner
Director of league operations

League counsel/attorney
Public relations director
Director of officials
Controller
Broadcasting and publications director
Marketing and sales promotions manager

Team positions:
General manager
Business manager
Operations manager
Ticket director
Head coach/assistant coach
Bookkeeper
Team physician/dentist
Trainer/physical therapist
Equipment manager
Traveling secretary
Stadium director
Concessions manager
Announcer
Sales and promotions director
Statistician

Sports-Medicine Opportunities

People in sports-medicine careers are concerned with injury prevention, rehabilitation techniques, and medical care. A complete sports-medicine program for a team or institution usually requires several individuals from different areas of specialization to work together to provide a wide range of services and programs for both healthy and injured athletes. A career in sports medicine usually requires specific health, physical-education, and medical training and often state or national certification.

Sports-medicine positions:
Sports physician
Physician's assistant
Sports-medicine clinic director
Physical therapist
Exercise physiologist
Nutritionist/dietition
Researcher
Athletic trainer

Coach John Thompson, Georgetown University. Coaching careers can be tremendously rewarding and can lead to additional careers in sports administration and business (courtesy of Georgetown University Athletics).

Recreational Sports Opportunities

Recreational sports careers are limited only by an individual's imagination and by the public's decisions about how to spend its leisure time. Recreational activities include everything from softball team competition to chess tournaments and horseback riding. Numerous sports and recreation career opportunities are made available through city, state, and federal government agencies. A city's parks and recreation department may need lifeguards and golf instructors, while the federal government may need a new director for a national park and recreation area. Recreational careers in the private sector may begin at a ski resort, a tennis camp, or a large amusement center. What these careers require is the ability to deal with a large number of people and to design and manage sports and recreation programs that meet their needs. Degrees in recreational sports and in business and recreation management are offered by many colleges and universities.

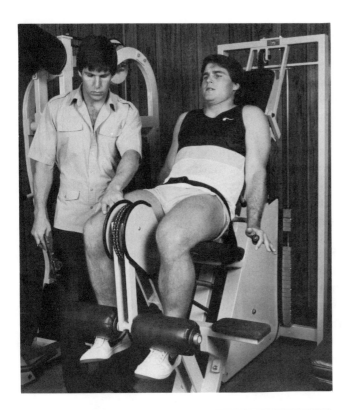

Careers in sports medicine are growing. Here, a physical therapist works with professional racquetball player Dave Peck at the Nautilus Orthopedic Clinic in Deland, Florida (courtesy of Nautilus Sports/Medical Industries).

Sports Organizations and Associations

There are dozens of sports organizations and associations that offer employment opportunities throughout the nation. These organizations range from one or two-person operations with few openings to national associations employing hundreds of people. Examples of these organizations are the United States Olympic Committee, the National Association for Girls and Women in Sports, the National Collegiate Athletic Association, and the United States Hang Gliding Association. Career possibilities include positions on the executive staff, in fund raising and promotions, in membership services and recruitment, and in the implementation of the organization's objectives. A degree in business management or administration, public relations, communications, accounting, or economics will help you sell yourself to a sports organization. You should let your sports interests be your guide as you explore these opportunities. A list of national sports organizations and associations is included in Appendix B.

Sports-Related Opportunities in the Media

Sports-career opportunities in the publishing, film, and broadcasting industries will continue to grow in the future for a number of reasons. These include the public's increasing appetite for sports news, the popularity and accessibility of cable television, the freedom which teams are gaining in the negotiation of individual radio and television contracts, and the popularity of new sports leagues and minor sports, which are demanding more and better media coverage.

Opportunities in the communications field include sports and play-by-play announcers, writers, columnists, editors, and photographers, as well as back-up personnel such as cameramen and headline writers. Requirements for these careers usually include a broad knowledge and interest in sports; practical experience working in the sports department of a school or local newspaper, or local radio or television station; and usually a degree in journalism, communications, or English. Because of the stiff competition for such jobs, a sports communications career requires many years of preparation if an individual is to move ahead of his or her peers and receive the best employment offers. The work is demanding, but the personal rewards and satisfaction of a sports-communications career are often as enjoyable and exciting as sports competition itself.

Sports-Business Opportunities

Sports, fitness, and health-related businesses (including sports equipment, clothing, shoes, food and vitamins, and books) account for over $30 million in sales each year. The business opportunities in these areas are almost unlimited. Potential purchasers for new products include interscholastic and intercollegiate sports programs, professional leagues and teams, amateur and professional athletes, and recreational sports participants who are attempting to shape up, stay healthy, and live longer.

You can begin planning a business career by examining all of the positions—from top to bottom—in a number of sports-related corporations. Career possibilities begin with the president's position at the top of the company and range through middle management and product assemblers to the shipping and receiving clerks. A smaller company, such as a sporting goods store, can be studied to determine possible career opportunities at the local level. As soon as your specific interests are matched with one or more career areas, your high school and college courses should be channeled in that direction. There are a number of courses and degree programs that will help you prepare for a sports-related business career. These include accounting, economics, business law, sports law, financial planning and management, advertising and marketing, public relations, and business administration.

Sports and Fitness Clubs and Services

Recent surveys have indicated that more than 50 percent of the people in the United States participate in one or more kinds of physical activity to improve their health and fitness. As a result, the market for exercise and fitness services is extensive. There are thousands of health clubs and fitness centers across the nation that cater to the exercising public. These centers offer everything from exercise machines, jogging tracks, and swimming pools to space-age medical analysis equipment and computer-operated exercise programs. The popularity of exercise programs such as Jazzercise and aerobics is steadily increasing. Sports and fitness specialty camps and centers are flourishing. These centers teach everything from specific sports skills and strategy (such as golf and tennis) to weight-reduction and stress-management techniques. Even retirement centers are discovering that they have a more fitness-conscious clientele and are providing sports and recreation programs for the elderly.

Careers in the sports and fitness industry require a broad knowledge of the fields of health and physical education. Good business skills in selling, public relations, and promotions are helpful and usually necessary. A creative approach will make these careers more interesting and profitable.

(Photo by Ken Litchfield, copyright © 1985).

Appendix A: Sports Conditioning

Dead lift (photo by Ken Litchfield, copyright © 1985).

Strength Training

DURING THE LAST DECADE THERE HAS BEEN AN INCREASED EMPHASIS ON strength training to improve the performance of both male and female athletes. The goal today is to engage in muscular conditioning that increases strength and endurance in all of the major muscle groups of the body. Athletes are beginning to zero in on the critical components that must be included in a total muscular conditioning program, but a great deal of confusion, misinformation, and wasted effort can still be found in high school and college weight rooms across the nation.

How Do Muscles Contract?

The human body is made up of three types of muscles: the smooth muscles found in the internal organs, the cardiac muscles found in the heart, and the skeletal muscles that are attached to the bones and produce movement. There are over 430 different skeletal muscles, each of which contains individual muscle fibers that run lengthwise from one end of the muscle to the other. The ends of a skeletal muscle are attached to bones by connective tissue called tendons. Just as hundreds of strands of thread can be joined together to make one rope, thousands of individual muscle fibers run parallel from tendon to tendon to make up a bundle of muscle fibers in a single muscle.

A muscle contraction is produced by electrical impulses and chemical reactions. A contraction begins when a specific number of muscle fibers, called a motor unit, are stimulated by a motor nerve impulse. During a contraction, each of the individual fibers within a muscle bundle will either contract with all of its force or rest while the other fibers around it contract to do the work. This is the principle of *muscle fiber recruitment:* the nervous system recruits or stimulates only the number of fibers needed to do the work — all of the fibers not recruited during the contraction will remain relaxed.

The skeletal muscles have a tremendous contracting potential, so much so that, if all the fibers in a muscle or group of muscles were to contract at the same time, the muscles could tear themselves from the bones. The sensory nervous system protects the body from injury by balancing the strength of each contraction and the tearing points of tendons, ligaments, and muscles. As a result, when an athlete is lifting all the weight he can possibly lift at one time, he is not using all of the fibers in the muscles doing the work; the sensory nervous system is forcing some fibers to remain relaxed for use later as reserve strength.

The point of this discussion about muscle fiber recruitment is that the nervous system stimulates the fibers of a muscle to contract in a staggered fashion. In a low-intensity contraction, only a few fibers will contract, producing a minimum amount of strength. In a high-intensity contraction, a larger percentage of the muscle fibers will contract, producing a maximum normal effort. As you might imagine, in a low-intensity contraction more muscle fibers will be relaxed or resting than in the case of a high-intensity contraction.

To apply this to weight lifting, assume that you can lift 100 pounds ten times before your muscles become completely exhausted. What happens is that, as you begin the exercise, only the minimum number of muscle fibers required will be recruited to lift the weight. As soon as these fibers begin to tire, other fibers will be recruited to add to the lifting effort. During the exercise, the working fibers will become tired and finally exhausted, and other fibers will be called into action to take their place in the contraction. At about the eighth or ninth repetition, the individual muscle fibers will be either exhausted or contracting in an all-out effort. At the end of the tenth repetition, all of the fibers will be exhausted, and you will not be able to lift the weight again without resting. Exercises, such as the one just described, that exhaust all of the muscle fibers in a short amount of time are called anaerobic or high-intensity-type exercises.

In a low-intensity or aerobic-type exercise, such as jogging, swimming, cycling, or cross-country skiing, the muscles will not become exhausted in a short period of time because a smaller number of muscle fibers is needed for each contraction and the resting fibers therefore have time to recover and can be recruited again later.

What Causes Muscles to Grow and Become Stronger?

Muscle growth is called *hypertrophy,* which is an increase in the diameter of a muscle bundle caused by an increase in the size of each individual muscle fiber within the bundle. Muscles grow after being stimulated by high-intensity exercises, such as weight lifting, or by low-intensity exercises, such as swimming or jogging. Exercise produces muscle growth *only* when the muscles are forced to do more work than they are accustomed to doing. What happens is that a series of chemical reactions occur that cause the individual muscle fibers to grow, which in turn increases the diameter of the entire muscle bundle. As the diameter of a muscle increases, it becomes stronger. In just the same way that a rope with a large diameter can pull more weight than a rope with a smaller diameter, a larger muscle can generate more pulling power than a smaller muscle.

It is not important for an athlete to understand the complex chemical reactions that make muscles grow stronger. But it is important for him or her to know that exercise starts the entire growth process. An individual muscle fiber will experience maximum growth only after being exhausted by exercise. A halfhearted effort produces only a mild chemical reaction and only a small amount of growth. Muscles automatically grow when they are stimulated to do so. A good example, which many athletes have heard, is everyday work that involves heavy lifting. If a person takes a job lifting heavy boxes in a warehouse, his muscles will grow both bigger and stronger until they are accustomed to the work being done, but after that, the muscles will not grow larger or stronger unless the work load is increased. The point is simple; muscles continue to grow as long as the work being done or the weight being lifted is progressively increased to put more demands on the muscles as they get stronger.

What Does This Mean to the Athlete?

This information means that each individual muscle fiber has to be exercised and exhausted for a muscle to experience the greatest amount of growth possible. All too often, athletes stop an exercise before they have completely exhausted a muscle or they overdo it with three, four, or five or more sets that overwork the muscles and actually retard the growth process. What this means for an athlete is that the most productive strength-training program he she can follow will be one in which progressive resistance/high-intensity-type exercises are used to exhaust all of the muscle fibers in a single muscle or a group of muscles with only one set of eight to fifteen repetitions per set.

What are Progressive Resistance/High Intensity Exercises?

Progressive resistance exercises are those in which more weight or more repetitions are added in each succeeding weight training session. If, for example, you can bench press 160 pounds ten times on Wednesday, you should try to press the same weight eleven or more times on Friday. Once you press 160 pounds fourteen or fifteen times, you will need to add 5 or 10 percent more weight during the next weight training session and do as many repetitions as possible. Progressive resistance exercise simply means stimulating the muscles to grow by continually increasing their work load.

High intensity exercises are weight training exercises that temporarily exhaust all of the muscle fibers in a particular muscle group with one set of eight to fifteen repetitions. Each repetition must be completed in a slow, controlled manner and with perfect form. There are no throwing, cheating, or jerking movements in high intensity exercise. A complete set should last approximately *forty to sixty seconds,* with each repetition requiring about *four to five seconds to complete.* In other words, you should take about two seconds to lower the weight and about two seconds to lift the weight. The repetitions have to be slow and precise and should continue until all of the muscle fibers in a muscle or group of muscles are exhausted and the weight cannot be lifted through another complete repetition. *The last complete repetition is the most important repetition because all of the muscle fibers are contracting to the point of exhaustion and all of them are being completely stimulated to grow.*

Is One Set Enough?

Many coaches and weight lifters advise from three to six sets per exercise with as few as one and as many as forty repetitions per set. When this many sets and reps are done, a workout can take up to three hours or more. That much work is not necessary. The natural growth process begins automatically after a muscle or group of muscles is exercised. The body can grow only so fast. As long as the muscle is completely exhausted in an exercise, the chemical reactions that cause growth will be essentially the same regardless of whether the muscle was exhausted in one set or five sets. The disadvantage of long workouts with many sets is that the athletes will be overworked and will begin avoiding workouts. Also, when several sets are completed per exercise, the muscles will require more recovery time and may not be

Kim Gillespie begins her first repetition on the leg-curl machine (photo by Ken Litchfield, copyright © 1985).

fully rested 48 hours later, when the next exercise session should take place.

One set per exercise is enough to produce the maximum possible gains as long as the exercises are performed in a slow and controlled manner and all of the muscle fibers are exhausted. When an athlete stops an exercise one or two repetitions early and fails to exhaust all of the muscle fibers, a second set will be necessary to achieve the best results. But it is a waste of time to complete a second set when just one or two more reps in the first set would have exhausted the muscle fibers completely. In almost every case, when an athlete has enough energy to complete two, three, or four or more sets per exercise, it probably means that, consciously or unconsciously, the athlete is loafing during most of the sets and saving strength to be able to get through the long workout. Both the research that has been completed and the actual results that have been obtained in the weight room clearly demonstrate that one set per exercise — coupled with a progressive-resistance/high-intensity-type program — will produce the greatest possible gains in the shortest amount of time.[1]

How Many Repetitions Should Be Completed Per Exercise?

The range of recommended repetitions per set often varies from coach to coach depending on the coaches' past weight-lifting experiences. Recommendations include six to nine, seven to twelve, eight to twelve, and eight to fifteen repetitions per exercise. Three basic guidelines can be drawn from these different programs and from the research that has been conducted over the past few years: 1) Young athletes between the ages of ten and thirteen and athletes just beginning to lift weights should work in the range of eight to fifteen or ten to fifteen repetitions per exercise. This range will require the athletes to use slightly less weight per exercise and, therefore, will allow them to concentrate on maintaining the correct lifting form and on lifting and lowering the weight slowly. At the same time, lighter weight and more repetitions will allow the athletes more time to develop strength before the weight is increased, will help the athletes avoid injuries that often accompany the use of excessive weights, and will help the athletes avoid burnout from being overworked early in their weight lifting program. 2) Older athletes and non-athletes may prefer to work in the range of eight to fourteen or eight to fifteen repetitions per exercise. And 3) Athletes aged fourteen through thirty should work in the range of eight to twelve repetitions per exercise. This range will produce highly intense workouts and lead to the fastest improvements. In *all* cases, only one set per exercise should be performed; an athlete should take at least two seconds to lift the weight and two seconds to lower the weight. A complete set should last about forty to sixty seconds from the first repetition to the last repetition, and the set should not be stopped until the athlete cannot lift the weight through another complete repetition.

Why Should the Exercises Be Done Slowly?

Anytime an athlete lifts a weight fast or jerks at it to start the weight in motion, he may be able to lift more weight, but he is making the exercise easier and losing many of the benefits of weight training. When a weight is lifted quickly, some of the muscle fibers needed to get the weight moving will relax once the bar is in motion. But during a slow, controlled repetition, all of the fibers will be recruited equally; when the working fibers become tired, other fibers will be recruited to add to the lifting effort. If the repetitions are done slowly (two seconds to lift the weight and two seconds to lower the weight), all of the fibers will eventually be involved in the contraction and will be stimulated to grow.

One of the biggest mistakes many weight lifters make is lowering the weight too quickly. When a muscle is forced to lower the weight slowly, it is making an eccentric contraction or doing what is called "negative work." If a slow repetition is maintained, the muscle is exercised in both the lifting and lowering movements. This requires the muscle to do more work and produces faster gains. Anytime an athlete drops the weight rather than lowering it slowly, he is wasting half of his effort. The most effective way to stimulate muscle growth is to work the muscles in both the lifting and lowering phases of a repetition through a slow, controlled movement. Many athletes refuse to work out this way because it hurts, it is harder work, and frankly, they cannot take it. If you will work out in a slow and controlled manner, you will have better results in less time and reduce your chances of a weight-training injury.

What Should Be the Goal of a Strength-Training Program?

The overall goal of a strength-training program should be to decrease the athlete's chances of injury in actual sports competition and to increase the athlete's chances of achieving his or her full athletic potential. This can be accomplished by improving the athlete's strength and endurance in all of the major muscle groups of the body and by reducing his or her percentage of body fat while increasing the percentage of muscle mass. These changes can be accomplished through high-intensity/progressive-resistance-type exercises.

Should Male and Female Athletes Follow the Same Weight-Training Program?

Yes. The factors that produce strength gains are the same for both male and female athletes. A female will not normally have high levels of the male hormone testosterone in her body and will, therefore, not experience large gains in muscle size, but she will be able to have substantial gains in muscle strength and muscle density.

What is the Difference Between Fast-Twitch and Slow-Twitch Muscle Fibers?

Research indicates that humans have two basic types of muscle fibers: fast-twitch fibers and slow-twitch fibers. Simply stated, the slow fibers are principally the source of endurance, while the fast fibers provide speed and a small amount of endurance. If a marathon runner has more slow fibers, he will have more total endurance, while a sprinter will be faster if he has more fast fibers. An individual's genetic make-up determines the amount of each type of muscle fiber he or she has. Exercise does not appear to cause one type of fiber to change into another type of fiber. But weight training does develop both strength and endurance in both fast-twitch and slow-twitch muscle fibers.

Despite the fact that researchers often suggest that certain athletes should participate in certain sports because of their muscle-fiber make-up, an athlete need not be concerned with what type of muscle fiber he or she has. If you will participate in many different sports, you will find the sports you like the best and the sports you are best suited to play. Regardless of your muscle-fiber make-up, if you do not like a sport and enjoy its challenges, you will not reach your full potential in it. Proper specialization is possible only when you like a sport and look forward to your improvement in it.

What Are Isometric, Isotonic, and Isokinetic Exercises?

Isometric exercises are exercises performed against an immovable object. If you put your hands under the chair you are sitting in and pull for six or seven seconds, you are doing an isometric exercise. Isometric exercises will build strength only at the specific point where the pressure is applied, and they will not cause a muscle to grow in size. Isometric exercises are best used in conjunction with isotonic and isokinetic exercises.

Isokinetic exercises are exercises performed on a machine that uses a friction or hydraulic device to produce resistance. In these exercises, the machine moves at a constant speed regardless of the pressure applied to it. Isokinetic exercises produce gains in both strength and muscle size and also work the muscles through the full range of motion around the joints. Isokinetic machines are often used to strengthen a muscle after an injury because the muscle itself provides the force against the friction device and therefore runs less risk of being overtaxed.

Isotonic exercises are those performed against a movable resistance such as a barbell or a stack of weights on a Nautilus or a Universal machine. Bench pressing 100 pounds ten times would be an example of an isotonic exercise. Isotonic exercises are usually referred to as weight lifting. These exercises will produce gains in muscle size, strength, power, and endurance. If a muscle is worked through the full range of its motion around a joint, the flexibility of the muscle

David Goodin demonstrates the biceps curl (photo by Ken Litchfield, copyright © 1985).

will be maintained.

Weight lifting is the most common type of strength training available to athletes. It can be done with $50,000 worth of Nautilus equipment or a $49 set of weights with one barbell and two dumbbells. You should not be overly concerned with the type of equipment you have to use during your workouts. It is true that some types of equipment produce more well-rounded gains in both strength and flexibility than other types of equipment, but that should not be your immediate concern. You have to make the most of whatever type of equipment you have to use. To reach your full athletic potential, you will have to make a decision that you are going to follow a regular, well-thoughtout weight-training program; the work that you do is more important than the type of equipment you use. The best weight-training program is the one that you will stick to on a year-round basis, all the while working to gain the greatest possible results.

At What Age May Weight Training Begin?

In most cases where there is good, intelligent supervision of an athlete, weight training can begin as early as 10 or 11 years of age. *The emphasis has to be on careful, intelligent supervision and strict adherence to correct form.* The gains that might be made from starting early will be completely erased if the program lacks good supervision and instruction and an injury occurs.

How Often Should an Athlete Work Out?

A cycle of stimulation and muscle growth requires 48 hours to be complete. An athlete should work out with weights three times a week on alternating days, such as a Monday-Wednesday-Friday or a Tuesday-Thursday-Saturday schedule. Then, after three weight training sessions, there should be two days of rest for the body to fully recover. To insure that proper flexibility is maintained, stretching exercises should be included in the program three to five times per week.

In What Order Should the Muscles Be Exercised?

Weight training sessions should always begin with exercises that work the lower body and legs. This means that the hips, legs, lower back, and upper back should be worked first, followed by the shoulders, chest, arms, neck and stomach. The stomach exercises should be added last so that the stomach muscles will be fresh and can provide adequate support for the body throughout the other exercises. The neck exercises can be added at the start or at the end of the program. Some athletes prefer to get their neck exercises out of the way first so they will not forget them at the end. If a neck machine is not available, isometric exercises should be used to work the full range of the neck muscles from side to side and front to back.

The following lists show the order in which the exercises should be completed for three different programs.

Free weights	*Nautilus*	*Universal Gym*
leg press	hip and back	leg press
leg extension	leg extension	leg extension
leg curl	leg press	leg curl
calf raises	leg curl	calf raises
dead lift	calf raises	lat bar behind neck
lat bar behind neck	pullover	seated overhead press
bent over rowing	lat bar behind neck	shoulder shrugs
seated overhead press	double shoulder	bench press
upright rowing	double chest	triceps press
bench press	triceps press	biceps curl
triceps press	biceps curl	inverted curl
biceps curl	neck	neck
neck	stomach	stomach
stomach		

An exercise program should have about twelve to eighteen different exercises and take about forty to sixty minutes to complete the full workout. Each exercise should consist of one set of eight to fifteen repetitions lasting about one minute per set (two seconds to lift the weight and two seconds to lower the weight per repetition). In order to avoid injury, you should skip the barbell squat completely because it is dangerous. If you decide to include squats in your workout, you should use lighter weights, wear a belt, and place a bench or a chair behind you to prevent yourself from going all the way to the floor. For the dead lift, start with a comfortable weight and work up slowly as you become stronger. Do not attempt maximum lifts in the dead lift or barbell squat. You can also avoid injuries by working out with a teammate or a coach who can help lift the weights into position and place them back after each exercise.

How Much Warming Up Should an Athlete Do Before Lifting Weights?

A few minutes of stretching and a few calisthenics are all that are needed. You should not warm up so much that you are tired before you start lifting. It is a good idea to begin *mentally warming up* several hours before your workout. You should prepare to give a total effort, to exhaust your muscles, and to do each exercise correctly.

What Kind of Diet Is Best for Muscle Growth?

Muscles will automatically grow in size, weight, and strength if you follow a regular, progressive-resistance type program. *Exercises* make your muscles grow, not diet. Many athletes think that if they add one or two thousand extra calories per day in the form of a protein supplement, they will gain bigger muscles. This is just not so. Your body will grow only "so fast." By pouring in extra calories, you will only gain additional body fat or have more calories to burn off in your daily activities. The best way to gain weight is to follow a three-day-a-week, progressive-resistance weight-training program (on a year-round basis if possible) and eat a *well-balanced* diet. Do not waste your money on protein supplements. Add a few hundred extra calories a day in the form of any kind of food, and be sure you are eating three to four servings of protein a day.

Should an Athlete Lift Weights During the Season?

Yes. A good in-season weight-training program should consist of *two workouts per week* lasting about thirty to forty-five minutes each. All of the major muscles should be exhausted in a dozen or so different exercises with one set per exercise. Each set should consist of eight to fifteen repetitions done slowly and with correct form. You should space your in-season workouts three to four days apart.

What Are the Components of a Good Weight-Training Program?

The program should include:
  A. Twelve to eighteen exercises that concentrate on the major muscles and muscle groups of the body.
  B. The exercises should be high-intensity, progressive-resistance-type exercises.
  C. Each exercise should consist of one set of eight to fifteen repetitions in which all of the muscle fibers being exercised are exhausted and no more complete repetitions can be performed without a rest. Once you can complete fifteen repetitions on an exercise, 5 to 10 percent more weight should be added for the next session.
  D. All repetitions should be done *slowly* (two seconds to lift the weight and two seconds to lower the weight) and with strict at-

Half squat completed with a belt, a spotter, and a bench below the lifter. Squats are dangerous! If you have the equipment, replace the barbell squat in your workout with leg presses, leg curls, and leg extensions. (photo by Ken Litchfield, copyright © 1985).

tention to *correct form*. There should be *no* jerking, throwing, or haphazard movement of the weight.

E. Regular workouts should be completed three times per week with approximately forty-eight hours rest between each workout.

F. Faster results can usually be realized when two or three athletes work out together. They can encourage each other to perform the exercises slowly and exhaust the muscles completely. At the same time, they can help each other by lifting and lowering the weight into position and removing the weight after each set is completed.

G. Weight training should be coupled with a three-to-five-day-a-week flexibility program and with regular speed and endurance training.

H. After you become a more experienced lifter, you may want to reduce the number of repetitions you are doing from eight to fifteen per set to eight to twelve per set. This change will require you to use slightly heavier weights, will make all of your sets more intense, and will produce slightly quicker gains in all three categories: strength, endurance, and bulk (size). With this change you should continue to perform only one set per exercise and avoid extra-heavy weights that prevent you from performing at least eight repetitions per set. You can increase the intensity of each repetition by taking two seconds to lift the weight and four to five seconds to lower the weight.

Lunge (photo by Ken Litchfield, copyright © 1985).

Holly Bashford. Take your time and enjoy your flexibility sessions.

Flexibility

FLEXIBILITY REFERS TO THE RANGE OF MOVEMENT POSSIBLE IN A SPECIFIC joint or a group of joints. Flexibility is determined by the ability or inability of muscles to stretch to their maximum length. Muscles work in pairs; as one muscle contracts to pull a bone in one direction, the other muscle in the pair relaxes and is stretched toward its full length. When you bend your arm at the elbow, for example, your biceps muscle contracts to pull your forearm toward your shoulder while your triceps muscle relaxes and is stretched. To straighten your arm, the biceps muscle relaxes and is stretched as the tricep muscle contracts, pulling your forearm from your shoulder.

If a muscle will not stretch to its maximum length, the range of motion around the joint will be restricted and flexibility will be reduced. A decrease in flexibility can affect the entire body or a specific joint. A runner may have flexible hip and leg joints, but he may lack a wide range of flexibility in his shoulders and back. An athlete's flexibility will affect his performance in both general abilities (running, jumping, agility) and specific skills (throwing, kicking, catching). As flexibility drops, so will an athlete's speed, reaction time, and endurance. A decrease in flexibility increases an athlete's risk of injuries because his muscles will be more susceptible to tear and pulls.

A total conditioning program should include a twenty- to thirty-minute session of stretching exercises that work to improve flexibility in the major muscles and muscle groups of the body. A short stretching session before a practice will help an athlete warm up, but it is usually not enough to maintain or improved flexibility.

You should set aside twenty to thirty minutes three to five days a week to devote to a series of flexibility exercises. A good time to do this is in the evening when you are watching television. Stretching and television go together; you can take your time and set your own pace through the exercises. The following guidelines will help you set up a good program using the exercises pictured in *The Sports Success Workout Book*.

A. Concentrate on the major muscles of the body: 1) hips, 2) hamstring, 3) quadriceps, 4) calves, 5) groin, 6) back, 7) stomach, 8) chest, 9) shoulders, 10) neck, and 11) wrist and ankles.

B. Stretching sessions should last about twenty to thirty minutes or longer. Take your time. Begin each exercise slowly, stretching the muscle until you feel the stretch; hold this position for fifteen to twenty seconds. At that point, increase the stretch slightly and hold this position for twenty to twenty-five seconds. Do not bounce up and down—all of your movements should be slow and easy.

C. Move from one exercise to another at a comfortable pace.

D. Your goal should be to improve your flexibility gradually and to maintain whatever level you reach. Do not try to increase your flexibility too quickly.

E. If pain develops during an exercise, release the stretch slowly. After a few seconds, repeat the exercise without stretching quite as far as before. If the pain continues, it could mean that you are aggravating an old injury; you should stop that exercise for the day and see your trainer or team doctor. Never force it. Stretching should be pleasant, not painful.

F. Do not compete with other athletes by trying to stretch farther than they can; follow your own pace.

G. Complement your stretching program with a regular program of weight training and speed and endurance conditioning.

Always lower the weight slowly (photo by Ken Litchfield, copyright © 1985).

Speed, Endurance, and Skills

Speed

Several factors work together to determine running speed: strength, flexibility, stride length, running form, anaerobic capacity, body fat, concentration, and proper training.

Strength provides the power to move the body—the stronger the muscles, the more potential there is for speed. Flexibility allows the muscles to move the legs and arms freely. Stride length determines how far you travel in one step. Running form deterines how efficiently you move your body.

Anaerobic means "working without oxygen." Full-speed sprinting requires such a burst of energy that the muscles run out of oxygen before the blood can resupply them. A good training program can improve your anaerobic capacity and allow you to run at your top speed for longer periods of time.

The amount of body fat a runner carries is only dead weight that will slow him down. Being ten pounds overweight is the same as running with a ten-pound weight strapped to your stomach. A good conditioning program and proper diet will reduce your body fat and improve your speed.

Check your running form.

1. *Arm movements.* Swing your arms forward and backward with your arms bent comfortably at the elbow. Do not let your hands move in front of your body; point your thumbs over your shoulders as you bring your arms forward. Bend your fingers; relax your hands, wrists, and forearms.

2. *Leg movements.* Lift your legs and knees high with your toes pointed ahead. Your toes should touch the ground below your center of gravity and catch your body as you learn forward. Contact with the ground should be light and quick; the longer your feet are on the ground the slower you will be running. Your trailing leg should push you forward with the full force of your leg muscles. Snap your foot off the ground with an extra push from your toes. Pull your leg forward with a high knee lift. When running for speed, always run on your toes.
3. *Lean forward for more speed.* Lean forward until you find a comfortable position that feels as if it is pulling you forward.
4. *Do not bounce up and down.* If you are bouncing up and down, instead of bursting forward, you are wasting energy. Make your legs push you forward rather than up and down.
5. *Head position.* Hold your head steady with little movement.
6. *Do not strain for speed.* The fast runners are usually the most relaxed runners. Relax your whole body—especially your face, neck, and shoulders.
7. *Mental form.* Concentrate on speed. Make your legs push harder. Review your form. Are you wasting any energy with sloppy movements?

Improving Your Speed

Running practice. Begin with a three-quarter pace and analyze your form; then accelerate quickly and review your form. Concentrate on good leg action, with a powerful push from each leg. Establish a long, comfortable stride. Move your arms quickly back and forth for more speed. How relaxed are you? Get a coach to critique your form.

Weight-training and flexibility exercises. A stronger muscle is a faster, more powerful muscle. The leg extension, leg press, and leg curl exercises on a weight-training machine will improve the strength of your quadricep and hamstring muscles. (Always lift and lower the weight slowly—in the weight room you are building strength, not speed.) Improve the flexibility of your entire body, not just your legs. Follow a complete stretching program three to five times per week.

Hill running. Running up and down a gradual hill will put extra stress on your muscles and cause them to develop faster. It is important for the hill *not to be too steep.* An incline of one degree is plenty—this

Derrick Wilson. Stretching should never be painful. Start slowly and gradually improve your flexibility with regular stretching sessions.

means that the hill should *not* rise more than six feet in 100 yards. Never run on a hill unless you are fresh and rested. Never run down a hill that is paved or that is so steep you have to fight the pull of gravity to keep from falling. You should check grassy areas for holes, sprinklers, and other hazards.

Run down the hill concentrating on good form and top speed. Work to develop fast leg action and try to improve your form. In running up the hill concentrate on powerful thrusts from your trailing leg. Push hard and try to improve your stride length. You should run five to eight all-out sprints both up and down the hill once or twice a week. Rest between sprints and quit running if your form becomes sloppy. Concentrate on speed, power, and quick leg action.

Acceleration practice. A steeper hill can be used for all-out acceleration drills because you will only be running up the hill in an all-out drive for power. This exercise is similar to running up the stadium bleachers, but your leg action can be more normal, and you don't have to worry about tripping on the steps. Force your trailing leg to push as hard as it can and then snap it to the front to catch yourself. Five to eight forty- to sixty-yard sprints once or twice a week should be enough.

Full-speed sprints. Run a series of full-speed sprints of about sixty to eighty yards in three or four sets of four sprints each. Run four sprints back-to-back, then rest two minutes and run another set. Such sets will isolate the fast-twitch fibers used in running and will build their strength and endurance. These drills should be the backbone of your speed-training program.

Anaerobic training. A series of long sprints will train the body to work more efficiently without oxygen. These sprints should be from 220 to 330 yards. You should start out as if you are running 100 yards as fast as you can possibly run. Do not hold anything back. Run as fast as you can for at least 220 to 330 yards. A series of four to six long sprints once or twice a week is enough.

Year-round training. No athlete should go out and try to complete all of the above exercises on the same day or even the same week. Together, these exercises make up a year-round program that is designed to let you alternate your training on a day-to-day basis. Your program should be built around three or four sets of four full-speed sprints run twice a week. These are your most important running exercises because they resemble actual running conditions. Hill running, acceleration practice, or anaerobic training should be sprinkled in once or twice a week depending on the time you have to work out. There is plenty of time for all these drills on a year-round basis. You cannot expect to improve your speed with just three or four weeks of running before your season starts.

Endurance

Cardiovascular conditioning improves the heart's ability to pump blood to the lungs and then circulate it throughout the entire body. The average resting heart rate for most high school and college students is about seventy to eighty beats per minute. A highly conditioned athlete will have a resting heart rate of about forty-five to sixty-five beats per minute. Because his heart is more efficient, a highly-conditioned athlete will have a tremendous advantage over any opponents who are not equally well conditioned.

The problem with most types of sports practices is that the cardio-vascular system is not thoroughly conditioned to meet the demands of actual competition, and a few wind sprints or laps at the end of practice will not be enough to improve the athlete's cardiovascular condition. In sports such as tennis, football, baseball, or golf, athletes spend more time standing around than they do actually practicing or building endurance. If you expect to be able to compete and perform with a total effort, you will have to develop a cardiovascular reserve that exceeds the maximum demands of your sport(s).

At the same time that you are developing your cardiovascular system, you will be developing the slow-twitch muscle fibers that will contribute to your overall endurance. These muscles fibers can continue contracting for long periods of time. Marathoners will run over seventy miles per week in an effort to build endurance in their cardiovascular and muscular systems. Enlargements of the slow-twitch muscle fibers are typical in long distance runners, swimmers, and bikers.

Research indicates that the minimum requirement for conditioning the cardiovascular system is thirty minutes of continuous, repetitive exercise in which the heart rate is elevated to between 65 and 85 percent of your maximum heart rate. You can calculate your maximum heart rate by subtracting your age from 220. If you are 20 years old, 75 percent of 200 (220 minus 20) would be 150 beats per minute. To condition your heart, you should exercise at least three times per week for thirty minutes or more at a pace that maintains your heart rate at about 150 beats per minute.

The best activities for cardiovascular conditioning are running or jogging, swimming, cycling, cross-country skiing, and rope jumping. To be the most efficient, you should exercise in an activity that makes use of the muscles that you will use in your sport. In other words, swimmers should swim, tennis players should run, and gymnasts should run or swim. Your endurance training should be continued on a year-round basis. Some weeks you will have more time for it and others you will not. But endurance training should be as much a part of your overall conditioning program as speed and weight training.

Skill Development

Your dedication and determination to excel in a sport will be directly reflected in the amount of time you spend developing your sports skills. The average athlete usually spends most of his time doing other things, while the exceptional athlete will follow a regular program devoted to developing the skills he needs for his sport. Most athletes have complete control of the quantity and quality of their free-time practices. A halfhearted effort will not get the job done, nor will one or two long sessions that are spread out over the summer. The following guidelines will help you organize a program to improve your skills.

1. Learn the importance of each of your skills. All of your skills are important, and all of them will affect your total performance at one time or another. For example, some baseball players want to practice hitting home runs, but they avoid bunting and sliding practice. Many soccer players will kick goals for hours but quickly lose interest in practicing their defensive skills. Do not get in the habit of only practicing the skills that you enjoy or the skills that you can already perform well. Develop an understanding of the importance of all your skills and work to improve each one of them.

2. Improve in a step-by-step process. All too often, athletes try to improve their skills too fast by cutting corners on their training. Design your practice sessions so that you improve in a step-by-step process that will result in better and better skills. Do not try to improve too quickly or be disappointed if you do not develop as rapidly as you think you should.

3. Get as much coaching as possible. When you are working to improve your skills, try to practice with a coach present as often as possible. Get the coach to critique your form and look for areas where you can improve. If a coach cannot help you, get a parent or a friend to watch what you are doing. If you can get some help at a YMCA or a Boy's or Girl's Club, do so. The more good coaching you can get, the better your chances will be of improving your skills.

4. Imagine that the competition is real. During each practice session, imagine that you are competing in a real game or contest and work as hard as you can to improve your performance. For example, you would not quit in the middle of a point, loaf, or take careless chances in a game, so avoid those things in practice. When you are practicing alone, imagine that you are competing against the best athletes in the world, like Magic Johnson or Cris Collinsworth, and at the same time, imagine that you are beating these invisible opponents. Anticipate your moves, develop new techniques, and improve your skills. Imagine that the score is close and that you have to make the winning jump shot or the game-saving interception. By imagining situations where you have to perform your best, you will be able to practice with more intensity and will be able to improve your skills at a faster rate.

5. Don't settle for average skills. There is a tremendous difference between being able to do something right most of the time and being able to do it right time and time again with never a miss. All too often, athletes become satisfied when their skills are about equal to or a little better than their teammates' skills, and they stop working hard to improve their skills further. Never settle for average or second best.

Those extra weeks of practice and improvements are the ones that will make the difference between an average performance and an excellent one.

6. Organize regular workouts against your teammates. Always try to compete against the best competition you can find. Playing against the kids in the neighborhood or a younger brother or sister will improve your skills only if you consciously try to improve and get some good out of the practice session. For better results, try to organize your practice sessions on a regular basis and get some of your teammates involved. Make them feel guilty when they do not show up, practice as hard as you can against the ones who do come, and improve as much as you can during each workout.

7. Tighten your skills with mental practice. Researchers have shown how important and helpful mental practice can be to an athlete. When you have some free time, try to visualize yourself practicing the skills connected with your sport. Imagine yourself making a free throw, hitting a baseball, or serving an ace. Coach yourself. Look for mistakes and critique your form. Where do you need to improve? What are you doing right? If you can perform your skills 100 percent perfect in your mind, your brain will transfer those mental patterns to actual practices and game conditions. Once you know every detail of what you are going to do and how to do it exactly right, you will be amazed at how well you can perform on the field, the course, or the court.

8. Stop practicing before you become mentally or physically exhausted. Practicing a skill when you are fatigued will improve your overall performance only if you will concentrate and work hard to improve. But if you are so tired that you are making mental mistakes or are working well below your physical capabilities, you will be better off if you stop for the day and practice some other time. Practicing improperly will only take away what you have already learned to do. Remember to strive for quality: perfect practice makes perfect.

9. Review your progress. After each practice session, review the progress that you have made and decide what you want to concentrate on during the next session. It is a good idea to keep a written record of your work and the progress you are making. Organize each session in advance, know what you want to improve, and contact several teammates to work out with you.

Dips are great for the triceps (photo by Ken Litchfield, copyright © 1985).

Total Conditioning

THE CONDITIONING PROGRAM DESCRIBED HERE WILL MEET THE NEEDS OF athletes in all sports. It is designed to increase muscular strength, endurance, and flexibility, to improve running speed and cardiovascular endurance, and to develop sports skills. The program follows a light-day/heavy-day routine that provides an ample amount of time to achieve all of these objectives. While this conditioning program is an excellent one, an athlete should remember that it is only a suggestion. You may want to follow it to the letter or use it as a guide for developing your own program. To do this, talk to your coach and get him to help you modify the program to meet your specific conditioning and training needs.

Off-Season Conditioning

Plan your program to include three heavy-training days that are separated by three light-training days. Alternate your heavy-training days on Monday-Wednesday-Friday or Tuesday-Thursday-Saturday.

STRUCTURE YOUR HEAVY-TRAINING DAYS AS FOLLOWS:

1. *Warm-up:* Easy stretching—all of the major muscles should be stretched and a few light calisthenics may be added. Total time: ten minutes.
2. *Weight-Training:* Exhaust all of the major muscle groups of the body with twelve to eighteen high-intensity exercises, each consisting of one set of eight to fifteen repetitions per set. (See instructions pages 197-210.) Each set should require about forty to sixty seconds to complete, with the athlete taking two seconds to lift the weight and two seconds to lower the weight. Time required: forty to sixty minutes.
3. *Speed and/or endurance training:* This part of the workout must be tailored to your particular needs. For speed training, the workout should include three to four sets of four top-speed

sprints of sixty to eighty yards run back-to-back, with one to three minutes rest between sets. Acceleration drills, anaerobic training, and hill running may be included in the program on an alternating basis. (See pages 216-219.) You may want to include some backward running (as in the case of a safety or outfielder) or lateral running (as in the case of a linebacker or infielder). A tennis player may want to include some short-distance sharts-and-stops running forward and backward as well as side to side. For endurance training, the workout should consist of thirty minutes or more of continuous training (such as running, biking, or swimming) to elevate the heart rate to between 65 and 85 percent of your maximum rate. (See pages 219-220.) Time required: thrity to sixty minutes.

4. *Skill development:* If time permits, an athlete may want to add some skill development training. But this training should not take away from the time that must be devoted to strength, speed, or endurance improvement. (See pages 220-222.)
5. *Cool down:* Easy stretching—five to ten minutes.

The time required for a heavy-day workout is about two hours. Strength training should be the major focus of a heavy-training day's workout. Your work in developing your speed and endurance should be balanced throughout the week and directed to the areas where you need the most improvement. Remember to include a regular three-to-five-day-a-week stretching program to round out your conditioning program.

THREE LIGHT-TRAINING DAYS PER WEEK (ALTERNATE WITH HEAVY DAYS)

1. *Warm-up:* Easy stretching—all of the major muscles should be stretched, and a few light calisthenics may be added. Jog one-quarter mile or more. Time required: ten minutes.
2. *Skill development:* One or two hours or more must be devoted to the specific skills of your sport. You may need to plan these sessions with a few teammates in order to get an effective work-out. Concentrate on improving all of the skills you need for your sport, and spend some extra time developing your weaker skills. (See pages 220-222.)
3. *Speed and/or endurance training:* If time permits, you may want to add a few minutes or more of speed and/or endurance training after your skill-development work. This additional work, however, should not take away from your skill training.
4. *Flexibility:* Your light-training days may offer you your best opportunities to improve your flexibility. Unless you are working to improve your flexibility in several separate sessions dur-

ing the week, you may want to use the time at the end of a light-day workout as a flexibility cool down. To do so, spend fifteen to twenty minutes stretching all of the major muscles of the body. (See pages 213-214).

A light-day workout must emphasize skill activities for all athletes and requires a minimum of one to two hours of work. Ask your coach to help you analyze your skills to determine what seem to be your weakest points; then work to improve those areas. Every activity that applies to your sport from catching passes, hitting a baseball, dribbling, shooting, kicking, putting, blocking, or serving to agility and hand-and-eye coordination drills must be included in your skill-development sessions. Tailor the sessions to fit your needs, and then, report to your first practice of the season ready to play your best and contribute to your team's effort to win.

In-Season Conditioning

It is ridiculous to spend a great deal of time in the off-season improving your overall performance and then let it all deteriorate during the season. Strength, endurance, flexibility, speed, and skill efficiency will slowly disappear if you do not work to maintain them. A few wind sprints and push-ups during each practice will not come close to maintaining top condition.

Each week during the season, you need two weight-training days seventy-two to ninety-six hours apart. The exercises must follow the high-intensity/progressive-resistance routine described on pages 200-210. It is also a good idea to plan at least one day a week for continuous endurance work to maintain your cardiovascular conditioning. Make it a point to notice how well you are competing and make your own adjustments when necessary. If your coach sends everyone to the showers after practice and you feel that you need extra skill training, running, or weight lifting, go ahead and do the work on your own. You are the best judge of your personal fitness and should know what you need to do to be able to play your best.

Injuries

THIS SECTION TAKES A BRIEF LOOK AT SPORTS INJURIES, INJURY PREVEN-tion, and immediate treatment for injuries. There are several factors that lead to athletic injuries: 1) poor conditioning, 2) lack of flexibility, 3) improper warm-up, 4) fatigue, 5) loafing, and 6) carelessness.

An athlete has a tremendous amount of control over all of these factors. By maintaining top conditioning and flexibility, you will be able to compete at your best level and avoid many of the injuries that plague other athletes. When you compete in both practices and games in a heads-up fashion, your chances of injury are reduced. But when you start cutting corners, slacking off on your warm-up, playing carelessly, or loafing, you will be leaving yourself open to any number of injuries that can knock you out of competition for anywhere from a few minutes to forever. You can reduce your chances of injury by controlling your participation at all times.

WHAT ARE THE MOST COMMON INJURIES?

The federal government's statistics indicate that minor injuries are the biggest hazards of sports competition. At the top of the list are aches and pains, pulls, strains, sprains, bruises, abrasions, and lacerations. These injuries, while they usually appear minor, can develop into major problems if they are ignored, treated improperly, or continually reinjured. Fractures, concussions, and dislocations are less common.

SHOULD ICE BE PUT ON SPORTS INJURIES?

Ice is the first treatment for most sports injuries. Strains, sprains, fractures, and muscle pulls all require a quick application of ice. An injury causes the tissue to be stretched or torn and to begin bleeding internally. Ice slows down the flow of blood to the injured area, retards swelling and pain, and shortens the recovery time. In most cases, heat *should not* be applied to an injury until forty-eight hours after the injury has occurred.

WHAT OTHER PRECAUTIONS SHOULD BE TAKEN WITH INJURIES?

Rest is required for sports injuries to heal. Playing with pain is never a good idea, and it can be dangerous if you are seriously hurt. Rest, elevation, compression wraps, and heat after forty-eight hours are usually the standard procedures with injuries that do not require special medical attention. There are a variety of treatments, such as ultrasound, whirlpools, and massage, that speed the healing process. In most cases, an athlete simply has to wait out the injury, allow himself time to recuperate, and then recondition himself to avoid any further injuries.

SHOULD ALL INJURIES BE REPORTED TO A DOCTOR?

The answer obviously depends on the severity of the injury. All injuries should be reported to the coaches and the trainer. Every injury should be examined and treated properly. You should not hesitate to go to the doctor when an injury does not seem to be healing. Anytime you have headaches or blackouts, experience internal pains or nausea, have an infection or a cut that may need stitches, or have pain in a joint, you should see a doctor. Common sense should prevail. Despite all of the sports medicine books that are available, an athlete should not try to diagnose and treat his own injuries without first showing the injury to his coaches and seeking medical advice when necessary.

WHAT IS THE BEST MEDICINE FOR INJURIES?

The best medicine is prevention. When an athlete is aware of the factors that lead to injuries, he can avoid them by using his good sense and a proper amount of preparation before competition. There are exceptions, but if all sports injuries are considered, few athletes are seriously injured when they are well prepared to play, are warmed up for competition, and compete in a heads-up, hard-nosed manner. If you expect to have a long, satisfactory sports career, you must manage your participation in such a way that you reduce your chances of injury, and when one does occur, allow yourself time to recuperate in order to avoid other related injuries.

Appendix B

Footnotes
Addresses

Notes

CHAPTER 1

[1]Pete Axthelm and Charles Leerhsen, quotation from Joe Montana in "Super Bowl: Duel of Wits," *Newsweek,* January 25, 1982, p. 66. Copyright 1982 by Newsweek, Inc. All Rights Reserved. Reprinted with the permission of Newsweek, Inc.

[2]Ira Berkow, quotation from Johnny Bench in *Beyond the Dream: Occasional Heroes of Sports,* Copyright © 1975 Ira Berkow (New York: Atheneum, 1975), p. 11. All Rights Reserved. Reprinted with the permission of Atheneum Publishers and John Bench.

[3]Quotation from Johnny Bench in "The Swinger from Binger," *Time,* July 10, 1972, p. 56. Copyright 1972 by Time, Inc. All Rights Reserved. Reprinted with permission of Johnny Bench.

[4]Steve Garvey, Calabasas, California, telephone interview, July 12, 1982.

CHAPTER 2

[1]BOB LILLY, WACO, TEXAS, TELEPHONE INTERVIEW, JANUARY 28, 1982.

[2]U.S. DEPARTMENT OF HEALTH, EDUCATION, AND WELFARE, FOOD AND DRUG ADMINISTRATION, OFFICE OF PUBLIC AFFAIRS, *A Primer of Four Nutrients: Protein, Carbohydrates, Fats, and Fiber,* by G. Edward Damon, HEW Publication No. (FDA) 75-2026. (Washington, D.C.: U.S. Government Printing Office, 1978). Also: U.S. Department of Agriculture, Consumer and Food Economics Institute, Science and Education Administration, *Nutrition: Food at Work for You,* Publication No. 779-020/15 (Washington, D.C.: U.S. Government Printing Office, 1978).

[3]Ann Meyers, La Habro, California, telephone interview, April 7, 1984.

CHAPTER 3

[1]Kyle Rote, Jr., with Basil Kane, *Complete Book of Soccer* (New York: Simon and Schuster: 1978), pp. 232-233. Copyright 1978 by Kyle Rote, Jr., and Basil Kane. Reprinted with permission of Simon and Schuster. All Rights Reserved.

CHAPTER 4

[1]Lorraine Borman, Edmonds, Washington, telephone interview, April 1983.

[2]Linda Sharp, Los Angeles, California, telephone interview, April 1983.

CHAPTER 5

[1]Fred Akers, Austin, Texas, interview, May 1982.

CHAPTER 6

[1]"National Collegiate Athletic Association Survey of Graduation Rates After Five Years for Males Entering College in Fall of 1975," Institutional Services Department, Research and Development Division, American College Testing Program, Iowa City, Iowa, April 1981.

[2]Ray Meyer, Chicago, Illinois, telephone interview, May 11, 1982.

[3]Bob Bass, San Antonio, Texas, telephone interview, June 22, 1982.

[4]Al Miller, Richardson, Texas, telephone interview, June 16, 1982.

[5]Moses Malone, Troy, Michigan, telephone interview, February 16, 1982.

CHAPTER 7

[1]Dennis Keegan, quotation from Bob Mathias in "Olympic Training Center," *The Olympian,* November 1981, p. 16. Reprinted with permission of the USOC and Bob Mathias.

[2]Frank Ryan, *Sports and Psychology,* (Englewood Cliffs, New Jersey: Prentice-Hall, 1981), p. 176.

[3]Bob Mathias, Colorado Springs, Colorado, telephone interview, June 17, 1982.

CHAPTER 8

[1]Vince Papale, Haddonfield, New Jersey, telephone interview, February 18, 1982.

APPENDIX A

[1]There is a growing number of books and articles that describe similar strength-training programs and the results that can be achieved with these progressive-resistance/high-intensity type workouts. Three excellent examples are listed below:

Joe Diange (Strenth Coach, U.S. Naval Academy), "Developing Maximum Strength With Maximum Intensity," *Scholastic Coach,* Vol. 53, No., 8, March 1984.

Dan B. Riley (Strength Coach, Washington Redskins), "Try PPE, The Best Way!" *Scholastic Coach*, Vol. 52, No. 2, September 1982.

Michael D. Wolf, Ph.D., *The Complete Book of Nautilus Training* (Chicago, Illinois: Contemporary Books, Inc., 1984).

Ordering Information

Additional copies of *The Sports Success Book* may be purchased from bookstores or ordered direct from the publisher. Write to:

Copperfield Press
Order Department
Post Office Box 15025
Austin, Texas 78761

Addresses

General Sports Organizations and Associations

AAU/USA Junior Olympics
3400 West 86th Street
Indianapolis, IN 46268

Amateur Athletic Union of the
United States
3400 West 86th Street
Indianapolis, IN 46268

National Association of
Intercollegiate Athletics
1221 Baltimore
Kansas City, MO 64195

National Association of Sports
Officials
1700 North Main Street
Second Floor
Racine, WI 53402

National Athletic Trainers
Association
P.O. Drawer 1865
Greenville, NC 27834

National Christian College Athletic
Association
1815 Union Avenue
Chattanooga, TN 37404

National Collegiate Athletic
Association
P.O. Box 1906
Mission, KS 66201

National Federation of State High
School Associations
P.O. Box 20626
Kansas City, MO 64195

National Handicapped Sports and
Recreation Association
P.O. Box 18664
Denver, CO 80218

National High School Athletic
Coaches Association
3423 East Silver Springs Blvd.
Suite 9
Ocala, FL 32670

National Junior College Athletic
Association
P.O. Box 1586
Hutchinson, KS 67501

National Little College Athletic
Association
P.O. Box 367
Marion, OH 43302

National Wheelchair Athletic
Association
2107 Templeton Gap Road
Suite C
Colorado Springs, CO 80907

Special Olympics
1701 K Street, NW
Suite 203
Washington, DC 20006

United States Olympic Committee
1750 East Boulder Street
Colorado, Springs, CO 80909

Women's Sports Foundation
195 Moulton Street
San Francisco, CA 94123

Specific Sports Organizations

The Abbreviation "NGB" indicates that the organization is one of the 37 National Sports Governing Bodies and is affiliated with the United States Olympic Committee.

ARCHERY

National Archery Association (NGB)
1750 East Boulder Street
Colorado Springs, CO 80909

ATHLETICS

Athletic Congress of the USA (NGB)
155 West Washington Street
Suite 220
Indianapolis, IN 46204

BASEBALL

American League Office
280 Park Avenue
New York, NY 10017

American Legion Baseball
P.O. Box 1055
Indianapolis, IN 46206

Little League Baseball
Williamsport, PA 17701

Major League Baseball Players
Association
1370 Avenue of the Americas
New York, NY 10019

The National Association of
Professional Baseball Leagues
P.O. Box A
St. Petersburg, FL 33731

National League Office
One Rockefeller Plaza
New York, NY 10020

The Office of the Commissioner
Major League Baseball
75 Rockefeller Plaza
New York, NY 10019

U.S. Baseball Federation (NGB)
4 Gregory Drive
Hamilton Square, NJ 08690

BASKETBALL

Amateur Basketball Association of
the U.S.A. (NGB)
1750 East Boulder Street
Colorado Springs, CO 80909

National Basketball Association
Olympic Tower
645 Fifth Avenue
New York, NY 10022

National Basketball Players
Association
15 Columbus Circle
6th Floor
New York, NY 10023

Women's American Basketball
Association
6400 East Broad Street
Columbus, OH 43213

BIATHLON

U.S. Biathlon Association, Inc.
(NGB)
Adjutant General's Office
Camp Johnson, Building 5
Winooski, VT 05404

BOBSLEEDING

United States Bobsled and Skeleton
Association (NGB)
P.O. Box 828
US Olympic Training Center
122 Main Street
Lake Placid, NY 12946

BOWLING

Ladies Professional Bowling Tour
7171 Cherry Vale Blvd.
Rockford, IL 61112

Professional Bowlers Association
1720 Merriman Road
Akron, OH 44313

Young American Bowling Alliance
5301 76th Street
Greendale, WI 53129

BOXING

Golden Gloves Association of
America
1704 Moon Avenue
Albuquerque, NM 87112

USA Amateur Boxing Federation,
Inc. (NGB)
1750 East Boulder Street
Colorado Springs, CO 80909

CANOEING

American Canoe Association (NGB)
P.O. Box 248
Lorton, VA 22079

CYCLING

U.S. Cycling Federation (NGB)
1750 East Boulder Street
Colorado Springs, CO 80909

DECATHLON

Deca
c/o Frank Zarnowski
Mount St. Mary's College
Emmitsburg, MD 21727

DIVING

United States Diving, Inc. (NGB)
901 West New York Street
Indianapolis, IN 46204

EQUESTRIAN

American Horse Shows Association
(NGB)
598 Madison Avenue
New York, NY 10022

FENCING

U.S. Fencing Association (NGB)
1750 East Boulder Street
Colorado Springs, CO 80909

FIELD HOCKEY

Field Hockey Association of America
(men — NGB)
1750 East Boulder Street
Colorado Springs, CO 80909

U.S. Field Hockey Association, Inc.
(women — NGB)
1750 East Boulder Street
Colorado Springs, CO 80909

FIGURE SKATING

U.S. Skating Association
(NGB)
20 First Street
Colorado Springs, CO 80909

FOOTBALL

Canadian Football League
1919 Scarth Street
Regina, SASK S4P 2H1

National Football League
410 Park Avenue
New York, NY 10022

National Football League Players
Association
1300 Connecticut Avenue, NW
Washington, DC 20036

United States Football League
52 Vanderbilt Avenue
New York, NY 10017

GOLF

Ladies Professional Golf Association
1250 Shoreline Drive
Suite 200
Sugar Land, TX 77478

National Golfers of America
Beaver Creek Golf and Country
Club
Lake Montezuma, AZ 86342

Professional Golfers Association
Sawgrass
Ponte Vedra, FL 32082

United States Golf Association
Golf House
Far Hills, NJ 07931

GYMNASTICS

U.S. Gymnastics Federation (NGB)
Merchants Plaza, Suite 1144E
101 West Washington Street
Indianapolis, IN 46204

ICE HOCKEY

Amateur Hockey Association of the
U.S. (NGB)
2997 Broadmoor Valley Road
Colorado Springs, CO 80909

National Hockey League
960 Sun Life Bldg.
Montreal, Quebec H3B 2W2

National Hockey League Players
Association
65 Queen Street West
Suite 210
Toronto, ON M5H 2M5

JUDO

U.S. Judo, Inc. (NGB)
P.O. Box 637
El Paso, TX 79944

LUGE

U.S. Luge Federation, Inc. (NGB)
One Wilmington Road
P.O. Box 651
Lake Placid, NY 12946

MODERN PENTATHLON

U.S. Modern Pentathlon Association
(NGB)
286 Lincoln Avenue
Hatboro, PA 19040

RACQUETBALL

American Amateur Racquetball
Association
815 North Weber Street
Colorado Springs, CO 80909

American Professional Racquetball
Organization
307 South Milwaukee Avenue
Suite 126
Wheeling, IL 60090

RODEO

The Professional Rodeo Cowboys
Association
101 Pro Rodeo Drive
Colorado Springs, CO 80919

ROLLER SKATING

U.S. Amateur Confederation of
Roller Skating (NGB)
7700 "A" Street
P.O. Box 83067
Lincoln, NE 68501

ROWING

U.S. Rowing Associaton (NGB)
#4 Boathouse Row
Philadelphia, PA 19130

SHOOTING

National Rifle Association of
America (NGB)
1600 Rhode Island Avenue, NW
Washington, DC 20036

SKIING

U.S. Ski Association (NGB)
1750 East Boulder Street
Colorado Springs, CO 80909

SOCCER

Major Indoor Soccer League
One Bala Cynwyd Plaza
Suite 415
Bala Cynwyd, PA 19004

North American Soccer League
1133 Avenue of the Americas
New York, NY 10036

United States Soccer Federation
(NGB)
350 Fifth Avenue
Suite 4010
New York, NY 10118

SOFTBALL

Amateur Softball Association of
America (NGB)
2801 N.E. 50th Street
R. R. #4, Box 385
Oklahoma City, OK 73111

SPEEDSKATING

U.S. International Speedskating
Association (NGB)
Beggs Isle
38235 Mainland Drive
Oconomowoc, WI 53006

SWIMMING

United States Swimming, Inc.
(NGB)
1750 East Boulder Street
Colorado Springs, CO 80909

SYNCHRONIZED SWIMMING

U.S. Synchronized Swimming, Inc.
(NGB)
901 West New York Street
Indianapolis, In 46202

TABLE TENNIS

United States Table Tennis
Association (NGB)
1750 East Boulder Street
Colorado Springs, CO 80909

TEAM HANDBALL

United States Team Handball
Federation (NGB)
1750 East Boulder Street
Colorado Springs, CO 80909

TENNIS

Association of Tennis Professionals
319 Country Club Road
Garland, TX 75040

United States Tennis Association
(NGB)
51 East 42nd Street
New York, NY 10017

VOLLEYBALL

U.S. Volleyball Association (NGB)
1750 East Boulder Street
Colorado Springs, CO 80909

WATER POLO

United States Water Polo, Inc.
(NGB)
1750 East Boulder Street
Colorado Springs, CO 80909

WEIGHT LIFTING

U.S. Weightlifting Federation
(NGB)
1750 East Boulder Street
Colorado Springs, CO 80909

WRESTLING

USA Wrestling (NGB)
405 West Hall of Fame
Stillwater, OK 74074

YACHTING

U.S. Yacht Racing Union (NGB)
Box 209
Goat Island
Newport, RI 02840

Index

Derrick Wilson (left) with Author Karl Woods (photo by Eric Hines).

ABOUT THE AUTHOR

KARL MORROW WOODS HAS HAD AN EXTENSIVE INVOLVEMENT WITH SPORTS. HE COMPETED IN HIGH SCHOOL FOOTBALL, BASKETBALL, TRACK, AND TENNIS AND WON A FOOTBALL SCHOLARSHIP TO OKLAHOMA PANHANDLE STATE COLLEGE. THERE HE EARNED A DEGREE IN COMMUNICATIONS AND PSYCHOLOGY AND LATER ATTENDED GRADUATE SCHOOL AT THE UNIVERSITY OF OKLAHOMA. AS A SPORTS-FITNESS TRAINER, WOODS HAS INSTRUCTED HIGH SCHOOL AND COLLEGE ATHLETES IN SPORTS FUNDAMENTALS, SKILLS, AND CONDITIONING. HE ALSO MANAGED A FITNESS CENTER THAT SPECIALIZES IN STRENGTH AND ENDURANCE TRAINING AND ORGANIZED THE NAUTILUS STRENGTH-TRAINING PROGRAM FOR THE FOOTBALL AND BASKETBALL TEAMS AT ABILENE CHRISTIAN UNIVERSITY. HE LIVES AND WRITES IN AUSTIN, TEXAS.